# Organisational Conflict and Its Management

# Organisational Conflict and Its Management

**Dr. Rabinarayan Samantara**
Associate Professor in Commerce
Shivaji College
University of Delhi

NEW DELHI

*Published and Printed by*
TechSar Pvt. Ltd.
4435-36/7, Ansari Road, Daryaganj
New Delhi-110 002 (India)
E-mail: tech_info@techsarworld.com
Website: www.techsarworld.com

ISBN 978-93-90620-12-8



Reprint 2025

Dedicated to my departed parents

Late Trinath Samantara

and

Late Hemalata Samantara

whose memories keep inspiring me ………….

# Preface

I have made an extensive study of the management literature available on various aspects of organisational conflict and its management. It has been observed that the traditional management writers and researchers regarded conflict as essentially negative or dysfunctional in character. However, the modern organisation theorists have come to view that conflict can have functional or dysfunctional effects within organisations depending upon its management. Therefore, the emphasis in the modern management literature has shifted from the elimination of conflict to its prudent management. Although the OB experts have suggested different approaches towards the management of organisational conflicts, I have noted that most of these conflict management approaches have been offered only at a theoretical or conceptual level without testing their validity in the actual organisational settings. A few empirical research studies have been conducted in the American industrial settings but such studies have been notably absent in the context of Indian industries. On account of these facts, I felt a special need to write a book on the subject of organisational conflict and its management, incorporating therein both the theoretical knowledge and perspectives available in the management literature and the valuable insights gained from certain empirical research studies conducted by me.

Management experts and thinkers have long been trying to find ways and means of enhancing organisational effectiveness or excellence. The effectiveness construct has indeed assumed different meanings such as productivity, adaptability, flexibility, employee satisfaction, community welfare, sustainable development, and so on. Nevertheless, the OB experts have always emphasized upon limiting the construct space of effectiveness so that it becomes easily measurable in terms of certain well defined dimensions or aspects. Although there are many organisational factors such as organisational structure, technology, policies, objectives, etc., which do contribute to effectiveness, a major objective of the present book is to assess the extent to which the conflict management behaviours of managers have an impact on organisational effectiveness. The management theorists have proposed certain methods or styles of managing or resolving interpersonal and intergroup conflicts within organisations. Therefore, attempts have been made in this book to examine the present conflict management behaviours of managers in terms of their utilisation of different conflict management methods or styles, and also examine the relative effectiveness or ineffectiveness of these conflict management styles in terms of their impact on certain well-defined measures of organisational effectiveness. Another important objective of this research is to suggest necessary modifications in the current conflict management behaviours of managers that would be required to enhance organisational effectiveness.

It may be noted that the empirical researches have been conducted by me in some organisations within the power generating and cement manufacturing industries. One chapter is exclusively devoted to the analysis of the results of a research study conducted in a power manufacturing and generating company. This study seeks to explore certain basic issues relating to organisational conflict such as issues and sources of superior-subordinate conflict, conflict management behaviours of Indian managers in terms of their utilisation of different conflict management methods or styles, and the effects of status differences on the management of interpersonal conflicts. More significantly, another chapter of the book has been devoted to analysing the empirical research findings or evidences obtained in the cement industry, regarding the relative effectiveness or ineffectiveness of different conflict management styles or methods. The underlying purpose is to obtain certain validated and generalizable research findings regarding the relative effectiveness of the conflict management styles. It is hoped that these research findings will help the managers to improve their conflict management skills and behaviour and enhance organisational effectiveness.

A noteworthy feature of the book is that it explores the utility of adopting the contingency approach to managing conflicts at the workplace. The normative theories of conflict management broadly suggested that there is one best style of conflict management. Therefore, many empirical research studies were conducted by researchers to determine the relative efficacy or effectiveness of conflict management methods or styles. These studies broadly suggest that problem solving is the best method or style of conflict management, and it seems to be followed by smoothing behaviour. In contrast to the normative approaches to conflict management, the contingency theorists view that different methods or styles of conflict management should be regarded as effective or ineffective depending upon the prevailing situational variables. Accordingly, a chapter of this book is devoted to a critical analysis of certain significant conflicts and conflict management issues within the contingency framework.

The last chapter of the book deals with ethical and cultural issues involved in conflict and conflict management. These ethical issues or challenges have emerged over organisational, environmental, and social issues including product safety, consumers' rights, adherence to government rules and regulations, conservation of natural resources and environment, fair treatment of employees, etc. The purpose of this analysis is to provide certain guidelines to managers so that they can ethically utilise different conflict management styles in different possible conflict situations. In addition, this chapter also deals with the role and importance of cultural issues relating to conflict and conflict management. These significant cultural issues have been examined especially in the context of management of multicultural conflicts arising in modern organisations.

**Rabinarayan Samantara**

# Acknowledgements

It must be brought to the knowledge of the readers that this research work has been the outcome of invaluable support and cooperation received by me from many sources. The biggest challenge for me came in the form of research efforts required to review and integrate the vast body of literature existing on various aspects of organisational conflict and its management. In the conceptualization of pertinent issues and ideas, the author received immense support from Dr R.A. Sharma who happened to be my great teacher and research supervisor during my M.Com., M. Phil. and Ph. D. studies in Delhi University. I am deeply indebted to him for having shared with me his authoritative knowledge and deep insights into the subject at various stages of development of this research work. My constant interactions with him helped me tremendously in formulating ideas and concepts relating to the subject chosen for the study.

Another formidable challenge came in the form of research efforts required to collect perceptual data from industry managers and executives on different aspects of organisational conflict and its management. Managers and executives in different departments and across hierarchical levels were contacted at their workplace personally and requested to provide perceptual data on the questionnaires that were specifically designed for the present study. Since the required data were sensitive from a competitive viewpoint, it was explicitly mentioned that the questionnaire data would be utilised for research purposes only, and the identities of the organisations studied and the respondents would be kept confidential. After receiving such assurances, the managers and executives working in one power generating firm in the public sector and two cement manufacturing firms operating in the private sector, volunteered to provide the much needed perceptual data on organisational conflict and its management aspects. In fact, the research studies would not have been possible without the active support and cooperation of all these managers and executives. I am immensely grateful to them for their great help in this research endeavour.

It must be mentioned that I was granted sabbatical leave by the Governing Body of Shivaji College, University of Delhi, for completing this research work which required full-time attention, especially at the finishing stage. I am grateful to Dr. Shashi Nijhawan, Principal, Shivaji College, for her constant support and inspiration during the course of this research. My thanks are due to Mr. Hemant Kumar, the Administrative Officer of Shivaji College, and his colleagues for completing necessary formalities relating to the sanction of leave to me. My thanks are also due to the staff of Shivaji College library who always cooperated with me during my frequent visits to the library for reference or consultation purposes.

As I had to consult many specialised books and journals for completing this research study, I visited certain well-known libraries in Delhi such as Ratan Tata Library in Delhi School of Economics, University of Delhi, South Campus library, University of Delhi, Indian Institute of Public Administration (IIPA) library in New Delhi, etc. from time to time. I do sincerely acknowledge and appreciate the cooperative attitude and help received from the staff of these libraries.

I am extremely thankful to Mr. Ratikant Samantray, Mr. D.K. Panda, Mr. B. Hota, and Mr. B. Parida who offered their valuable suggestions and ideas during this research work and also provided their knowledge and deep insights into the actual functioning of industries and the industrial environment in general. I gratefully acknowledge the helpful attitude and cooperation of Mr Y.M. Dua who turned my handwritten pages into a beautiful book through his typographical skills. My sincere thanks are due to Ms. Vineeta, Assistant Professor in the Department of Commerce, Shivaji College, who provided help in statistical analysis of data obtained from managers and executives. In general, all my colleagues in the department of commerce provided the much needed encouragement to me during the completion of this book.

Last but not the least, my heart felt indebtedness is ever due to my departed parents who have always been blessing me from their heavenly abode. I must express my gratitude to my wife Mrs. Nandini, for bearing with my preoccupations during the course of this arduous research work. I must also acknowledge that she has always stood as an encouraging force behind my academic achievements. My love and appreciation are also due to my children, Shrikant and Shriya, who have always lent their helping hands at the time of need.

**Rabinarayan Samantara**

# Contents

# 1
# Introduction

Conflict is an integral part of human life. It may be regarded as a natural outcome of human interactions. The notion of conflict arises from the fact that individuals, groups, and organisations engage in antagonistic behaviours as they interact with one another. Conflict is thus concerned with situations that involve contradictory or irreconcilable interests between two opposing individuals or groups. Conflict involves a process in which efforts are made by one party to block or obstruct the attainment of goals by the other. It would be apt to say that individuals or groups develop differences among themselves as they compete for scarce resources, status, power, etc., and to maximize their individual share of it at the cost of one another. Conflict can also arise between two parties over a number of individual, organisational, and social factors. In the organisational context, conflicts can occur among individuals, between individuals in a group and between groups. These conflicts may have significant implications from the viewpoint of individual, inter-individual, intra-group, and intergroup effectiveness in organisations. A manager often experiences great anxiety while dealing with differences or disputes among individuals or groups at the work situation. The presence of conflict often complicates a manager's job in many different ways depending upon the nature and intensity of conflict. Therefore, it is of utmost importance for managers to understand the basic dynamics and processes of conflict existing at various levels of an organisation so as to handle it effectively. It may be mentioned that the understanding of organisational conflict and its management aspects is important not only to managers but also to academicians, researchers, and practitioners. Therefore, the present book represents a modest endeavour to cater to the needs and interests of all these individuals or parties.

In this introduction chapter of the book, attempts have been made to present explanations of the development of the theory of social conflict. This chapter includes a detailed analysis of contributions made to this end by many famous social scientists and scholars representing diverse disciplines such as sociology, psychology, philosophy, political science, economics and so on. This chapter also discusses as to how the concept of organisational conflict has gained prominence over time with the contributions of classical, neo-classical, and modern organisation theorists. The detailed explanations of these viewpoints subsequently presented in this chapter highlight the fact that the views regarding conflict in organisations have undergone significant changes over time. Finally, this chapter provides details of the organisation of the book including the abstract of different chapters contained in it.

## 1.1 CONTRIBUTIONS OF SOCIAL SCIENTISTS

Conflict as a social phenomenon has influenced human thinking and behaviour since the dawn of civilization. The theory of social conflict has developed due to many significant contributions made by social scientists in different disciplines such as philosophy, sociology, psychology, political science, economics, and so on. While the famous classical philosophers such as Plato, Aristotle, Locke, Hegel, Marx, and Dewey contributed significantly to the development of the social conflict theory, the sociologists who contributed in equal measure in this field were Simmel, Mayo, Parsons, and Coser. The contributions of these social scientists towards the development of the social conflict theory have been discussed by Rahim in a succinct manner.

Plato was of the view that tension in a society is natural and, therefore, some conflict is inevitable. Plato, however, suggested that such social conflict can be minimised if a proper balance of different parts of the society can be attained which, he thought, is possible only with appropriate leadership. Plato further suggested that private property should be abolished especially for those who provide political leadership so that the leaders were not motivated by private interests and they could do their job properly. Although Aristotle[1] did not subscribe to Plato's views on private property and on the form of government, he agreed with Plato's emphasis on the need for order in the state. In fact, both Plato and Aristotle viewed social conflict as a pathological concept and accepted that the absence of conflict is an essential prerequisite for attaining the just form of human life in the city state.

The social contract theories of Thomas Hobbes and John Locke propagated that the objective of the government should be to establish order in social relations, in the absence of which there would be constant violence or conflict among human beings. Hobbes argued that the sovereign must control human beings and decide or make laws which must be obeyed by all citizens. Locke disagreed with Hobbes's form of political order or the type of government and viewed that the government should be formed by people through their common consent. In fact, the government's duty was to protect and preserve the lives, liberties and estates of people.

G.W.F. Hegel's philosophy is based on the fundamental notion of the dialectic which conveys four different meanings: (1) arriving at the truth; (2) dialogue or debate; (3) process of ascertaining the unrestricted truth; and (4) process of change through the conflict of opposing forces. The notion of dialectic that every finite concept known as the thesis has within itself its own opposite known as the antithesis. In order to overcome this opposition or conflict, the dialectical method tries to reconcile the opposite concepts by arriving at a third position, known as the synthesis.

Karl Marx perceived the human history as being full of class struggle, i.e., conflict between the bourgeoisie (business class) and the proletariat (working class), which leads to change and development. Marx was a revolutionary thinker who wanted that the capitalists relinquish their power. Marx's dialectic is thus associated with class conflict arising due to economic disparities. According to Marx, this class struggle will finally result in a classless society which is devoid of suppression of human rights and liberties and where the human beings will become truly free from any conflicts whatsoever. Marx and his associate Angel were quite frank about their opinions on social revolution and ended their famous treatise *The Communist Manifesto* with these words: "The Communists .... openly declare that their ends can be attained only by the forcible overthrow of all existing social conditions. Let the ruling classes tremble at a Communist revolution. The Proletariates have nothing to lose but their chains. Working men of all countries, unite!"

John Dewey's[2] ideas on conflict were significantly influenced by Darwin's evolution theory and Hegel's process of dialectic. Dewey suggested that when the relationship between human beings and the environment is disrupted by conflicts or obstacles, people must readapt themselves through a process of change. In other words, people must examine the conflict situations, discover different possible courses of action in the changed situations, and choose the one that is most effective.

Charles Darwin was a naturalist and is well known for his theory of evolution,[3] which suggests that biological species survive and grow by confronting environmental challenges. Darwin and his associates recognised the significant role of environmental conflict in human growth and development, which led to the formulation of the doctrine of the survival of the fittest. Darwin observed that the growth of human beings depends on their ability to confront or handle their conflicts with the environment. If conflict was altogether absent as idealized by the classical philosophers, the growth and development of human beings would be checkmated. In the words of Darwin, " man.... has no doubt advanced to his present condition through a struggle for existence consequent on his rapid multiplication and if he is to advance still higher, it is to be feared that he must remain subject to a severe struggle. Otherwise, he would sink into indolence and the more gifted men would not be more successful in the battle of life than the less gifted."

George, Simmel,[4] a German sociologist, hypothesized that a certain amount of conflict is necessary for the effective functioning of groups. He viewed that conflict served a social purpose in ensuring the unity and stability of groups even if it was at the cost of the annihilation of one of the parties. Conflict facilitates the socialization processes within a group and reduces the tension among group members. Simmel suggested three different ways to resolve conflict: (1) victory of one party over another; (2) compromise; and (3) conciliation.

Elton Mayo's[5] studies during the late 1930s and onwards led to the human relations movement. These studies led to certain important discoveries within the organisational system such as the existence of informal groups, informal communication system known as the grapevine, positive effects of informal group processes on employee's moral and productivity. Thus, the human relations movement emphasized upon the need for cooperation between employees and managers for attaining maximum possible organisational effectiveness. According to Mayo, conflict was a necessary evil in organisations and therefore, it needs to be minimised or eliminated altogether if possible. Child[6] concluded that Mayo had a "deep abhorrence of conflict in any form .... Mayo and his colleagues .... assumed that ordinary employees were largely governed by a "logic of sentiment", which was of a different order from managers' rational appraisal of the situation in terms of costs and efficiency. Conflict with management was thus an aberration that threatened the effectiveness of organisations."

Talcott Parson's[7] development of the structural functional theory has had a considerable influence on social science thoughts. His theory is based on the assumption that society is inherently stable, integrated, and functional and, as a result, conflict is to be viewed as abnormal and dysfunctional. It may be noted, however, that a number of social scientists including Coser,[8] Bernard,[9] Mills,[10] Dahrendorf[11] proposed their viewpoints opposite to Parson's analysis. This development led to the growing interest in the study of conflict as a social phenomenon.

Lewis Coser's[12] famous treatise, *The Functions Social Conflict*, focused on the productive potential of conflict. According to Coser, conflict seemed to serve the useful function of using the society and led to new technology, institutions and economic systems. Coser's most significant contribution to conflict resolution was in the form of his presentation of two opposite viewpoints regarding the outcomes of conflict, i.e., the functional and dysfunctional roles of conflict. A synthesis of these viewpoints is necessary to enhance the usefulness of conflict in organisations.

## 1.2 VIEWS ON ORGANISATIONAL CONFLICT

Organisation theorists have taken interest in the study of conflict only in recent times. After having accepted conflict as a significant social phenomenon, the organisation experts have come to recognise that conflict is certainly one of the major organisational phenomena. According to Pondy,[13] organisation theories "that do not admit conflict provide poor guidance in dealing with problems of organisational efficiency, stability, governance, and change, for conflict within and between organisations is intimately related as either symptom, cause or effect, to each of these problems". Similarly, Baron[14] has observed that "organisational conflict is an important topic for both managers and for scientists interested in understanding the nature of organisational behaviour and organisational processes". Therefore, it would be no exaggeration to state that the study of organisation theory and behaviour cannot be complete without an adequate study and understanding of the phenomenon of conflict. In this context, it would be appropriate to discuss as to how the concept of organisational conflict has evolved over time with the major contributions of the classical, neoclassical, and modern organisation theorists or experts.

### 1.2.1 The Classical View

The classical organisation theorists assumed that conflict is essentially dysfunctional in character or detrimental to the attainment of organisational objectives. Therefore, they viewed that conflict should be minimised or avoided at all costs. This approach to the management of organisations suggested that cooperation, harmony, and the absence of conflict were necessary for attaining optimum organisational effectiveness. The classicists believed that conflict is the result of such factors as lack of trust among people, poor communication, management's failure to fulfil the needs and expectations of employees, etc. Therefore, the classical organisational structure included hierarchy of authority, chain of command, rules and procedures, rationality, and efficiency so that the organisational members would restrain themselves from conflict and conflictful behaviour. According to this view, there is a need to identify the causes of conflict and correct them in order to improve group's and organisation's performance.[15] The classical school of thought included such famous scholars as F.W. Taylor, Henry Fayol, Max Weber, Mooney and Reiley, Gullick and Urwick, and Mary Parker Follett. The views of these scholars may be discussed as follows.

#### *1.2.1.1 Taylor*

Taylor,[16] known as the father of scientific management, believed that increasing productivity was the means through which profits can be increased and higher wages paid to workers. Taylor and his associates asserted that the application of the principles of scientific management will lead to improved organisational functioning and effectiveness. Some of the basic principles of scientific management may be stated as follows:

1. Scientific approach to the study of tasks in place of rule of thumb work methods.
2. Scientific selection, training, and development of workers.
3. Cooperation with workers to ensure that they actually perform the scientific methods of work.
4. Equal division of responsibility between managers and workers so that planning of work and its performance are separated.
5. Development of each person to the best of his capabilities.
6. Mental revolution on the part of both management and workers.

Taylor asserted that labour and management disputes will disappear if the above principles of scientific management were applied. Although scientific management led to significant benefits in terms of enhanced productivity and efficiency, it was criticized especially by the workers. Scientific management led to speed up of workers, determination of wages without collective bargaining, and made no provision for management of conflicts in organisations.

#### 1.2.1.2 Fayol

Henry Fayol,[17] a French executive, is well known for his concept of functional management. Fayol enunciated 14 principles of management such as division of work, unity of command, span of control, etc., which are applicable in the industrial situations even today. In addition, Fayol emphasized that the management functions of planning, organising, command, coordination, and control have relevance to all organised human activities. Although Fayol offered a more systematic approach to management than Taylor, it must be pointed out that both of them assumed that conflict was detrimental to the attainment of organisational objectives. Therefore, they prescribed mechanistic forms of organisational structure with division of work, hierarchy of authority, unity of command, and so on, in order to encourage cooperation and harmony and eliminate conflicts in organisations.

#### 1.2.1.3 Weber

Max Weber[18] proposed a bureaucratic form of organisation which, he believed, was the most efficient form of organisation. The bureaucratic organisation has the following distinguishing features:

1. A well-defined hierarchy within the organisation.
2. A formal system of rules and regulations.
3. Division of work based on functional specialisation.
4. Impersonality in the application of rules.
5. Selection and promotion of employees based on technical competence.

Weber believed that there was no scope for conflict in his bureaucratic model. Although he was aware of certain limitations of this model, he emphasized that the bureaucratic structure was most appropriate for achieving organisational effectiveness.

#### 1.2.1.4 Follett

Mary Parker Follett,[19] another prominent classical organisation theorist, was well known for her advanced ideas and insights into management and organisational processes. She emphasized upon the value of constructive conflict in management and recommended the use of integrative or problem solving method for managing organisational conflict. According to her, the other methods of handling conflict such as dominance, compromise, avoidance and suppression were ineffective in resolving or managing conflicts.

### 1.2.2 The Neo-Classical View

The studies conducted by Elton Mayo[20] at the Hawthorne plant of the Western Electrical Company during the 1920s and 1930s led to the human relations movement. These studies were designed to study the effects of working conditions on productivity and led to certain important discoveries regarding organisational functioning. It was observed that physical conditions alone did not lead to higher productivity of workers. In fact, the positive relational factors such as teamwork among employees, employee recognition, informal social relations, etc., played a significant role in ensuring employee productivity or job satisfaction. In the course of time, the human relations theory of Mayo gained prominence and was supported by other management theorists including Lewin,[21] White,[22] and Likert.[23]

In regard to the role of conflict in organisations, Mayo suggested that conflict was a necessary evil and needed to be minimised or eliminated for enhancing organisational effectiveness. According to Mayo, cooperation rather than conflict was the essential symptom of organisational health. While the classical theorists such as Taylor, Fayol, and Weber attempted to reduce conflict through suitable alterations in the techno-structural system of the organisation, Mayo attempted to achieve this objective by changing its social system. Thus, Mayo's views on organisational functioning including the role of conflict led to significant changes in management thoughts and practices.

### 1.2.3 The Modern View

The modern view of conflict emerged on account of the contributions made by some prominent management thinkers especially after the first half of the 20$^{th}$ century. Litterer[24] argued that "tension is normal even desirable with the thought growing that healthy personalities actually seek to increase tension" Whyte[25] (1967) summarised the functions of organisational conflict as follows : "since conflicts are an inevitable part of organisational life it is important that conflict resolution procedures be built into the design of organisations". Now, there is a paradigm shift in the views of management thinkers on organisational conflict and increasing emphasis on management of conflict rather than its elimination. In fact, the healthy organisations not only resolve conflicts but also seek to stimulate conflict so as to realise its potential benefits. This balanced approach to organisational conflict is no longer considered as on organisational weakness, as implied by the classicists or human relationists. It is important to note that Robbins has presented three philosophies of organisational conflict as mentioned below:

1. The philosophy of conflict of the classicists or traditionalists discussed above, was based on the assumption that conflict was detrimental to an organisation and must be reduced or eliminated.
2. The classical stage was followed by the behaviourists' philosophy which can best be described as the recognition that conflict is inevitable in organisations.

Behaviourists accept the presence of conflict and even occasionally advocate the enhancement of conflict for increasing organisational effectiveness. But they have not actively created conditions that generate conflict in organisations.

3. The philosophy of conflict of the interactionists is the third philosophy, which differs significantly from the previous two. It is characterized by the following:
   (a) recognition of the absolute necessity of conflict;
   (b) explicit encouragement of opposition;
   (c) defining conflict management to include stimulation as well as resolution methods; and
   (d) considering the management of conflict as a major responsibility of all administrators.[26]

Conflict is now considered both inevitable and legitimate in organisations. It is now being increasingly recognised that conflict, if managed properly, can be beneficial to an organisation in terms of creative problem-solving and productivity, improved organisational effectiveness, etc., while little or no conflict in organisations can lead to stagnation, poor decision-making, and ineffectiveness. It is also to be noted that conflict, left uncontrolled, can have serious dysfunctional consequences within organisations. Therefore, it is generally accepted that a moderate amount of conflict, handled in a constructive manner, is essential for attaining and maintaining an optimum level of organisational effectiveness.[27] The details regarding the functional effects of moderate conflict in organisations have been addressed more systematically in the subsequent chapters.

## 1.3 ORGANISATION OF THE BOOK

The present book has been divided into ten chapters. The details of the organisation of the study including an abstract of each chapter are given below.

**Chapter 1** is introductory in nature. It includes a critical analysis of contributions from different disciplines such as philosophy, psychology, sociology, political science, economics, anthropology, etc., towards the evolution of the theory of social conflict. This chapter includes a review of the scholarly writings of some famous social scientists such as Aristotle, Hobbes, Locke, Hegel, Marx, Dewey, Darwin, Simmel, Mayo, Parsons, and Coser, on the subject of social conflict. Although these scholars have different perspectives on the nature and dimensions of social conflict, their viewpoints have been carefully synthesized and analysed in the broader perspective of the development of a theory of social conflict. The discussion of conflict has been extended further to include different views on organisational conflict including the classical, neoclassical, and modern viewpoints. As discussed earlier, the classical organisation theorists implicitly viewed conflict as a negative phenomenon in organisations and therefore sought to avoid or eliminate conflicts by prescribing organisation structures based on division of work, hierarchy of authority, chain of command, rules and regulations, efficiency in administration, rationality, etc. They believed that the organisational structure based on these classical pillars would lead to harmony, cooperation, and the absence of conflict, which were necessary for maximizing organisational effectiveness. In this context, the contributions of famous classical authors such as Taylor, Fayol, Weber, and Follett on the subject of organisational conflict have been critically analysed. It may be noted that the neoclassical or human relations theorists also assumed that conflict is dysfunctional in character, but they sought to eliminate conflicts in organisations through appropriate changes in their social systems. This chapter includes an analysis of Mayo's research findings and ideas on various aspects of the social system such as teamwork among employees, informal social relations, employee recognition, etc., which contributed significantly to employee satisfaction and productivity. Finally, this chapter includes a discussion on the modern view of organisational conflict which posits that conflict is not necessarily dysfunctional for organisations. According to this view, conflict, if handled constructively, can lead to enhanced productivity, organisational effectiveness and creative problem-solving in organisations. While little or no conflict can result in stagnation and ineffectiveness, conflict, left uncontrolled, can lead to many serious dysfunctional effects in an organisation. Therefore, the modern perspective on organisational conflict emphasizes that a moderate amount of conflict is most appropriate or desirable for enhancing organisational effectiveness.

**Chapter 2** provides an overview of various concepts and issues relating to organisational conflict. In addition to exploring the conceptual meaning of conflict, the chapter focuses on the inevitability of conflict in organisation's life, the need for constructive management of conflicts, and the potential benefits of conflict to organisations. It emphasizes upon the fact that conflict, if managed constructively, can lead to many positive outcomes in an organisation. The potential benefits of conflict, as discussed in this chapter, include organisational change and creativity, release of tension of group members, cohesiveness, enhanced group and organisational effectiveness, productive challenges for individuals and groups, higher and more constructive level of tension, etc. It has also been pointed out that if conflict is not properly managed, it can lead to several unintended consequences such as increased employee turnover, dissatisfaction of the losing parties, creation of mutual suspicion or mistrust, goal displacement, weakening of the organisation, etc. Regarding the relationship between intensity of conflict and organisational performance, it is stated that both too little and too much of conflict are detrimental to the attainment of organisational effectiveness. As suggested by the modern organisation theorists, a moderate amount of substantive or task related conflict is most essential for enhancing organisational effectiveness. The chapter provides a critical analysis of conflict as a dynamic process as suggested by Pondy, which includes five stages of conflict such as latent conflict, perceived conflict, felt conflict, manifest conflict, and conflict aftermath. A discussion of some of the major sources as well as issues of conflicts existing within the organisations has also been included in this chapter. This chapter discusses different types or levels of conflicts such as intra-individual, inter-individual. intra-group, and intergroup conflict as well as their causal factors. The last part of this chapter highlights the negotiation skills that can be utilised for resolving interpersonal and intergroup conflict in organisations. In this context, the role and functionality of integrative bargaining versus distributive bargaining involved in the negotiation process have been explained. It is also suggested that the negotiators must try to consider or understand certain contemporary issues in negotiation in order to improve their bargaining strength and problem solving skills. These significant issues relate to the role of personality traits in negotiation, gender differences in negotiation, cultural differences in negotiation, and the role of third party negotiators in the negotiation process.

**Chapter 3** includes a conceptual approach to the study of conflict and conflict management in organisations. In nutshell, this chapter analyses the available literature on some significant aspects of organisational conflict such as the changing perspective on conflict, antecedents to conflict, outcomes or consequences of conflict, and the management of conflict. It may be mentioned that the above-discussed aspects of organisational conflict have been dealt with only in a cursory manner in this chapter as these significant issues have been explored quite extensively in the subsequent chapters. As discussed previously, the views on the functionality of organisational conflict have undergone significant changes with the passage of time. Conflict is no longer viewed as being essentially dysfunctional in character in the present times. In fact, conflict can have many beneficial outcomes if it is handled constructively. Therefore, the modern organisation theorists have come to emphasize upon the management of conflicts rather than their elimination in the organisations. The antecedents to organisational conflict as analysed include task interdependence, organisational differentiation, competition for scarce resources, performance criteria and rewards, task ambiguities, hierarchical differences in prestige, power and knowledge, identity concerns, barriers to communication, personality attributes, role dissatisfaction, drive for autonomy, and the need for tension release. In regard to the outcomes or consequences of organisational conflict, the review of literature has shown that conflict can have both positive and negative effects. In regard to the management of conflicts, the available research findings of some empirical studies have been briefly reported in this chapter as these aspects have been discussed in greater detail in Chapter 7. In addition, the contingency viewpoints regarding conflict management put forth by some of the leading organisation experts have also been briefly analysed. In fact, Chapter 8 deals with these contingency perspectives on conflict management in a comprehensive manner.

**Chapter 4** attempts to define conflict management and analyse various approaches to conflict management as suggested by the social scientists. This chapter also explains the conflict management process as well as certain conflict management strategies that may be adopted by managers so as to maintain a desirable level of conflict in an organisation. It has been noted that the management of organisational conflict has generally moved in two directions. In the first approach, the researchers have attempted to measure the intensity or degree of organisational conflict existing at various levels in terms of stress, tension, anxiety, hostility, etc., and also find out the sources of such conflict. The underlying idea is to ensure that a moderate amount of conflict is maintained by altering the sources of conflict with a view to enhancing organisational effectiveness. The second approach to conflict management involves the researchers' efforts to examine the effectiveness of different conflict handling methods or styles in terms of their impact on various criteria of organisational effectiveness. In regard to various approaches to conflict management, it has been observed that these approaches are essentially based upon different methods or styles of handling conflicts in organisations and point to the functionality or effectiveness of different conflict management methods or styles in different possible conflict situations. An analysis of conflict management approaches suggested by leading organisation theorists such as Blake and Mouton, Thomas, Rahim, Pareek, Blake, Shepard and Mouton, Walton, Likert and Likert, Luft and Ingham, Hall, Pruitt and Filley have revealed that every manager has a preference for using a particular style of managing conflicts and tends to fall back upon a backup style when the dominant method of managing conflicts fails to work in a particular situation. The broad consensus is that the problem-solving approach is most effective in managing conflicts in industrial situations. The managers following this approach need to achieve the production targets while at the same time maintaining harmonious working relations with employees. As regards the process of managing conflicts discussed in this chapter, it has been pointed out that conflict management does not mean avoidance or reduction of conflict alone; it involves designing effective macro-level strategies to enhance the positive effects of conflict and reduce its negative effects, and also to increase learning and effectiveness in an organisation. In this context, the intervention strategies suggested include process intervention and structural intervention. While process intervention is designed to help the organisation's members to match their styles of managing conflicts with the demands of specific situations, structural intervention seeks to manage conflict by altering the perceptions or the intensity of conflict at various levels of the organisation. The general strategies suggested for managing conflicts include minimising or reducing affective conflicts in an organisation and maintaining a moderate amount of substantive conflict, which leads to more efficient problem-solving, better decision-making, and higher levels of individual and group performance.

**Chapter 5** has been devoted to an empirical study of certain basic issues relating to conflict in organisations. More specifically, this chapter attempts to explore or investigate issues and sources of superior-subordinate conflict, managers' utilisation of various conflict management methods or styles, and compares the conflict management behaviours of senior managers and their subordinates with a view to finding out both similarities and differences between them in this regard. The investigation of these important issues was conducted with the help of perceptual data collected from 52 managers of a public sector electricity producing and distributing company operating in the NCR region of Delhi. Since the sample managers belonged to different hierarchical and different functional departments of the organisation such as production, finance, engineering, HR, IT, etc., it can be said that the managers contacted for this empirical study were truly representative of the entire organisation. The issues of superior-subordinate conflict examined within this organisation include conflict over job objectives, work standards to be accomplished, planning of activities, utilisation of equipment and facilities, time spent on the job, errors, misinterpretation of orders, carelessness, etc., supervision, direction, and control, performance appraisal, administration of wages and salary, promotions and sanction of leave, and physical work environment. At the same time, some important issues of superior-subordinate conflict have been explored such as personality differences, differences in basic values, beliefs or opinions, differences in knowledge, skills, and expertise, unreasonable policies, procedures or rules, barriers to interpersonal communication, hierarchical differences in status, power, and rewards, competition for position, power or recognition, drive for autonomy, and need for tension release. Another significant aspect of the study is that it attempts to analyse the conflict management behaviours of both senior managers and their subordinates in terms of their utilisation of conflict management methods or styles such as problem-solving, smoothing, compromise, forcing, and withdrawing. Subsequently, attempts have also been made to make a comparative analysis of the conflict management behaviours of senior managers and their subordinates so as to find out the role of status differences in this regard, if any.

**Chapter 6** highlights the fact that organisational effectiveness as a concept has always occupied a pivotal place in almost all theories and studies of formal organisations. Despite the importance of the effectiveness concept, the literature available on this subject is plagued with problems of definition, circumspection, and criteria identification. The chapter explores the above-mentioned problems and issues regarding the effectiveness construct and also examines certain important issues in relation to the measurement of organisational effectiveness. It has been observed that the organizational behaviour experts have made both theoretical and empirical attempts to define or limit the construct space of effectiveness. This chapter discusses some of the significant theoretical research works done by leading authors such as Price, Steers, and Campbell. Since these theoretical attempts have met with little success in delineating the construct space or boundaries of effectiveness, subsequent authors proceeded to make certain empirical approaches to the study of organisational effectiveness. Some of the significant empirical approaches to the study of effectiveness as discussed in this chapter, include those of Georgopoulos and Tannenbaum, Seashore and Yutchman, Mahoney *et al.,* and Quinn and Rohrbaugh. It is noteworthy, however, that the empirical approaches too have failed to bound the construct space of effectiveness. The reasons for discrepancy in the results obtained by these empirical models include the study of limited organisations, study of limited number of constituencies or stakeholders, differences in the level of analysis and in the focus of activities being studied, and different conceptualizations of organisations being accepted by the researchers. This chapter attempts to make a critical appraisal of certain important models of effectiveness such as Rational Goal model, Systems model, Strategic Constituencies model, Competing Values model, Likert's model and Cunningham's model. In addition, this chapter discusses some of the integration efforts made by Scott, Seashore, and Cameron to find out how various effectiveness models relate to one another. In the end, this chapter addresses some of the significant issues concerning the measurement or assessment of organisational effectiveness.

**Chapter** 7 reports the findings of a comprehensive empirical research study conducted by the author in two private sector cement manufacturing firms operating in the north-eastern part of India. Although this study attempts to examine the conflict management behaviours of Indian managers, the primary thrust of the study has been on determining the relative effectiveness of different conflict management methods or styles used by senior managers in resolving work related conflicts with their subordinates. Therefore, these conflict management methods as used by managers such as problem solving, smoothing, compromising, forcing, and withdrawing were evaluated in terms of their impact on certain well-defined measures of organisational effectiveness: (1) productivity, (2) adaptability, and (3) flexibility. It may be mentioned that for conducting this study, perceptual data were obtained from 60 and 57 managers of two cement manufacturing organisations, respectively. These managers belonged to different hierarchical levels and different functional departments of their respective organisations. A comparative study of these two manufacturing firms was made as these two organisations showed certain common characteristics in terms of ownership, industry-affiliation, nature of production, etc. The analysis of research data revealed that the managers of both these organisations made considerable use of problem solving, compromise, and smoothing behaviour together with their low degree of utilisation of forcing and withdrawing behaviours. The multiple regression results indicated that 'conflict management' was a significant organisational variable in both the organisations, having significant impact on various organisational effectiveness dimensions. With regard to the comparative effectiveness of conflict management methods or styles, the findings of the study indicated that problem solving is the most effective method of conflict management while the forcing mode of resolving conflicts was found to be the most ineffective one. The smoothing and compromising modes seemed to have mixed effects on certain effectiveness aspects while the compromising mode was found to be related to none of the effectiveness aspects. In the light of these research findings, attempts have been made to put forth some useful suggestions for the improvement of the conflict management behaviours of Indian managers so as to enhance organisational effectiveness. The fact that the managers are making maximum use of problem solving in resolving work-related conflicts with their subordinates augurs well and needs to be enhanced further. Although the smoothing mode was found to have mixed effects on certain effectiveness dimensions in the present study, the empirical studies previously conducted by the author have shown the positive effects of this mode of managing conflicts. Therefore, maximum use of smoothing behaviour in resolving conflicts seems to be justified although there is no specific need to enhance it further. The compromising mode indicated no significant relationship with any of the effectiveness aspects and accordingly, there is a paramount need to discourage the managers' frequent utilisation of this mode as is being done by them at present. The findings of the present study have amply demonstrated the negative effects of forcing behaviour on several effectiveness dimensions. In this context, it is quite heartening to know that the Indian managers are making infrequent or negligible use of this mode of managing conflict with their subordinates. Since the withdrawing behaviour was found to be having mixed effects on certain organisational effectiveness aspects, the managers should not be encouraged to make frequent use of this mode of resolving conflicts.

**Chapter** 8 points out that the contingency approach to management has developed basically due to certain limitations of the classical organisation theories that were based upon universalistic principles of management. The contingency approach clearly recognises the fact that organisation's structure, processes, technology, etc., are influenced by environmental or situational factors. The present chapter examines the evolution of the contingency concept and discusses certain contingency approaches to conflict management as suggested by some leading management experts. In addition, this chapter focuses on the role of certain process and structural contingencies that influence conflict and its management in certain situations. It may be mentioned that some of the classic contingency approaches to management were developed by such famous scholars as Woodworth, Burns and Stacker, Thompson, and Lawrence and Lorsch. These classical contingency studies and the subsequent studies highlight the changes in an organisation's structure, processes, technology, etc., that do take place in response to the changing demands of its internal and external environments. In contrast to the normative approaches to conflict management that emphasize upon one best style of conflict management, the contingency approaches are based on the premise that conflict management methods or styles should be regarded as effective or ineffective depending upon the prevailing situational factors or variables. Some of the well-known contingency approaches to conflict management include those of Blake and Mouton, Rahim, Pareek, Philip and Cheston, and so on. This chapter explains Beres and Schmidt's analysis of certain conflict and conflict management issues within a contingency framework. This contingency analysis includes a description of both process contingencies and structural contingencies prevailing in a conflict situation that have a profound influence on the conflict process itself and on various conflict management issues. While the process contingencies include the parties and the stages of discord, the structural contingencies include the causes of conflict, the social context, and the values. It may be pointed out that these contingency perspectives on conflict management have been supported by both theoretical knowledge and empirical research evidences obtained by researchers on the effectiveness of conflict management styles or methods. Despite this vast body of knowledge existing on the contingency perspective on conflict management, the fact remains that it has not been possible so far to develop a well accepted contingency model of conflict management in the management literature. In fact, there is a need to conduct many more research studies on the efficacy or effectiveness of conflict management methods or styles in the light of various organisational, psycho-social and other contingency variables.

**Chapter 9** includes a critical analysis of both ethical and cultural issues involved in conflict and conflict management. Although the ethical aspects of conflict management have been found to be associated with positive results for organisations, it has been observed that ethical values in the area of conflict management have not been adequately explored. Therefore, this chapter explains certain conflict related issues such as individual values and value systems, personality types and styles, and individual differences in conflict. This chapter also attempts to provide some ethical guidelines so that the organisation's members can handle interpersonal and intergroup conflicts more effectively and more ethically. In this regard, the decision-tree model of Buller, Kohls, and Anderson has been discussed, which have relevance for managing cross-cultural ethical conflicts. It may be noted that the decision tree model is intended to serve as an extremely useful aid to decision makers to handle conflicts in an ethical manner. According to this model, the important variables to be considered in the choice of appropriate strategies for handling cross-cultural ethical conflicts include power urgency and moral significance. Another pioneering research effort was made by Rahim who discussed the ethical appropriateness or inappropriateness of different conflict management styles in different possible situations. The specific methods or styles of conflict management discussed by Rahim in this regard included integrating, obliging, dominating, avoiding, and compromising. As viewed by Rahim, the integrating style of managing conflicts should be used by the organisation's members to the maximum possible extent while their utilisation of dominating and avoiding styles should be discouraged as much as possible. In regard to cultural issues involved in conflict management, this chapter emphasizes upon the fact that the formation of multicultural task groups in MNCs and international organisations has led to multicultural group conflicts in organisations. Since the task groups are composed of people with different national, ethnic and racial backgrounds, the managers must try to realise the benefits of cultural diversity rather than view it as a negative phenomenon within organisations. This chapter includes a review of the relevant literature on these aspects of multicultural group conflict and its management. The review of literature pointed to the fact that national cultures have significant effects on the utilisation of different conflict management styles. Therefore, it is important to study how multicultural group members interact to promote cross-cultural collaboration among themselves. In this chapter, attempts have also been made to study the relationship between culture and cultural diversity as well as between cultural diversity and conflicts in organisations. In this regard, it is observed that cultural differences among group members have a profound influence on group life, group development, and group processes in organisations. It is also noted that cultural diversity in groups plays a significant role in the perception and resolution of conflicts. Finally, this chapter includes a discussion of the management aspects of multicultural group conflicts existing in organisations. It has been broadly suggested that the managers need to adopt an open minded approach and be flexible enough so as to promote collaborative behaviour among group members while managing multicultural group conflicts in organisations.

**Chapter 10** deals with certain major conclusions derived from the analysis of various research issues connected with organisational conflict and its management. This chapter highlights the criticality of such important aspects of organisational conflict as its gradual evolution as an independent area of enquiry, the changing views of conflict, the need for constructive management of conflict, its potential benefits to organisations, the relevance of negotiation skills and processes in conflict management, etc. In addition, this chapter discusses the practical utility of various conflict management approaches as suggested by the organisation theorists and the valuable insight gained therefrom. It emphasises upon the adoption of macro-level intervention strategies to enhance the positive effects of conflict and minimise its negative effects and also to increase learning and effectiveness in an organisation. Attempts have also been made to underline the importance of the contingency approach to conflict management which is based upon the fundamental assumption that the conflict management methods or styles should be viewed as effective or ineffective depending upon the situational factors or variables. This contingency viewpoint regarding conflict management is in sharp contrast to the normative approaches to conflict management that emphasise upon one best style of managing conflicts. Finally, a critical analysis of some ethical and cultural issues involved in organisational conflict and its management has been made in this chapter. Attempts have been made to provide certain ethical guidelines to organisation's members so that they can handle both inter-personal and inter-group conflicts more effectively and more ethically. In regard to cultural issues involved in conflict and conflict management, this chapter highlights the phenomenon of multicultural group conflicts in MNCs and other organisations. It is broadly suggested that the managers should try to promote collaborative behaviours among group members while managing multicultural group conflicts and thereby realise the benefits of cultural diversity existing in organisations. As it was pointed out earlier, the empirical research studies were conducted in a public sector electricity generating and distributing company in the NCR region of Delhi and two privately owned cement manufacturing organisations operating in the north-eastern region of India. These empirical studies were not only intended to investigate the issues and sources of senior-subordinate conflict, and the present conflict management behaviours of Indian managers but also examine the relative effectiveness of conflict management methods or styles in terms of their effects on various dimensions of organisational effectiveness. In addition to drawing meaningful inferences from the findings of these studies regarding various significant issues or aspects of conflict and its management, this chapter provides valuable suggestions and guidelines to the practising managers and researchers.

## REVIEW QUESTIONS

1. Discuss the contributions made by social scientists towards the development of the social theory of conflict.
2. Explain the term conflict. Is it that the views regarding organisational conflict have significantly changed over time?
3. The concept of organisational conflict has gained prominence over time due to contributions made by classical, neoclassical, and modern organisation theorists. Discuss.

## REFERENCES


1. Aristotle, Politics (trans. B. Jowett), J. Barnes (Ed.), *The Complete Works of Aristotle: The Revised Oxford Translation,* Princeton University Press, Princeton, NJ, 1984.
2. Dewey, J., Human Nature and Conduct, Modern Library, New York, 1957.
3. Darwin, C.R., The Descent of Man and Selection in Relation to Sex, Modern Library, New York, 1871.
4. Simmel, G., Conflict (trans. K.H. Wolf), *The Web of Group Affiliation* (trans. R. Bendix), Free Press, Glencoe, IL, 1955.
5. Mayo, E., *The Human Problems of an Industrial Civilization,* Macmillan, New York, 1933.
6. Child, J., Follett: Constructive conflict, P. Graham, (Ed.), *Mary Parker Follett – Prophet of Management: A Celebration of Writings from the 1920s,* Harvard Business School Press, Boston, 1995.
7. Parson, T., *Essays in Sociological Theory: Pure and Applied,* Free Press, Glencoe, IL, 1949.
8. Coser, L.A., *The Functions of Social Conflict,* Free Press, Glencoe, 1956.
9. Bernard, J., The Sociological study of conflict, International Sociological Association (Ed.), *The Nature of Conflict Studies on the Sociological Aspects of*

*International Tensions*, UNESCO, Tensions and Technology Series, Paris, 1957, pp. 33-117.

10. Mills, C.W., *The Sociological Imagination*, Oxford University Press, New York, 1959.
11. Dahrendorf, R., *Class and Class Conflict in Industrial Society* (trans. from German, revised and expanded), Stanford University Press, Stanford, CA, 1959.
12. Coser, L.A., 1956, *op. cit.*
13. Pondy, L.R., Organisational conflict: Concepts and models, *Administrative Science Quarterly*, 12, 1967, 296-320.
14. Baron, R.A., Conflict in organisations, K.R. Murphy and F. E. Saal, (Ed.), *Psychology in Organisation: Integrating Science and Practice*, Erlbaum, Hillsdale, NJ, 1990, pp. 197-216.
15. Robbins, S.P., *Managing Organisational Conflict: A Non-traditional Approach*, Prentice-Hall, Englewood Cliffs, NJ, 1974.
16. Taylor, F.W., *The Principles of Scientific Management*, Harper and Row, New York, 1911.
17. Fayol, H., *General and Industrial Management* (trans. from French), Pitman, London, 1949.
18. Weber, M., *The Theory of Social and Economic Organisation* (trans. from German, A.M. Henderson and T. Persons), Oxford University Press, New York, 1947.
19. Follett, M.P., Constructive conflict, H.C. Metcalf and L. Urwick, (Ed.), Dynamic Administration: The Collected Papers of Mary Parker Follett, Harper and Row, New York, 1940, pp. 30-49.
20. Mayo, E., 1933, *op. cit.*
21. Lewin, K., *Resolving Social Conflicts: Selected Papers on Group Dynamics*, (Ed. By G.W. Lewin), Harper and Row, New York, 1948.
22. White, H., Management conflict and sociometric structure, *American Journal of Sociology*, 67, 1961, pp. 185-199.
23. Likert, R., *The Human Organisation: Its Management and Value*, McGraw-Hill, New York, 1967.
24. Litterer, J.A., Conflict in organisation: A re-examination, *Academy of Management Journal* , 9, 1966, pp. 178-186.
25. Whyte, W.H., Models for building and changing organisations, *Human Organisation*, 26, 1967, pp. 22-31.
26. Robbins, S.P., 1974, *op. cit.*
27. Rahim, M.A. and Bonama, T.V., Managing organisational conflict: A model for diagnosis and intervention, *Psychological Reports*, 44, 1979, pp. 1323-1344.

# 2

# Organisational Conflict: Concepts and Issues

## 2.1 INTRODUCTION

Conflict is an integral part of human life and human behaviour. The term 'conflict' is often used to express such negative connotations as antagonism, aggression, hostile or negative attitudes, rivalry, misunderstanding, etc., which is often not correct. In fact, the concept of conflict has different meanings for different persons depending upon one's frame of reference being used. When a person is experiencing conflict in his mind, we can say that the individual is having dilemma over a particular issue and is not able to reach to any decision. At the interpersonal or intergroup level, conflict refers to differences of opinion or views between two or more persons or groups. In this situation, each party is competing with and is trying to outwit the other or is trying to obstruct the attainment of goals by the other. Thus, conflict is associated with situations that involve contradictory or conflicting interests between two opposing groups. At this point, it is noteworthy that conflict must be distinguished from competition. Conflict is always directed against another group and, actions are taken by one group to obstruct the other group's goal attainment. In competition, however, each team is trying to achieve a common goal, and one group does not obstruct or interfere with the efforts of another group.

Organisation theorists agree that conflict is endemic to every organisation irrespective of its nature, objectives or the functions it is performing. At the individual level, conflict denotes certain incompatible response tendencies in an individual, e.g., goal conflict, role conflict, role ambiguity, etc. Such intra-individual conflict is often attributed to a mismatch between an individual's needs and expectations and an organisation's requirements or expectations. For instance, an employee's desire for autonomy often conflicts with the organisation's need for coordination or cooperation. Similarly, an employee may be expected by his senior manager to maximize output while the labour union may expect him to restrict or lower output. These dual sets of expectations often tend to cause incompatible response tendencies in the individual concerned and leave him in a state of anxiety, stress or conflict. When the term 'conflict' is extended to situations where two or more parties are involved, these situations lead to interpersonal, intergroup or even inter-organisational conflicts. Every organisation requires the coordination of human efforts or activities for the achievement of certain explicit goals or objectives, e.g., profit maximisation, productivity, efficiency, sound human relations, employee satisfaction, etc. Alongside such cooperation among employees or coordination of their work activities, it is to be expected that conflicts may arise among them due to incompatible goals, attitudes, emotions or behaviours that lead to disagreements or differences of opinion. Such conflicts between two persons or groups may take the forms of goal conflict (incompatible goals), cognitive conflict (incompatible ideas or thoughts), affective conflict (incompatible emotions and feelings), procedural conflict (differences in the processes or procedures to be used for resolving conflict), etc.

## 2.2 CONFLICT DEFINED

It is noteworthy that so far there has been no consensus among organisational behaviour experts on a specific definition of conflict. Therefore, conflict has been defined in various ways by different authors. In a review of conflict literature, Fink[1] found that 14 different criteria were used for simply distinguishing conflict from competition. Within the organisational conflict literature, Pondy[2] noted a number of divergent definitions that related to antecedent conditions, emotions, perceptions and conflictful behaviour. Instead of classifying any one of these specific definitions as conflict, Pondy recommended that conflict should be defined or understood in a broader sense to include all these phenomena.

Since conflict has been defined by experts in many different ways, it is quite natural that the term conflict has acquired divergent meanings. In spite of this, Robbins[3] noted a few common themes of conflict underlying most definitions of conflict: perception of conflict, opposition or incompatibility, and some form of interaction. A few common definitions of conflict which provide some indications as to the meaning of conflict may be presented here. As would be discussed in detail later, Pondy[4] defined the term 'conflict' so as to include (1) antecedent conditions, i.e., competition for resources, drives for autonomy, differences in subunit goals; (2) cognitive states of individuals, i.e., their awareness or perception of conflict situations; (3) affective states of individuals, i.e., tension, anxiety, hostility, etc.; (4) manifest conflict, i.e., changing behaviour from passive resistance to overt aggression; and (5) conflict aftermath, i.e., outcomes or consequences of conflict. Pondy viewed that these different aspects of conflict represent different stages in the development of a conflict episode and, therefore, it would be appropriate to describe conflict as a dynamic concept or process.

March and Simon[5] defined conflict as a breakdown in the standard mechanism of decision-making. When an individual is experiencing intra-individual conflict, he is unable to take any decision in the prevailing situation. Similarly, in the case of interpersonal, intra-group, inter-group conflict, there is a breakdown of the decision making mechanism since the individual concerned or the members of the group or the groups are not able to reconcile their conflicting views and reach any particular decision in the given situation.

Follett[6] defined conflict as the appearance of difference, difference of opinions, of interests. As soon as differences appear between the parties in conflict, these differences are perceived as friction-producing and are transformed into a conflict experience. Follett views integration as an orientation towards conflict management and as an attitude towards the potential for cooperation inherent in conflict situations.

"Conflict is a process in which an effort is purposefully made by one person or unit to block another that results in frustrating the attainment of the other's goals or the furthering of his or her interests".[7]

"Conflict is the process which begins when one party perceives that the other has frustrated or is about to frustrate some concern of his".[8]

Two systems (persons, groups, nations) are in conflict when they interact directly in such a way that the actions of one tend to prevent or compel some outcome against the resistance of the other".[9]

"Conflict refers to the struggle between incompatible or opposing needs, wishes, ideas, interests or people; it arises when individuals or groups encounter goals that both parties cannot obtain satisfactorily".[10]

"Conflict is the result of incongruent or incompatible relationships between members of a group or dyad".[11]

"Organisational conflict occurs when members engage in activities that are incompatible with those of colleagues within their network, members of other collectivities, or unaffiliated individuals who utilise the services or products of the organisation".[12]

"Conflict may be defined as any situation in which incompatible goals, attitudes, emotions and behaviours lead to disagreement or opposition between two or more parties".[13]

"Conflict is the process by which individuals or groups react to other entities that have frustrated or are about to frustrate their plans, goals, beliefs or activities".[14]

"Conflict refers to differences between individuals or groups relating to interests, beliefs, needs and values".[15]

Rahim[16] conceptualizes conflict as "an interactive process manifested in incompatibility, disagreement or dissonance within or between social entities (i.e., individual, group, organisation, etc.)". According to Rahim, conflict may occur when:

1. A party is required to engage in an activity that is incongruent with his or her needs or interests.

2. A party holds behavioural preferences, the satisfaction of which is incompatible with another person's implementation of his or her preferences.
3. A party wants some mutually desirable resource that is in short supply, such that the wants of everyone may not be satisfied fully.
4. A party possesses attitudes, values, skills and goals held by others that are salient in directing his or her behaviour but are perceived to be exclusive of the attitudes, values, skills, and goals held by the other(s).
5. Two parties have partially exclusive behavioural preferences regarding their joint actions.
6. Two parties are interdependent in the performance of functions or activities.

## 2.3 CHANGING VIEWS OF CONFLICT

The classical or traditional view of conflict assumed that conflict is inherently bad and must be avoided at all costs. The classicists believed that conflict indicated malfunctioning within the organisation, resulting from inadequate or poor communication, lack of faith or trust among employees, and the management's failure to respond to the needs or expectations of employees. According to the classicists, conflict is caused by troublemakers within the organisation, and it must be prevented and controlled through the use of legalistic forms of authority. They emphasize upon an organisational structure that would not allow conflicts to appear or arise at all. This can be achieved through a clear-cut delineation or specification of authority and responsibility, policies, procedures, rules, etc., thus leaving no scope for conflicts to arise in the organisation.

The human relations approach to management posited that conflict is a natural occurrence in all groups and organisations. This approach viewed conflict as inevitable in individual, group or organisational life. According to the human relations experts or neoclassicists, there is a basic incongruence or contradiction between the characteristics, needs or aspirations of adult, mature employees and the requirements of the modern formal oganisations. In other words, the formal organisation system is based upon certain premises or expectations which militate against the goals and aspirations of individuals and, therefore, cause dissatisfaction in them. The neo-classicists, therefore, emphasized upon the understanding of individual psychology, informal groups, informal leadership, democratic or participative style of leadership, and so on. Since conflict is perceived as both inevitable and functional in the organisation, the neo-classicists, therefore, emphasise upon the amicable resolution of conflicts with a view to achieving sound human relations and higher levels of productivity.

The interactionist or modern viewpoint goes further to state that conflict is not only inevitable in organisational life but also necessary and even desirable under certain specific circumstances. A certain degree of conflict must be encouraged by the group leader so as to keep the group viable, self-critical, and creative. However, conflicts must be controlled and kept within reasonable limits to avoid their dysfunctional effects. According to the modern organisational theorists, conflict is not always caused by troublemakers; rather, conflict is determined by structural factors and is integral to the nature of change. Thus, it would be inappropriate to classify conflict as being good or bad. The effects or consequences of conflict from the organisational viewpoint will depend upon whether such conflict is functional or dysfunctional. While functional conflict encourages the group to achieve its goals and improve its performance, dysfunctional conflict is destructive or harmful in nature and, it obstructs the attainment of group objectives or performance.

## 2.4 POSITIVE ASPECTS OF CONFLICT

The modern management thinkers and writers view that a minimum level of conflict is necessary in the organisation to keep its members, creative and innovative. Therefore, the current management thoughts or perspectives emphasize upon the management of conflict rather than its elimination so as to realise its potential benefits to the organisation and its members. Considered from this perspective, conflict serves the following useful functions in the organisation:

**Conflict stimulates change and creativity:** Conflict stimulates change within the organisation. In the face of conflict, the organisation's members tend to change their attitudes, beliefs or work habits in order to meet the demands or requirements of the new situation. In conflict, the managers, executives or employees display their creativity in identifying various alternative courses of action and in choosing the best alternative out of the whole lot. Conflicts among individuals and groups often result in innovations in organisation's policies, procedures, methods, etc.

**Conflict helps release the tension of group members:** When the individuals or group members are placed in conflict situations, they are able to ventilate their thoughts and emotions over certain organisational issues. This process helps the group members to reduce their stress or tension and thereby derive some psychological satisfaction.

**Conflict facilitates group cohesiveness:** It is noteworthy that while conflict increases antagonism or animosity between groups, it is also true that external threats and challenges cause the group members to unite among themselves and pull together as a unified entity or unit. Thus, inter-group conflict motivates the members to identify themselves with their own group and thereby increase their feelings of solidarity.

**Conflict enhances group and organisational effectiveness:** Conflicts can lead to search for new goals and means, and thus pave the way for new innovations within the organisation. Effective resolution of a conflict leads to greater openness and trust among group members and greater effectiveness of group processes and outcomes.

**Conflict creates challenges for individuals and groups:** The abilities or capacities of individuals and groups are often tested when they are confronted with conflict situations. If they are able to overcome such challenges, they derive immense satisfaction at the workplace and their motivation to work harder is enhanced.

**Conflict leads to higher and more constructive level of tension:** In the absence of conflict among individual employees or groups, they are likely to suffer from apathy, antagonism, stagnation and other weaknesses. In this situation of extremely low tension or stress level, the individuals or groups are not sufficiently motivated to achieve higher levels of productivity or performance in the organisation.

## 2.5 NEGATIVE ASPECTS OF CONFLICT

Just as conflicts offer certain potential benefits to the organisation and its members, conflicts in certain situations may prove to be detrimental to the attainment of individual goals or organisational productivity. The undesirable aspects of conflict at various levels in the organisation may be discussed as follows.

**Increased employee turnover:** If some of the organisation's employees are not able to resolve conflicts in their favour, they might ultimately leave the organisation. This phenomenon of employee turnover may result from both intra-individual and inter-individual conflict existing in the organisation. In this situation, the organisation will be the ultimate loser due to huge expenditure already incurred by it on selection, training and development of employees.

**Source of dissatisfaction:** Conflict is likely to be a source of great dissatisfaction for the losing party who develops feelings of injury, anger or humiliation. This situation will have an adverse impact on the moral and motivation of the concerned employees, and cause their productivity to suffer.

**Creation of mutual suspicion or trust:** It is often observed that the conflict situation leads to mutual suspicion or mistrust between the conflicting parties in the organisation. The concerned parties try to avoid interactions among themselves. This situation is likely to spoil the climate of trust, cooperation and harmonious work culture in the organisation.

**Displacement of goals:** Conflict consumes a great deal of time and energy of the parties concerned and distracts their attention from the principal goals or objectives of the organisation. Personal victory of the parties in conflict becomes their main concern rather than the organisational goals. This phenomenon has been described by Organisational behaviour experts as the displacement of organisational goals.

**Weakening of the organisation:** The persistence of conflicts may weaken the organisation due to its unintended consequences. If the management doesn't make concerted efforts to resolve conflicts or channelise them in the desired direction, then they may assume gigantic proportions at a later stage and become unmanageable. In any case, frequent occurrence of conflicts is not a healthy sign as it leads to an atmosphere of ill-will, distrust and lack of cooperation among the members of the organisation.

Thus, it can be concluded that conflict is not necessarily an evil in an organisation. According to the organisation theorists and experts, the functionality or dysfunctionality of conflict depends upon the way in which it is managed. If conflicts are managed amicably and to the satisfaction of the conflicting parties, this will bring tremendous benefits to the organisation. Although conflict may appear to threaten the emotional well-being of executives or employees, it may prove to be a positive factor in their personal development. It may generate a challenging situation for the managers and make them pool both material and human resources to accelerate the pace of development within the organisation. Conflicts, therefore, should not be viewed as bad in themselves. If handled properly, they can lead to problem-solving, creativity and innovations in the organisation.

## 2.6 INTENSITY OF CONFLICT AND PERFORMANCE

It is now clearly recognized that conflict in certain limits is essential to attain optimum performance of individuals, groups or the organisation. While little or no conflict leads to such unintended consequences as stagnation, weak decisions and ineffectiveness. Organisational conflict beyond certain limits will hamper productivity, employee's satisfaction and human relations in the organisation, etc. In the words of Rahim,[17] "too little conflict may encourage stagnation, mediocrity, and group think but too much conflict may lead to organisational disintegration". Therefore, it would be apt to say that too little or too much conflict are both dysfunctional from the viewpoint of organisational effectiveness. As viewed by Rahim and Bonama,[18] "a moderate amount of conflict, handled in a constructive manner, is essential for attaining and maintaining an optimum level of organisational effectiveness."The authors further argued that a moderate degree of substantial or task-related conflict (but not affective or emotional conflict) is required for achieving and maintaining optimum organisational effectiveness. In regard to the specific relationship between the intensity of conflict and performance, a low degree of conflict leads to low performance on account of monotonous, routine nature of jobs, apathy or complacency on the part of employees, lack of commitment to achieve higher productivity, etc. Therefore, a certain degree of conflict should be stimulated so as to enhance organisational activities or processes. As a consequence of conflict stimulation, performance increases and reaches a particular stage beyond which any further stimulation of conflict becomes counter-productive. If the intensity of conflict goes on increasing, it leads to decrease in performance and, therefore, conflict becomes dysfunctional. A high degree of conflict pulls down the performance level, disrupts the normal functioning of the organization, and ultimately leads to chaotic conditions in the organisation. This situation calls for resolution of conflict or, at least, reduction of conflicts. Schmidt[19] pointed out that managers spend about 20% of their time in handling conflicts. This fact signifies the importance of conflict management so as to enhance individual, group or organisational performance.

## 2.7 CONFLICT AS A DYNAMIC PROCESS

As noted by Pondy[20] and Walton and Dutton,[21] conflict in a dyadic relationship tends to occur in dyadic cycles. In other words, a conflict relationship between two individuals or other social units can be analysed as a sequence of conflict episodes. Each conflict episode is partially shaped by the results of previous episodes and in turn, leaves an aftermath that affects the course of succeeding episodes. Pondy[22] noted five stages of a conflict episode as can be seen from Figure 2.1. These stages are (1) latent conflict (antecedent conditions), (2) perceived conflict (cognition), (3) felt conflict (affective stages, e.g., stress, tension, anxiety, hostility, etc.), (4) manifest conflict (conflictful behaviour ranging from passive resistance to overt aggression), and (5) conflict aftermath (outcomes or consequences).

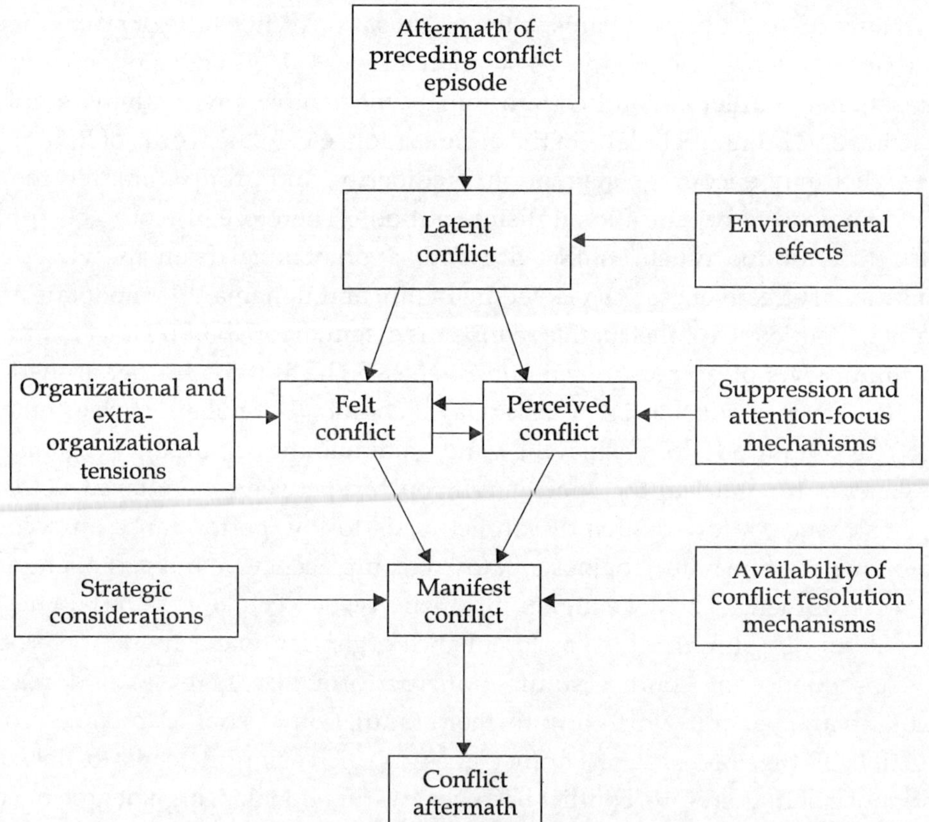


**Figure 2.1:** Potential sources of conflict and orientations

*Source:* L. R. Pondy, Organisational Conflict: Concepts and Models, Administrative Science, Quarterly, (12), 296-320.

**Latent conflict:** Although the literature on organisational conflict includes several underlying sources of conflict, Pondy highlighted three basic types of conflict:

(1) competition for scarce resources; (2) drives for autonomy; and (3) divergence of subunit goals. According to Pondy, competition forms the basis of conflict when the aggregate demands of participants for resources exceed the resources available. Autonomy needs form the basis of conflict when one party either seeks to exercise control over some activity that another party regards as his domain or seeks to insulate himself from such control. Goal divergence becomes the source of conflict when two parties or subunits need to cooperate on some joint activity but are unable to arrive at a consensus on some coordinated action.

**Perceived conflict:** Perceived conflict involves the cognitive states of individuals, i.e., their perception or awareness of conflict situations. It may be noted that conflict may sometimes be perceived when no latent conditions of conflict exist while it is also possible that latent conflict conditions may be present in a relationship without any of the participants perceiving that conflict. The fact that conflict may be perceived even though no latent conflict conditions exist in reality, is best explained by the "semantic model" of conflict. According to this model, conflict is said to result from the parties' misunderstanding of each other's position. It is argued that such conflicts can be resolved by improving communications between the parties. In fact, the semantic model has been the basis of a variety of management techniques aimed at improving interpersonal relations. The fact that some related conflicts fail to reach the level of awareness may be attributed to two important mechanisms: the suppression mechanism, and the attention focus mechanism.[23] Individuals tend to block conflicts that are only mildly threatening out of awareness. However, when the conditions relate to values central to the individual's personality, these conflicts really become strong threats and, therefore, must be acknowledged. The attention focus mechanism, on the other hand, is related more to organisational behaviour than to personal values. In view of time and capacity constraints, organisations are generally confronted with more conflicts than they can possibly handle. Therefore, every organisation focuses its attention only on those conflicts for which short-run, routine solutions are available, thus relegating frequently the less programmed conflicts to the background.

**Felt conflict:** It is important to distinguish between perceived conflict and felt conflict. A conflict may be perceived by the conflicting parties but it will have no effect on their emotions and feelings unless the conflict is personalized by them. There are two explanations for the personalization of conflict. In the first place, the organisation's members often experience anxiety due to the conflicting demands of efficient organisation and individual growth.[24] They may also experience anxiety arising from identity crisis or from extra-organisational pressures. The individuals often tend to ventilate these anxieties against suitable targets in order to maintain their internal equilibrium. In the second place, conflict becomes personalized when the entire personality of the individual is involved in his relationship with the other party. Hostile feelings giving rise to conflicts are commonly found in the intimate relations that characterize total institutions such as residential schools and colleges, families, etc.

**Manifest conflict:** Manifest conflict results when an individual member of an organisation consciously engages in behaviour that blocks another member's goal achievement. Manifest conflict may mean different varieties of conflictful behaviour ranging from passive resistance to overt aggression. It should be noted, however, that open aggression or violence as a form of manifest conflict in organisations is rare since it is usually prohibited by organisational norms. Organisational behaviour experts have observed the covert attempts to sabotage or block an opponent's plans through aggressive and defensive coalitions. They have also described the tactics of conflicts used by lower level participants such as apathy or rigid adherence to the rules, to resist mistreatment by the upper levels of the hierarchy.

**Conflict aftermath:** It may be reemphasized that each conflict episode is nothing but one of a sequence of such episodes that constitute the relationships among organisational participants. If the conflict is genuinely resolved to the satisfaction of all participants, the basis for a more cooperative relationship may be laid. On the other hand, if the conflict is merely suppressed but not resolved, the latent conditions of conflict may be aggravated and explode in more serious form until these are rectified or until the relationship dissolves. This legacy of a conflict episode is known as conflict aftermath.

## 2.8 SOURCES OF CONFLICT

Sources of conflict refer to the underlying factors that give rise to conflicts in an organisation. According to management experts, there are two sources of conflict: (1) internal sources; and (2) external sources. Internal sources of conflict refer to factors which are inherent within the organisation structure or framework e.g. clash of interests among organisation members, power relationship between two parties, etc. External sources, on the other hand, exist outside the limits or boundaries of the organisation. A good example of such external source of conflict exists in a situation where the government as the third and regulatory party enacts laws or formulates policies that favour one party to the conflict at the cost of the other.

Pareek[25] viewed that the sources of conflict "depend on the mode (mindset) of the parties involved in a situation - conflict escalation mode or conflict avoidance/ resolution mode". As shown in Table 2.1, there are seven main sources of interpersonal and intergroup conflicts which have implications in terms of possible perceptions of these sources, and the resultant orientations under the conflict-escalation and conflict-prevention or resolution modes. If the members of a group perceive their own concerns as more important, want their goals to be fulfilled at any cost, fight over available resources, have no faith or trust in people having power positions, stereotype the parties with conflicting ideologies, refuse to tolerate varied norms and try to dominate in the group, then naturally conflicts will escalate or increase in these situations. On the other hand, conflicts will not occur in the group if the group members value the broader group concerns, understand that different goals can be mutually complementary, consider their own goals as being subordinate to group goals or objectives, share resources with others, have trust or faith in persons having power positions, value or understand different ideologies, attempt to tolerate varied norms, have empathy for others and cooperate with them.

**Table 2.1:** Potential sources of conflict and orientations

| Potential source of conflict | Conflict-escalation mode | | Conflict-prevention/resolution mode | |
|---|---|---|---|---|
| | Perception | Resultant orientation | Perception | Resultant orientation |
| Concern with self | Narrow (own) | Short-term perspective | Broader | Long-term perspective |
| Different goals | Conflicting | Individualistic | Complementary | Superordination |
| Resources | Limited | Fighting | Expandable | Sharing |
| Power | Limited | Lack of trust | Shareable | Trust |
| Ideologies | Conflicting | Stereotyping | Varied | Understanding |
| Varied norms | Undesirable | Intolerance | Useful | Tolerance |
| Relationship | Depending | Dominance/ submission | Interdependent | Empathy and cooperation |

*Source*: U. Pareek, *Understanding Organisational Behaviour*, Oxford University Press, New Delhi, 2011, p. 416.

The organisation theorists or experts have suggested a number of sources of conflict. These sources of conflict increase the possibilities or chances of interpersonal or intergroup conflict in an organisation. As long as the sources of conflict tend to promote or stimulate constructive conflict, these can be allowed to exist in the organisation. However, when the symptoms of destructive conflict appear, necessary steps must be taken to eliminate or correct the sources of conflict. Some of the major sources of conflict may be discussed as follows.

**Competition for scarce resources:** It may be noted that resources in an organisation include finance, personnel, material resources, valuable information, power, authority, etc. These resources often become the basis for competition and conflict among the participants. As such conflicts often lead to unintended consequences, these can be avoided through the enlargement of the resource base such as increasing budgetary allocations, hiring additional personnel, increasing promotional avenues, etc.

**Ambiguous or overlapping jurisdictions:** Lack of clear-cut delegation of authority and responsibility relationships often creates scope for conflict among various position holders in the organisation. The officials often compete among themselves for resources and controlling powers. If such conflict becomes really problematic, then reorganisation can be immensely useful for clarifying or defining job boundaries.

**Communication breakdown:** The formal communication system is extremely complex and has many barriers which often provoke conflict. If the two-way communication flow is disrupted or interrupted in some way, it is likely to lead to mistrust and misunderstanding among the members of the organisation. Therefore, the channels of communication must be clearly defined to ensure smooth flow of information, both vertically and horizontally.

**Time pressure:** Although time pressure or deadlines may lead to prompt performance of employees, these deadlines can trigger destructive emotional reactions too. Therefore, while imposing such deadlines for the completion of specific jobs by employees, managers must consider individual employees' capabilities and their ability to cope with emergency situations.

**Unreasonable policies, procedures or rules:** Unreasonable policies, rules, procedures, etc., often lead to conflicts between the seniors and their subordinates. Therefore, the managers must try to convey an impression of fair play to their subordinates and try to correct extremely unfair decisions before these lead to undesirable consequences.

**Status differentials:** Hierarchical differences among managers, executives and employees often lead to interpersonal and intergroup conflicts in the organisation. However, the managers can avoid such conflicts through the appreciation of subordinates' ideas, suggestions and feelings. A democratic work culture can be developed through the participation of subordinate employees in the decision-making process.

**Personality clashes:** Personality clashes among participants are bound to exist due to differences in individual personality, culture, background, etc. These differences contain ample scope for conflict at both the vertical and the horizontal levels of the organisation. Therefore, the practical remedy for such personality clashes is to separate such conflicting parties and reassign them to new jobs or different jobs.

**Unrealised expectations:** Conflicts arise among individual participants due to non-fulfilment of their expectations or aspirations in the organisation. These conflicts can be avoided by making people realise how far their expectations from the organisation are truly justified or realistic. Any unrealistic expectation can be corrected through open discussions with the concerned parties before they trigger undesirable conflicts.

## 2.9 ISSUES OF CONFLICT

While the underlying sources of conflict may be attributed to both organisational and individual factors, the issues of conflict are manifestations of real conflict situations and are more specific in nature. As suggested by organisational behaviour experts, most of the conflict issues in organisations can be classified under the following six headings: status inconsistencies, conflicting goals, overlapping authority, task interdependence, incompatible reward systems, and scarce resources. All these six types of conflict-producing situations or factors have been presented in Figure 2.2.

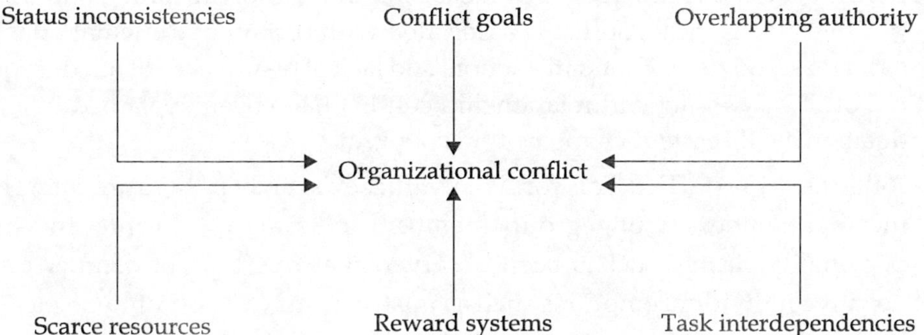


**Figure 2.2:** Sources of organisational conflict

*Source*: U. Pareek, *Understanding Organisational Behaviour*, Oxford University Press, New Delhi, 2011, p. 418.

Status inconsistencies signify that individuals or groups enjoy higher organisational status than others due to such factors as job position in the organisational hierarchy, expertise, access to resources, ability to identify with the top management, etc. These status differentials contain ample score for conflict in the organisation. In a business organisation, for example, the marketing group is considered to be very important as it generates revenue for the organisation. On the other hand, other groups such as the human resource (HR) group, the research and development (R&D) group, etc., are not considered so much significant as their work activities are not directly related to profits. Conflicting goals of various organisation members may be the cause of conflicts as different members will work at cross purposes for achieving their individual interests and will lose sight of the broader organisational objectives or missions. Similarly, when two or more managers exercise authority over the same activities, this will lead to conflict between the managers and the employees. Task interdependence among different groups or group members may also lead to conflicts. If a particular group or person is not able to finish his part of the task, it will affect the completion of the entire task, thus causing conflict among the parties involved. Some conflicts also arise due to incompatible evaluation or reward systems as the organisation's members often feel that they deserve more than what they actually received.

## 2.10 CLASSIFICATION OF CONFLICT

Conflict has been classified into various types by the management theoreticians. A major form of classification of conflict is as follows:

1. **Task conflict:** It refers to disagreements among group members over the task contents, work goals, distribution of resources, interpretation of facts and procedures,[26] etc. Task conflict thus includes differences in ideas, opinions or

viewpoints regarding task related and organisational issues. Task conflict has been found to have positive effects in organisations in terms of the quality of debate within a team, quality of ideas, and innovation. In spite of having these positive effects, task conflict is associated with certain detrimental effects such as increased anxiety,[27] job satisfaction, and lack of teamwork.[28] The consequences of both task conflict and relationship conflict have been explained in a greater detail in a subsequent chapter of this book.

2. **Relationship conflict:** This form of conflict exists when there are interpersonal incompatibilities among group members in terms of tension, anxiety, and personality clashes. It has been observed that this type of conflict produces negative individual emotions such as mistrust, anxiety, resentment, etc.[29] It also leads to tension, frustration, and the fear of being rejected by other team members.[30]
3. **Process conflict:** This type of conflict refers to differences arising among group members over delegation of authority, individual members' responsibilities for the performance of specific tasks, and the ways in which various tasks are to be completed. Process conflict has been found to be associated with lower employee morale, decreased productivity,[31] and poor performance of teams.[32]

In addition to the aforesaid basis of classification of conflict, some organisation theorists have made attempts to distinguish between functional and dysfunctional conflicts as described below:

1. **Functional or constructive conflict:** The interactionist's viewpoint regarding conflict does not suggest that all conflicts are beneficial for organisations and its members. Rather, those conflicts that help in achieving group objectives and improving group performance are functional or constructive forms of conflict. According to Robbins,[33] functional conflict is the conflict that supports the goals of the group and improves its performance. In fact, functional conflict helps foster healthy competition among group members and thereby motivates them to work harder and produce higher levels of output. Thus, functional conflict is beneficial for the task group, its members, and the organisation as a whole.
2. **Dysfunctional or destructive conflict:** Dysfunctional conflicts refer to those conflicts that hinder group performance and the attainment of organisational goals. Although conflict is inevitable in organisational life and can prove to be beneficial on some occasions, it can have detrimental effects if it is not handled properly. Conflict can affect interpersonal relationships and disrupt the smooth exchange of information, ideas, and resources within groups as well as between departments. Dysfunctional conflict has been found to hamper organisational performance and can lead to decreased productivity.

## 2.11 LEVELS OF CONFLICT

Conflicts may be envisaged at various levels in an organisation. Conflicts may exist within one individual, between two individuals or between two or more groups within an organisation. These conflicts, have been described as intra-individual, inter-individual, intra-group and inter-group conflicts, respectively. In addition to these different forms of intra-organisational conflict, conflicts may also exist between two or more organisations. These are known as inter-organisational conflicts. Intra-individual conflict takes place when an individual is confronted with a problem in decision making. Such conflict often involves some form of goal conflict, role conflict, or cognitive conflict. Intra-individual conflict may arise due to three types of goal conflict: approach-approach conflict, avoidance-avoidance conflict and approach-avoidance conflict. While the approach-approach conflicts and the avoidance-avoidance conflicts do not pose serious problems for individuals, the approach-avoidance conflicts need to be very carefully handled or managed. Intra-individual conflict may also arise due to role conflict within the organisation. There are three major types of role conflict: conflict between the person and the role, intra-role conflict and inter-role conflict. All these aspects of goal conflict as well as role conflict have been discussed in detail at a later stage.

Intra-individual conflicts have also been attributed to cognitive dissonance which takes place due to incongruencies in an individual's attitudes, thoughts, values, etc. It has been observed that the intensity of intra-individual conflict increases if two or more coping mechanisms are available for handling that conflict, if their positive and negative outcomes are approximately equal, or if the source of conflict is considered significant. In real-life situations, many of the important personal decisions made by individuals are affected by both goal conflict and cognitive conflict. As viewed by Sharma,[34] the greater the goal conflict before decision, the greater will be the cognitive dissonance following the decision.

Inter-individual conflict takes place when at least two persons belonging to the same group or different groups are in conflict. When two or more persons of the same group are involved in conflict, it is often described as intra-group conflict. If, for instance, some members of a group are not observing certain group norms, this may be negatively viewed by the other group members, thus giving rise to intra-group conflict. Inter-individual conflict may also develop when two or more members of different groups do not agree over the meaning or implications of a particular organisational policy, procedure, rule, etc. Let us suppose that there are two individuals of the same department, and they are placed in senior-subordinate relationship. Conflict between these two individuals will be considered intra-departmental or intra-group conflict. If these two individuals are of the supervisory and non-supervisory groups, conflict between them will be regarded as inter-individual conflict which, if blown up further, may lead to intergroup conflict too.

Intergroup conflict occurs when two or more units or groups in the same organisation are involved in conflict. Intergroup conflicts within an organisation are often noticed in the form of line and staff conflict, labour-management disputes, etc. In such conflicts, the groups are found to focus only on their self-interest, refuse to listen to one another's viewpoints, do not have faith in each other, and so on. An intergroup conflict may assume serious proportions and lead to an organisation-wide conflict if necessary steps are not taken to localise it. Then, the whole organisation will be affected by this conflict syndrome. Inter-organisational conflict takes place when a particular organisation is involved in conflict with one or more organisations in the environment. A business enterprise may be engaged in a cut-throat competition with other enterprises manufacturing the same product or supplying the same service to customers. A political party is engaged in electoral fight with other political parties at the time of elections. These inter-organisational conflicts may lead to intra-organisational conflicts too.

### 2.11.1 Intra-individual Conflict

Intra-individual conflict arises primarily due to incongruence between individual goals and organisational goals. As an individual joins an organisation, he seeks to satisfy not only his economic needs but also many other higher level psychosocial needs. As he works for the organisation, he elaborates his behaviour beyond the formally required one. Gradually, however, he finds that he is not able to fulfil his individual needs and aspirations within the organisational setting. This is because there is often a mismatch between his individual needs and the rewards provided to him by the organisation. An individual's need or desire for autonomy, for example, is not consistent with the organisation's requirement for rationality and coordination. As argued by the individual proponents, this incongruence between individual goals and organisational goals is due to the basic characteristics of a formal organisation that inevitably violates the basic given of his healthy and mature personality. This incongruence between individual goals and organisational goals is often a conflict-producing situation, at least, for some of the individuals working in the organisation.

Intra-individual conflicts also develop because the individuals feel dissatisfied with the alternatives provided to them by the organisation. As viewed by March and Simon,[35] individual dissatisfaction is the outcome of disparity between aspiration levels and achievements. The greater the disparity between aspiration levels and achievements, the higher is the probability of intra-individual conflict. A proper match between the two depends upon favourable environmental conditions. If the environmental conditions are good, individuals will be able to satisfy their needs or aspirations. If, however, the environment is not conducive, a gap or mismatch between aspiration levels and achievements develops, thus causing intra-individual conflicts in the organisation.

**Goal conflict:** Intra-individual conflict often arises due to two or more competing goals or due to a goal having both positive and negative features. The Organisational behaviour experts have generally identified three types of goal conflict as discussed below.

*Approach-approach conflict*: This type of goal conflict refers to a situation where the individual is motivated to approach two or more positive but exclusive goals. Thus, the individual can choose only one goal at the cost of the other. If, for example, both personal goals and organisational goals are attractive to the members, they will choose between these two sets of goals quickly and resolve their conflicts. Similarly, an executive or an employee may have to choose between accepting a promotion within the same organisation and taking up an attractive job in another organisation. Another example is the case of a college graduate who has been offered two excellent job opportunities and he has to make a choice between the two. Although these situations often cause some anxiety or conflict in the individual, these are quickly resolved.

Approach-approach conflict can be explained in terms of the famous theory of cognitive dissonance. Dissonance refers to the psychological discomfort or conflict that is created in individuals when they are faced with two equally attractive goals or decision alternatives. According to the theory of cognitive dissonance, the individual facing or experiencing dissonance will be highly motivated to reduce it or eliminate it. The individual will try to avoid situations or information that are likely to increase such dissonance within himself. For instance, the college graduate provided with two attractive job opportunities will experience dissonance and will also actively try to reduce it. He may rationalise that one job is really better than the other one and make the choice accordingly. After making such choice, the individual will try to remain convinced that this is the right choice and will avoid any argument, evidence or information to the contrary.

*Approach-avoidance conflict*: In this type of conflict situation, an individual is motivated to approach a goal and at the same time, he is motivated to avoid it as this single goal has both positive and negative features. Organisational goals often have positive and negative aspects for members and, therefore, tend to cause greater degree of conflicts in them. It may be mentioned that the positive features or aspects of a particular organisational goal appear to be stronger from a distance than the negative aspects. However, as the individual reaches nearer to the goal, the negative features become pronounced and cause him to hesitate or stop progressing any further. For example, the top level managers might have developed some strategic plan or goal as a part of long-term planning. However, as the time approaches to commit resources and implement the plan, the negative consequences appear to be more and more pronounced. In this situation, the top level managers are likely to reach a point where approach equals avoidance and thus experience a great deal of internal stress and conflict.

*Avoidance-avoidance conflict*: This type of goal conflict refers to a situation in which an individual is motivated to avoid two or more negative but mutually exclusive goals. Avoidance-avoidance conflict is usually easily resolved as the individual provided with two negative goals may not choose any of them or simply leave the situation. In certain cases, however, the individual concerned may be unable to leave the situation. This is true of certain persons such as patients in a hospital, inmates in a prison, members of armed services, and so on. These circumstances may continue to cause great deal of approach avoidance conflict within the individuals concerned.

**Role conflict:** A role is defined as a position that has expectations evolving from the established norms.[36] According to Sarbin,[37] "a role is a set of activities expected of a person holding a particular position in a group or organisation". People who have these expectations regarding the behaviour of the role player are regarded as members of the role set. In the organisational context, managers are part of the role sets of their subordinates. The role expectations from subordinates may be communicated by their senior managers in the form of instructions regarding desirable work related behaviour, undesirable behaviour to be avoided, allocation of resources, performance evaluation, etc. As and when such communications regarding role expectations are distorted, role ambiguity and role conflict may result.

Role ambiguity takes place when an individual has no clarity regarding the role expectations which other members are having about him. For example, role ambiguity arises either when the manager has not communicated the subordinate's duties properly or the subordinate is not able to understand his superior. In this situation, the subordinate is not clear about his duties or responsibilities and, therefore, the consequent role ambiguity can be extremely stressful for him.

Role conflict occurs when an individual in a role is not able to fulfil the expectations of other members of the role set. A supervisor, for example, is often expected to fulfil the expectations of both the managers and the workers. However, he cannot comply with such conflicting expectations due to some reason or the other. Such role conflict is a potential source of tension or stress that can lead to job dissatisfaction, decreased confidence in one's superior, or a desire to avoid the unpleasant work situation.

There are four kinds of role conflict which may arise in the organisational setting. These may be discussed as follows:

1. **Intra-sender role conflict:** This conflict occurs when an individual employee is asked to do a certain job which he is not capable of doing or when the material resources and time allocated are not sufficient to complete the job. A purchasing agent, for example, may be asked by his superior to buy materials which are not easily available in the market and is also asked not to purchase such materials in the black market.
2. **Inter-sender role conflict:** It is quite possible that different members of a role set may have different and conflicting expectations from a particular member

in the organisation. While, for example, a superior might ask the supervisor to exercise strict control over his subordinates, the subordinates often expect liberal supervision from the supervisor. These dual sets of role expectations can be a source of great deal of role conflict in the individual member concerned.

3. **Inter-role conflict:** Such conflict arises when an individual is expected to fulfil the requirements of multiple roles that are to be played at the same time. A company executive may have to work for unusually long hours at the workplace which may cause his family members to be upset about it.
4. **Person-role conflict:** This type of role conflict occurs when a person is expected to do a particular job which is incompatible with his personality and value system. A production executive or an employee with sufficient expertise and capability may be appointed to lead a new production team. Although he is expected by his superiors to exercise strict control over his team members, he may be unable to do so as it goes against his personal ethics or value system.

Thus, it can be stated that role conflicts and role ambiguities always do exist in the organisational setting. This can cause great deal of stress and conflict among individual members and affect their attitudes and behaviours adversely. Therefore, the managers must make efforts to resolve or manage such conflicts by maintaining effective two-way communication among the members of particular role sets.

### 2.11.2 Inter-personal Conflict

Although interpersonal conflict has been attributed to a number of factors, such conflict arises primarily from divergent choices made by different individuals in the organisation. Each individual has a separate, acceptable alternative course of action, and different individuals prefer different alternative courses for choices. At one extreme, conflicts are embedded in divergent and incompatible interests among organisation members. Any victory or gain for one party means defeat or loss for the other party. In game theory, this limiting case is described as a zero-sum game. At the other extreme, conflicts may be inherent, indifferent or divergent interests of individuals which are not necessarily incompatible. It is quite common that people often have different opinions over certain issues or facts regarding the functioning of the organisation.

There are a number of factors which contribute to interpersonal conflicts in organisations. These may be discussed as follows:

**Role incompatibility:** Interpersonal conflict arises from both intra-individual role conflict and intergroup conflict in the organisation. Although the managers' functions or tasks in modern organisations are highly interdependent, it is sometimes found that their individual roles are incompatible or conflicting. For example, the production manager and the sales manager are supposed to work in harmony with each other. In spite of this interdependent relationship, the production manager may try to minimise costs by maintaining minimum inventory level which hampers the sales manager's efforts to make timely delivery of goods to customers and thereby maximize sales and sales revenue. This conflict arising from role incompatibility has to be resolved by top management or systems development manager through advanced information technology.

**Informational factors:** Interpersonal conflict may arise due to communication breakdown in the organisation. This may be due to the fact that the conflicting parties are either using different information or having misinformation about certain organisational issues. As they have different viewpoints or different perceptions of certain facts or issues, conflicts are bound to arise among them.

**Competition for scarce resources:** Conflicts may develop among individuals when they compete for limited or scarce resources. Managers of individual departments may compete for maximum possible budgetary allocations. Two or more employees may compete for a single higher level promotion. Similarly, common telecommunication facilities such as telephone, fax, etc., may be available for a number of departments or executives. These different situations contain ample scope for interpersonal conflict in the organisation.

**Differences in status:** It is noteworthy that each job holder or position holder enjoys a certain degree of status or importance in the organisation. These status differentials often tend to obstruct interpersonal interactions and free flow of communication among various position holders within the organisational system. A higher level official or executive, for example, may consider it below his status to approach a junior level executive to seek some information or clarification. This status difference blocks communication and thereby leads to interpersonal conflict.

**Differences in perceptions:** Individuals perceive the same fact, information or situation in different ways due to the role of various perceptual factors. Each individual tends to selectively perceive or focus his attention upon certain limited items out of the whole lot of information available, and then interpret such limited items or information in a way that suits him. Thus, it is not surprising that the same basic facts or information may produce divergent perceptions in the minds of different persons and thus cause interpersonal conflict.

**Differences in value systems:** Individuals may have misunderstanding among themselves on account of differences in their upbringing, cultural and family traditions, and value systems. These differences often lead to disagreements that might become highly sensitive and take on moral overtones. A production manager may, for example, suggest that the product quality ought to be lowered so as to increase profits whereas the marketing manager views it as unethical.

**Environmental stress:** The present-day environments are characterized by depleting resources, competitive pressures and a higher degree of instability or uncertainty. These stressful environmental factors can lead to conflict among individual members of the organisation. For example, a top management decision to engage managers to support a new night shift work in the factory or office may lead to conflicts or infighting among them due to the fear of a possible disruption of family routines and social relations.

Irrespective of the sources of interpersonal conflict, it must be handled or resolved in a constructive manner so as to create an atmosphere of harmony, mutual trust and openness in the organisation. Although a number of conflict resolution techniques or methods have been suggested by organisational behaviour experts, the major ones include counselling, effective communication, win-win negotiation and transactional analysis (TA).This will not only minimise the dysfunctional aspects of conflict but also lead to significant increase in the morale, motivation, and productivity of organisation members.

### 2.11.3 Intra-group Conflict

Intra-group conflict involves clashes or differences among the group members over organisational issues which affect the group's processes and outcomes. Intra-group conflict may arise when the group faces a novel problem, or when new values are imported from the social environment into the group, or when a person's extra-group role comes into conflict with his intra-group role.[38] It is quite common that individuals act as members of different groups for achieving different purposes or objectives. Conflicts between different persons may gradually lead to an intra-group conflict. If the intra-group conflict is of serious nature, the members of the group may be divided in two groups with the result that the intra-group conflict is converted into inter-group conflict.

It may be noted that intra-group conflict is similar to interpersonal conflict except for the fact that the individuals involved in the conflict situation belong to a common group. Intergroup conflicts are commonly observed in family-run businesses especially when the succession issue becomes very crucial due to the retirement or death of the owner-founder. The successful continuity of the family business depends on the mutual respect shown by family members towards one another, their willingness to accept work rules or responsibilities according to the business requirements, and their ability to manage conflicts.

### 2.11.4 Inter-group Conflict

Intergroup conflict refers to differences between different groups in an organization. Some common examples of intergroup conflict are union-management conflict, line-staff conflict, conflict between production and marketing teams, etc. According to March and Simon,[39] intergroup conflicts arise when there is existence of a positive felt need for joint decision making, or when there is differentiation of goals (i.e., different persons have different views regarding goals), or when there is difference in the perceptions of reality. These conditions or factors are considered essential prerequisites for intergroup conflicts to arise in an organisation. In addition to these three factors, intergroup conflict may also be caused by certain other factors such as task ambiguity, differentiation in work orientation, organisational reward structure, and status struggles. All these factors may be discussed as follows.

**Need for joint decision-making:** The need for joint decision-making contains ample scope for conflict among different groups or departments in an organisation. Such need for joint decision-making has been attributed to certain organisational factors such as sharing of resources, task interdependence, and the need for coordination. Most organisations have limited resources at their disposal, and these resources have to be shared by different groups or departments. Conflicts often arise because every department or group competes for a higher share of organisational resources such as budget funds, personal space, support services, etc. Task interdependence among different groups in certain areas such as fixation of work schedules, sharing of office facilities, etc., often give rise to inter-departmental conflicts. The more diverse the objectives, policies, personnel and priorities of the inter-departmental groups, the more will be the conflicts among such groups. Coordination at the top level requires inter-departmental cooperation and joint decision making by various department heads. If they are not able to pull their resources, expertise and knowledge effectively, conflicts are likely to arise.

**Difference in goals:** The process of organising leads to division of work and to the creation of specialised departments on the basis of functions, products, territories served, etc. As these departments or subunits of the organisation become specialised, they tend to develop divergent goals and may not be able to relate their group goals to the overall goals or objectives of the organisation. These different goals can lead to different expectations of members of each department or group and thereby lead to conflicts among such groups. In addition, it may be noted that the pattern of interaction among the group members may have its effects on goal differentiation. If, for example, the members of a group do not interact frequently, differentiation of goals is bound to occur. However, if the group members interact quite frequently, they are likely to share some goals with the members of other groups. In this case, the sources of intergroup conflict are minimised.

**Difference in perceptions:** Another important cause of intergroup conflict is difference in perceptions of members of different groups in the organisation. People tend to have differences in perceptions due to differences in their value system, family and cultural background, education, training, etc. People may also have different perceptions if adequate information is not shared with some persons, or if the flow of communication is not smooth. The different perceptions of reality have also been attributed to such other factors as different time horizons or perspectives of different groups, status incongruencies among groups, inaccurate perceptions, etc.

**Task ambiguity:** Task ambiguity refers to a situation in which there is lack of clarity as to which group is responsible for certain work activities. This situation frequently leads to hostility or clashes between different work groups. Task ambiguity often arises due to the growth and expansion of organisational activities, the changes in structure, technology and processes resulting therefrom, the rapid changes in the external environment, etc. For instance, conflict may arise due to task ambiguity when one group attempts to exercise undue control over organisational activities, or claims credit for desirable activities and disclaims its responsibility for undesirable activities. Similarly, conflict occurring due to task ambiguity may be noticed in the recruitment of new employees. It may be noted that both the personnel department and the specific functional departments such as production, finance, marketing, etc., have responsibilities in the recruitment and selection of new employees. Conflicts often arise as to which department has the final authority to decide upon the selection of employees and also execute such employee selection decisions.

**Differences in work orientation:** It has been observed that employees of different functional departments differ widely in the ways in which they handle their work activities and deal with others. First, the functional groups or departments differ in their time perspectives. For example, the research and development group has long range goals or objectives as compared to the manufacturing, marketing, or finance group. Second, the functional groups or departments vary greatly in their goals and objectives. While, for example, the research and development department has much broader and less quantifiable goals such as developing new products, making new innovations, etc., the manufacturing department has more specific production targets in terms of volume of output, cost savings, permissible level of defectives, etc. Third, people in different functional departments differ quite significantly in their interpersonal orientations or approaches. While the research and development (R&D) department encourages informal social relations and an organic structure, these features might prove to be dysfunctional in the production department.

Thus, conflicts are likely to arise between different work groups as the differences in their goals, time and interpersonal orientations become more and more pronounced. These differences in work orientation lead the groups to misunderstand the behaviour of other groups and thus are frustrated with their behaviour.

**Organisational reward structure:** Intergroup conflict may also arise due to the ways in which an organisation evaluates group performance and distributes economic and non-economic rewards. If the reward structure is such that it allows only one group to achieve its goals at the cost of other groups, it will naturally lead to intergroup conflicts and power struggle.[40] For example, the top management of an organisation may provide rewards or incentives only to the marketing department for enhanced sales and sales revenues, and ignore the contributions made by other departments such as production, advertisement, etc. This will lead other departments or groups to develop conflicts with the marketing department and even try to sabotage its marketing efforts.

**Status struggles:** Conflicts arise among different groups when one group attempts to enhance its status, and it is viewed by another group as a threat to its position in the organisational status hierarchy. One group may also feel that it is not being equitably treated in comparison with other groups in terms of job assignments, working conditions, rewards, privileges, etc. Personnel departments, for example, often feel that they are being inequitably treated in relation to production, finance, and marketing departments.

## 2.12 NEGOTIATION

As it has been observed earlier, conflict can have functional or dysfunctional effects in an organisation depending upon its management. According to the management experts, a minimum level of conflict is necessary to enhance organisational effectiveness. Thus, various conflict resolution techniques can be used to reduce or resolve conflict if conflict is too high while conflict stimulation techniques or methods can be utilised to increase conflict if the conflict level is too low. Another approach to the management of conflict involves examining different conflict handling methods or modes, and their impact on various aspects of individual, group, and organisational effectiveness. All these different aspects of conflict management will be discussed in the next chapter.

In the present section, an attempt has been made to throw light on the negotiation skills and processes that have moved from the field of industrial relations to the forefront of managerial skills. Although some organisation experts have viewed that there are similarities between negotiation strategies and conflict management, it may be noted that negotiation often moves beyond resolving conflicts and can be utilised as an effective managerial skill for achieving both individual and organisational success. Walton and McKersie define negotiation as "deliberate interaction of two or more social units in an attempt to reach a jointly acceptable position on some conflicting issues.[41] Negotiation is the process through which two or more parties make attempts to reach some common agreement although they have different preferences. Neale and Bazerman[42] viewed that negotiation in its various forms is a common mechanism for resolving differences and allocating resources. As defined by them, negotiation is a "decision making process among interdependent parties who do not share identical preferences. It is through negotiations that the parties decide what each will give and take in their relationship."Although some organisation experts have noted that there are similarities between negotiation strategies and conflict management.[43] Negotiation can move beyond conflict resolution and can be useful as a managerial skill for achieving personal and organisational success. In fact, the negotiation process pervades the interactions of almost all members in groups and organisations. Managers negotiate with employees, peers and bosses; sales persons negotiate with customers; purchasing agents negotiate with suppliers, and so on. In the present-day organisations, negotiation skills have become very critical as the members have to interact with various colleagues with a view to carrying on various team works and processes.

**Bargaining strategies:** Walton and McKersie[44] used the terms negotiation and bargaining interchangeably and suggested that there are two general approaches to negotiation: distributive bargaining and integrative bargaining. The essence of distributive bargaining is that it operates under zero-sum conditions, i.e., the gain made by one party is at the cost of the other party. In other words, distributive bargaining assumes a "fixed pie" and focuses on negotiating over who gets what share of the fixed pie. Distribution bargaining is essentially concerned with the distribution of benefits such as wages, bonus, commission, etc., between individuals or parties. Research studies have shown that teams, more than individuals, developed mutually beneficial trade-offs among issues in the negotiation and discovered compatible interests. However, the common assumption that teams have a comparative advantage over individual opponents in negotiations was not supported by the actual findings.[45] The conflict management strategies of accommodating, forcing, compromising, and avoiding tend to be associated with a distributive negotiation strategy.

As against distributive bargaining, integrative bargaining represents an alternative approach that seeks to "expand the pie" in order to find win-win outcomes.[46] Integrative bargaining is generally concerned with issues of common interest to both the parties such as allocation of work, design of more satisfying or challenging jobs, provisions for greater employee freedom and control over work, quality of work life, etc. The integrative approach is based on collaborating strategy(rather than on accommodating, forcing, compromising or avoiding strategy) and requires the negotiator to utilise the skills as described below:

1. **Establishing superordinate goals:** In the negotiation process, the establishment of superordinate goals involves developing and adopting certain common goals and objectives that cannot be achieved without the cooperation of the parties involved. In fact, these common goals and objectives cannot be attained by any one party individually and supersede the individual goals of the parties involved. In this process, the negotiating parties feel motivated or driven towards achieving those mutually beneficial goals and objectives rather than focusing on their individual goals.
2. **Separating the people from the problem:** Another major way to arrive at a mutually accepted solution is to separate the substantive negotiation issues from the issues related to the inter-personal relationships between the parties and handle these two sets of issues separately. The negotiators should engage themselves in the bargaining process in a constructive manner and deal with the substantive problems or issues rather than attacking each other.
3. **Focusing on interests, not on positions:** People in negotiating positions tend to be driven by their ego. In addition, the negotiators have been seen focusing

only on their stated positions which often obscures their real needs or wants. Therefore, instead of focusing only on the negotiators' respective positions, a much more effective strategy would be to highlight the underlying purposes and needs that caused them to take these positions.

4. **Inventing options for mutual gain:** It is observed that devising optimal solutions in the presence of a rival often tends to narrow down people's horizon of thinking. The search for the best possible solution inhibits their creativity especially when the stakes involved are too high. These obstacles can be overcome by establishing a forum in which a wide variety of possible solutions can be generated before deciding about the most ideal one to be chosen.
5. **Using objective criteria:** The negotiating parties should discuss the terms and conditions of the negotiation in terms of some reference standard such as established custom, law, expert opinion, etc. This will divert the negotiators' attention away from their personal whims or desires. The use of objective criteria of negotiation will ensure that the parties are not required to yield to each other's wishes and thereby, it becomes easier for them to arrive at a reasonable solution.

The negotiation process comprises five steps:

1. preparation and planning;
2. definition of ground rules;
3. clarification and justification;
4. bargaining and problem-solving; and
5. closure and implementation.[47]

In the first place, it is necessary for the negotiator to do some homework before the negotiation process begins. He should have a clear-cut understanding about such important aspects as the nature of the conflict, the background facts leading up to the present negotiation, the parties in conflict, their perception of the conflict, etc. In any case, the negotiator must know precisely what he expects from such negotiation. If, for example, a purchasing agent seeks to get a significant cost reduction from a supplier, he must ensure that this goal remains paramount throughout the negotiation process and doesn't get overshadowed by other issues. It is also equally important to know about the other party's goals and objectives so that a suitable strategy can be designed to counter the opponent's arguments.

After having done necessary groundwork and developing an appropriate strategy, the negotiator starts defining the ground rules or procedures with the other party over the negotiation itself. These ground rules relate to the persons or parties to act as negotiators, the place of negotiation, specific issues of negotiation, time constraint, if any, etc.

When the ground rules of negotiation have been defined, and the parties have exchanged their initial proposals or demands, they will explain, clarify or justify their initial demands and also try to educate each other about how each of them arrived at their initial or original demands. At this point, each party may also provide the other party with any documentary proof that helps him support his position.

The next stage of the negotiation process involves the actual bargaining and problem solving, i.e., the actual give-and-take in trying to reach an agreement. At this stage, necessary concession will be made by both the parties till they reach a point of compromise or agreement.

The final step in the negotiation process involves formalizing the agreement that has been worked out and developing any procedures that are required for implementing such agreement. All the specific details must be put in black and white in the form of a formal contract.

### 2.12.1 Traditional Versus Modern Negotiation Approaches

In the process of negotiating, the managers and other members of an organisation have certain prejudices that prevent them from negotiating rationally and get the most out of a conflict situation. These biased negotiation approaches commonly followed by managers and non-managers have been described as traditional negotiation approaches. As stated by Luthans,[48] the research findings have revealed certain common mistakes made by negotiators following the traditional approach to negotiation as mentioned below:

1. Negotiators tend to be overly affected by the frame or form of presentation of information in a negotiation.
2. Negotiators tend to non-rationally escalate commitment to a previously selected course of action when it is no longer the most reasonable alternative.
3. Negotiators tend to assume that their gain must come at the expense of the other party and thereby miss opportunities for mutually beneficial trade-off between the parties.
4. Negotiator judgements tend to be anchored on irrelevant information, such as an initial offer.
5. Negotiators tend to rely on readily available information.
6. Negotiators tend to fail to consider information that is available by focusing on the opponent's perspective.
7. Negotiators tend to be overconfident concerning the likelihood of attaining outcomes that favour the individual(s) involved.[49]

It is significant to point out that the traditional approaches to negotiation are being challenged by contemporary management experts who have suggested certain alternative negotiation skills. These contemporary negotiation approaches have been classified into two different categories in terms of degree of risk to the users as given below:[50]

1. **Low risk negotiation techniques**
   (a) Flattery – subtle flattery usually works best but the standards may differ by age, sex, and cultural factors.
   (b) Addressing the easy point first – this helps build trust and momentum for the tougher issues.
   (c) Silence – this can be effective in gaining concessions, but one must be careful not to provoke anger or frustration in opponents.
   (d) Inflated opening position – this may elicit a counter offer that shows the opponent's position or may shift the point of compromise.
   (e) "Oh, poor me" – this may lead to sympathy but could also bring out the killer instinct in opponents.
2. **High risk negotiation techniques**
   (a) Unexpected temper losses – erupting in anger can break an impulse and get one's point across, but it can also be viewed as immature or manipulative and lead opponents to harden their position.
   (b) High balling – this is used to gain trust by appearing to give in to the opposition's position but when overturned by a higher authority, concessions are gained based on the trust.
   (c) Boulwarism ("take it or leave it") – named after a former vice president of GE who would make only one offer in labour negotiations, this is a highly aggressive strategy that may also result in anger and frustration in the opponents.
   (d) Waiting until the last moment – after using stall tactics and knowing that a deadline is near, a reasonable but favourable offer is made, leaving the opponent with little choice but to accept."[51]

**Issues in negotiation:** It must be really emphasized that the successful negotiators must possess necessary negotiation skills and also understand the specific aspects of the negotiation process. At the same time, however, they should have an understanding of certain contemporary issues in negotiation so as to enhance their bargaining strength and problem-solving abilities. These contemporary issues include the role of personality traits, gender differences in negotiation, cultural differences in negotiation, and the use of third parties to help resolve differences or disputes.

**The role of personality traits in negotiation:** It has been observed that the negotiators have significant differences in terms of their varied personalities, attitudes, risk-taking abilities, and so on. Although it is generally assumed that knowing all these personality traits of the opponents on the negotiation table may help in predicting their negotiating tactics or strategies, the research evidence doesn't support this assumption or intuition.[52] It has been found that personality traits have no significant effect on the bargaining process or negotiation outcomes. Therefore, the negotiator should focus on the negotiation issues and situational factors in each bargaining episode rather than on the opponent's personality traits.

**Gender differences in negotiation:** A common view held by many is that women are more cooperative and relationship-oriented than men in negotiations. Comparisons between experienced male and female managers indicate that women are neither better nor worse than men in terms of negotiation skills, cooperation and persuasiveness. The stereotype that women are nicer than men in negotiations is perhaps due to lesser power held by women in many of the large-sized organisations. Research has shown that managers with less power, regardless of gender, use persuasive tactics with the opponents rather than direct confrontation and threats. Where men and women have approximately equal level of power, their negotiation styles do not vary significantly.

**Cultural differences in negotiation:** It has been observed that the negotiating styles of managers and executives vary significantly depending upon their cultural background. In other words, the negotiating styles clearly vary across cultures in different nations.[53] The cultural factors tend to influence the preparation for bargaining, the relative emphasis placed on task versus interpersonal relationships, the negotiation tactics or strategies used, etc.

**Third-party negotiation:** It is quite possible that the individuals or group representatives, on certain occasions, may be unable to resolve their differences through direct negotiations and thus reach a deadlock situation. In such cases, they may approach a third party to help them find a solution to their differences or conflicts. As mentioned by Wall and Blum,[54] there are four types of third-party roles: mediator, arbitrator, conciliator, and consultant.

A **mediator** is a neutral third party who facilitates a negotiated settlement by using reasoning and persuasion, suggesting alternatives, and so on. Mediators are widely used in labour-management negotiations, civil court disputes, etc. The effectiveness of mediated negotiations depends on certain essential prerequisites or conditions. First, the conflicting parties must be motivated to bargain and resolve the conflict. Second, the intensity of conflict should not be too high as mediation is most effective when model levels of conflict are present. Finally, the mediator must be perceived or seen as a neutral and non-coercive person so that he can play an effective role.

An **arbitrator** is a third party having the authority to dictate an agreement. Arbitration may be voluntary as requested by the negotiating parties, or it may be compulsory being forced on the parties by law or contract. The authority of the arbitrator varies according to the rules set by the negotiators. An advantage of arbitration over mediation is that it always results in a settlement. However, arbitration may not always lead to completely fair or impartial decisions for both the parties. If one party feels defeated, he will be certainly dissatisfied and is unlikely to happily accept the arbitrator's decision. Therefore, the conflict may surface again at a later stage.

A **conciliator** is a trained third party who establishes informal communication links between the two conflicting parties. Conciliators also engage in fact-finding, interpreting messages, and persuading the conflicting parties to develop agreements. It has been found that conciliation is extensively used in labour, family, community, and international disputes.

A **consultant** is a skilled and impartial third party who facilitates problem-solving through communication and analysis of facts or information. A consultant is not expected to settle the issues; rather, he tries to improve relations between the conflicting parties so that they can arrive at a settlement on their own. Instead of suggesting specific solutions, the consultant tries to help the parties understand and work with each other. Therefore, this approach has the long term objective of building positive perceptions and attitudes between the conflicting parties.

## 2.13 SUMMARY AND CONCLUSION

The present chapter has examined organisational conflict in a broader framework in view of its inevitability in organisational life, the need for conflict management, and the potential benefits of conflict to an organisation. The classical or traditional notion of conflict assumed that conflict is bad and destructive. According to the modern viewpoint, however, conflict is not only inevitable in organisations; rather, a moderate level of conflict should be considered necessary and even desirable for achieving individual, group, and organisational effectiveness. The potential benefits of conflict to an organisation include organisational change and creativity, release of tension of group members, group cohesiveness, group and organisational effectiveness, productive challenges for individuals and groups, constructive level of tension, etc. It must be pointed out that if conflict is not managed properly, then it can lead to certain unintended consequences including increased employee turnover, dissatisfaction, mutual suspicion of trust, displacement of goals, weakening of organisation, etc. All these positive and negative effects of conflict have been discussed in the present chapter. In regard to the relationship between intensity of conflict and performance, it has been stated that too little conflict and too much of conflict are dysfunctional from the organisational viewpoint. As viewed by the modern organisation experts, a moderate amount of conflict is most essential for attaining optimum organisational effectiveness. It has been further argued that a moderate degree of substantive or task-related conflict (but not affective or emotional conflict) is necessary for achieving and maintaining optimum organisational effectiveness. Therefore, conflict stimulation techniques must be used to increase conflict in situations of low degree of conflict whereas conflict resolution techniques must be utilised to reduce conflict if a high degree of conflict is existing.

As noted by Pondy[55] and Walton and Dutton,[56] conflict between two individuals or social units can be viewed as a sequence of conflict episodes. The present chapter includes a critical analysis of the five stages of conflict as noted by Pondy.[57] These stages include latent conflict (antecedent conditions), perceived conflict (cognition), felt conflict (affective stages such as tension, anxiety, stress, hostility, etc.), manifest conflict (conflictful behaviour ranging from passive resistance to overt aggression), and conflict aftermath (conflict outcomes or consequence). An analysis of some of the major sources of conflict has been made in this chapter, which includes competition for scarce resources, ambiguous or overlapping jurisdiction, breakdown of communication, time pressure, unreasonable policies, procedures or rules, status differentials, personality clashes, and unrealised expectations. Similarly, the issues of conflict (representing real conflict situations) have been classified and discussed under six conflict producing situations such as status inconsistencies, conflicting goals, overlapping authority, task interdependence, incompatible reward systems, and scarce resources.

In regard to the levels of conflict existing in an organisation, it has been stated that conflict may exist in an individual, between two individuals, or between two or more groups in an organisation. These conflicts are known as intra-individual, inter-personal, intra-group, and inter-group conflicts, respectively. In addition, conflict may also exist between two or more organisations, and it is known as inter-organisational conflict. Intra-individual conflict may involve some form of goal conflict, role conflict, or cognitive conflict. While intra-individual conflict may arise due to approach-approach, approach-avoidance, or avoidance-avoidance situations, role conflict and ambiguity may emanate from various forms of role conflict, intra-role conflict or inter-role conflict. All these details of goal conflict, role conflict and ambiguity have been analysed in the present chapter. The various factors contributing to inter-personal conflict and inter-group conflict have also been discussed in order to provide a clear-cut picture regarding the intricacies of conflict and conflict episodes occurring within the organisational setting.

The last part of the chapter throws light on negotiation skills that have moved beyond the fields of industrial relations and that can be utilised for resolving differences and disputes arising between individuals or groups in organisations. Traditionally, negotiators have depended upon distributive bargaining that involves "division of the existing pie" between the conflicting parties, i.e., the gain made by one party is at the cost of the other party. As against distributive bargaining, an alternative approach has been suggested in the form of integrative bargaining which uses problem-solving or collaborative strategy, and attempts to "expand the pipe" in order to find win-win outcomes for both the parties. In addition, the negotiation process has been explained in the present chapter as consisting of certain steps such as 1) preparation and planning; 2) definition of ground rules; 3) clarification and justification; 4) bargaining and problem-solving; and 5) closure and implementation. All these steps involved in the negotiation process, if followed properly and adequately, will lead to a successful resolution of differences or conflicts existing between individuals or groups in an organisation. As discussed in the final section of this chapter, there are certain significant contemporary issues in negotiation that must be understood by the negotiators in order to enhance their bargaining strength and problem-solving skills or abilities. These issues include the role of personality traits in negotiation, gender differences in negotiation, cultural differences in negotiation, and the role of third-party negotiators to help resolve differences or disputes. In regard to the third-party negotiators, it has been mentioned that their role is extremely useful in situations where the individual negotiators or group representatives are unable to solve their differences through direct negotiations and, therefore, reach a deadlock. In this context, the roles of four types of third-party negotiators have been discussed such as those of a mediator, an arbitrator, a conciliator, and a consultant.

## REVIEW QUESTIONS

1. Explain the meaning and nature of conflict. What are the essential features of conflict?
2. State the positive and negative aspects of conflict in organisations.
3. Conflict evolves through certain processes or stages. Discuss.
4. Explain the major sources of inter-personal conflict. Which ones are most relevant in today's organisations?
5. Conflicts occur at various levels of an organisation. What are the causes of these conflicts?
6. Explain approach-avoidance conflict with the help of suitable examples.
7. What are different types of conflicts commonly found in organisations? Discuss with suitable examples of each.
8. What is role conflict? Explain different types of role conflict.
9. What are the causes of inter-group conflict in organisations? Discuss.
10. Discuss suitable strategies that may be adopted to reduce goal conflict in an organisation.
11. Explain the various steps involved in the negotiation process.
12. Explain the role and importance of integrative bargaining as against distributive bargaining.
13. Define the term 'negotiation'. Also describe the general approaches to bargaining in organisations.
14. Discuss the contemporary issues relating to negotiation.
15. Discuss the role of third-party negotiators in the negotiation process.

16. Compare between the traditional and the contemporary approaches to negotiation. Which approach do you think is the better one and why?

## REFERENCES


1. Fink, C.F., "Some conceptual difficulties in the theory of social conflict", *Journal of Conflict Resolution*, December 1968, pp. 412-460.
2. Pondy, L.R., "Organizational conflict: Concepts and models", *Administrative Science Quarterly*, Vol. 12, 1967, pp. 296-320.
3. Robbins, S.P., *Organizational Behaviour*, Prentice Hall, New Delhi, 2001.
4. Pondy, 1967, *op. cit.*
5. March, J.G., and Simon, H.A., *Organizations*, John Wiley and Sons, 1958, p. 112.
6. Follett, M.P., *Creative Experience*, Peter Smith, New York, 1958.
7. Robbins, S.P., *Managing Organizational Conflict: A Non-traditional Approach*, Prentice Hall, Upper Saddle River, NJ, 1974.
8. Thomas, K., "Conflict and conflict management", in M.D. Dunnett, ed., *Handbook of Industrial and Organisational Behaviour*, Rand McNally, Chicago, 1976.
9. Katz D. and Kahn, R.L., *The Social Psychology of Organizations*, Wiley, New York, 1978.
10. Chung, K.H. and Megginson, L.C., *Organisational Behaviour: Developing Managerial Skills*, Harper and Row, New York, 1981.
11. Kabanoff, B., "Potential influence structures as sources of inter-personal conflict in groups and organisations", *Organizational Behaviour and Human Decision Processes*, 36: 115.
12. Roloff, M.E., "Communication and conflict", in C.R. Berger and S.H. Chaffee, ed., *Handbook of Communication Science*, Sage Publications, CA, 1987.
13. Hellreigel, D., Slocum, J.W. and Woodman, R.W., *Organizational Behaviour*, St. Paul, Minn. West, 1992.
14. Steers, R.M. and Black, J.S., *Organisational Behaviour*, Harper Collins, New York, 1994.
15. De Dreu, C.K.W., Harinck, F. And Van Vianen, A.E.M., "Conflict and performance in groups and organisations", *International Review of Industrial and Organisational Psychology*, 14, 1999.
16. Rahim, M.A., *Managing Conflict in Organisations*, Quorom Books, London, 2002, p. 18.
17. *Ibid.*, p. 12.
18. Rahim, A. and Bonoma, T.V., "Managing organisational conflict: A model for diagnosis and intervention", *Psychological Reports*, 44(3), 1979, pp. 1323-1344.

19. Schimdt, W.H., "Conflict: A powerful process for (good or bad) change", *Management Review*, Vol. 63, December 1974.
20. Pondy, 1967, *op. cit.*
21. Walton, R.E. and Dutton, J.M., "The management of inter-departmental conflict; A model and review", *Administrative Science Quarterly*, 14, March 1969, pp. 73-84.
22. Pondy, 1967, *op. cit.*
23. Cyert, R.M. and March, J.G., *A Behavioural Theory of the Firm*, Englewood Cliffs, NJ, 1963.
24. Argyris, C., "The individual and organisation" Some problems of mutual adjustment", *Administrative Science Quarterly*, 1957, pp. 1-24.
25. Pareek, U.N., *Conflict and Collaboration in Organisations*, Oxford and IBH Publications, New Delhi, 1992.
26. Jehn, K.A., "A multi-method examination of the benefits and detriments of intragroup conflict", *Administrative Science Quarterly*, 40, 1995, pp. 256-282; Jehn, K.A., A qualitative analysis of conflict types and dimensions in organisational groups, *Administrative Science Quarterly*, 1997, pp. 530-557.
27. Jehn, K.A., 1997, *op. cit.*
28. *Ibid.*
29. Jehn, K.A., 1995, *op. cit.*
30. Murnigham, J.K., and Conlon, D.E., "The dynamics of intense workgroups: A study of British sting qualets", *Administrative Science Quarterly*, 36, 1991, pp. 165-186.
31. Jehn, K.A., 1997, *op. cit.*
32. Jehn, K.A., Northcraft, G.B., and Neale, M.A., "Why differences make a difference: A field study of diversity, conflict, and performance in work groups", *Administrative Science Quarterly*, 44 (4), 1999, pp. 741-763.
33. Robbins, S.P., *Organisational Behaviour*, Prentice Hall of India, New Delhi, 2001.
34. Sharma, R.A., *Organisational Theory and Behaviour*, Tata Macgraw-Hill, New Delhi, 2000.
35. March and Simon, *op. cit.*
36. Luthans, F. *Organisational Behaviour*, McGraw Hill, Boston, 2002, p. 407.
37. Sarbin, T.R., "Role theory", *Handbook of Social Psychology*, Addison-Wiley, Cambridge, 1954, pp. 223-258.
38. Kelly, J., *Organisational Behaviour*, Richard D. Irwin, Homewood, 1974.
39. March and Simon, *op. cit.*
40. Schein, E.H., *Organisational Psychology*, Prentice Hall, Englewood Cliffs, N.J., 1970.

41. Walton, R.E., and McKersie, R.B., *A Behavioural Theory of Labour Negotiations: An Analysis of a Social Integration System*, McGraw Hill, New York, 1965.
42. Neale, M.A. and Bazerman, M.H., "Negotiating rationally: The power and impact of the negotiator's frame", *Academy of Management Executive*, August, 1992.
43. Whetton, D.A. and Cameron, K.S., *Developing Management Skills*, Harper Collins, New York, 1999, p. 402.
44. Walton, R.E. and McKersie, R.B., 1965, *op. cit*.
45. Thomson, L., Peterson, E., and Brodt, S.E., "Team negotiations: An examination of integrative and distributive bargaining", *Journal of Personality and Social Psychology*, Cameron, *op. cit*., p. 404.
46. Whetton, D.A. and Cameron, K.S., 1999, *op. cit*., p. 404.
47. Robbins, S.P., 2001, *op. cit*.
48. Luthans, F., *Organisational Behaviour*, McGraw Hill, New Delhi, 2002, p. 419.
49. Neale, M.A., and Bazerman, M.H., 1992, *op. cit*.
50. Luthans, F., 2002, *op. cit*.
51. Adler, R., Rosen, B., and Silverstein, E., "Thrust and parry: The art of tough negotiating", *Training and Development Journal*, 50 (3), 1996, pp. 42-48.
52. Robbins, S.P., 2001, *op. cit*.
53. *Ibid*.
54. Wall, J.A. and Blum, M.W., "Negotiations", *Journal of Management*, 17(2), 1991, pp. 273-303.
55. Pondy, 1967, *op. cit*.
56. Watton and Dutton, 1969, *op. cit*.
57. Pondy, 1967, *op. cit*.


## CASE STUDIES

**Case 1:** Abhishek completed his graduation in Commerce recently from an affiliated college of Delhi University. Although he had studied courses in Organisational Behaviour, Human Resource Management, etc., and completed assignments and projects, he had little exposure to teamwork in a true sense. He appeared an interview for a job in an educational software firm which made extensive use of cross-functional teams. During the interview, Abhishek confessed that he had limited experience in teamwork but mentioned that he had developed interpersonal skills that would help him as an effective group or team player. Abhishek joined as an assistant marketing manager in the software company that developed and marketed software programs especially for the high school students to learn mathematics subjects such as calculus, algebra, geometry, etc. Abhishek had to work with other group members such as the marketing manager, advertising specialist, senior programmer, strategic marketing expert, educational consultant, etc. After working with the group members for a few days, Abhishek seriously thought of quitting the job. In fact, Abhishek found it difficult to work with all these team members who were highly competitive and expressed their rigid opinions about various issues and problems. Abhishek faced severe difficulties as his job responsibilities were not clearly defined and every other team member always interfered in his work.

**Questions**

1. Would it be right to say that the above situation involves intra-group conflicts among the members?
2. What techniques or skills would you recommend for Abhishek to improve his effectiveness as a cross-functional team member?

**Case 2:** Help Age India Ltd., a registered national level voluntary organisation, is actively engaged in the task of helping the elderly and disadvantaged persons and improving their quality of life. Help Age India works with Senior Citizens Associations at the national, state, and societal level and attempts to address the elders' needs such as quality healthcare, universal pension, action against elders' abuse and so on. Abhay has been working as a coordinator in South (i.e., one of the five defined zones in Delhi such as South Delhi, North Delhi, East Delhi, West Delhi, and Central Delhi) for the elders' needs and had a team of 20 persons including 5 program managers and 15 supervisors working under the program managers.

Suddenly, Abhay was informed by three of his supervisors (all of them working under one particular project manager) that they were very much upset with the continuous intolerable behaviour of their project manager. In fact, it was very difficult for the supervisors to continue working with him if this misbehaviour on his part continued further. In order to find a solution to this problem, Abhay called a meeting of all the project managers and supervisors and asked them to carry out a small activity. Three questions were given to each group: What is the meaning of a team? Is a team really necessary for carrying on work activities? How is it possible to build an efficient team? The group members were asked to first discuss each question within their respective group or team and then write down the answer to each question when they arrived at a consensus. They were given an hour's time for completing this task or activity. After an hour, the groups presented their responses to these three questions. After analysing their responses to the questions, Abhay observed that members of all the groups knew the meaning of a team. Then, he asked the group members to answer honestly as to how many of these points they actually followed in their day-to-day activities. The group members replied that they applied about 40 per cent of these points in their daily works and ignored the remaining 60 per cent of points. The group members' acceptance of their weaknesses or limitations made them to realise the need for self-assessment of their team behaviour. Then, they decided as to how they will work with their respective teams effectively in the future.

**Questions**

1. What kind of conflict is involved in the above situation?
2. Suggest some measures to be taken by each project manager to improve his group members' approach to teamwork. Present your answer as a HR manager.

**Case 3:** Tata Motors established its Tata Nano car manufacturing plant in in 2008 in the city of Sanand, Gujarat, India. Nano is India's most fuel efficient petrol car with a seating capacity of four passengers and has the lowest price in the market in India. Nano has a CNG variant as well with a relatively lower price level. Since Nano has not been able to establish itself really well in the domestic market, it has started focusing on sales in foreign markets too. Although the Nano project was the brainchild of Ratan Tata who promised to deliver the lowest priced affordable motorcar to the Indian buyers with certain distinctive features, this car has not been successful in terms of actual sales and profit figures. In fact, this car project has been running at losses for so many years due to a number of factors such as cost escalation, the consequent increase in market prices, delays in production, product deficiencies, attitudinal issues, and so on.

The problems of Nano project have multiplied due to continuous warfare between Mr Ratan Tata and Mr Cyrus Mistry, the former Chairman of Tata Sons. Although during Cyrus Mystry's tenure as Chairman of Tata Motors, some significant product improvements were made in the Nano versions based on market feedback, all these initiatives did not bear fruits. Therefore, an unanimous decision was made by the Board of Directors of Tata Motors to discontinue the production of Nano a few years ago. In spite of this, the Nano production continues with heavy losses leading to depression in market share prices, retrenchment of employees, and inability of the company to pay dividend to its shareholders. According to sources close to Mr Ratan Tata, the Tata Nano constitutes only a very small portion of Tata Motors, i.e., out of Rs. 2,00,000 crore revenue, only about Rs. 9000 crore is generated from the personal vehicle market and of that, Nano contributes a very small amount. The Ratan Tata and Cyrus Mistry conflict has been going on for quite a long time. Allegations and counter-allegations have been levelled by both the parties concerned. Tata Sons has said that Mistry is busy in creating a parallel power structure for himself and his relatives. In his defence, Mistry says that the Nano project has been a complete failure but even then production has continued only due to Tata's personal interest. Although the Nano project was launched with Ratan Tata's mission of a people's car with the lowest price tag of Rs. 1 lakh, the fact remains that this car project has not been really successful in the Indian car market due to a number of factors including cost escalation, low sales volume, and continuous losses.

**Questions**

1. Identify some of the possible causes of interpersonal conflict between Mr Ratan Tata and Mr Cyrus Mistry in the above case.
2. Do you think that the above conflict situation involves both inter-personal and inter-group conflict? Discuss in brief.

**Case 4:** The labour unrest at Maruti Suzuki India Ltd's (MSIL's) Manesar plant began as early as 2000 in which employees of MSIL went on an indefinite strike demanding higher wages, incentives and pension. As a result of this strike, Maruti vehicle sales and net profit fell quite significantly. In 2012, a worker at MSIL's Manesar Plant was suspended for misbehaving with a shop floor supervisor. This led to a violent clash between the workers and the management staff and the burning of the administration division of the plant that led to the death of Mr. Awanish Kumar Dev, the general manager of HR, due to burn injuries. In the course of this conflict, the workers injured 9 policemen and about 100 managers. The company declared a lockout and several of its employees were arrested. The company stated that none of the workers would be paid for the lock-out period. More than 90 workers were arrested and the company dismissed 500 workers accused of perpetrating violence in the factory. Although the issue has been partially reserved, it continues to simmer off and on.

The major reason for the labour-management dispute in the MSIL Manesar plant was the fact that the company had hired several workers on contract basis. In this way, the company not only paid lesser compensation and benefits to the contractual workers but was also able to limit the scope of applicability of labour law provisions. As against permanent employees of MSIL, the company did not provide medical benefits, paid leave, and transport facility to its contractual workers even though the nature of work remained the same for both categories of employees. In addition, the general working conditions in the MSIL Manesar plant were not congenial enough with huge deductions in pay for leave, no time for breaks, and no payment for overtime work. Therefore, the MSIL labour union demanded for increase in salary, cheaper house loan, paid vacation leave, and several allowances. None of these demands made by the workers was acceptable to the management team of MSIL.

**Questions**

1. Explain some of the important issues and sources of labour-management conflict at the Manesar plant of MSIL in 2012.
2. Would you say that this conflict falls within the category of inter-group conflict? Analyse some of the causes of intergroup conflict in this case.

# 3

# A Review of Organisational Conflict Literature

## 3.1 INTRODUCTION

In the realm of organisational behaviour, a large volume of literature is available on the subject of organisational conflict, its management and other related aspects. In spite of this, the subject of organisational conflict has continued to draw the attention of academicians, researchers and practitioners. Although the researchers accept the inevitability of conflict in organisational life and also agree on the need to manage conflict constructively, it must be noted that the literature available on organisational conflict is somewhat fragmented and is specialised, pertaining to specific organisational areas such as line staff conflict,[1] labour-management disputes,[2] senior-subordinate conflicts,[3] inter-departmental disputes,[4] etc. It may be noted, however, that the dynamics of conflict behaviour in one area have immense relevance in other areas as well. In addition, researches undertaken outside the limits of orgnisations such as small group research, experimental gaming, international relations, social conflict, etc., have produced immense knowledge and insights that have relevance to the understanding of conflict in organizations.

Against the backdrop of the above-mentioned observations, an attempt has been made in the present chapter to make a conceptual and generic approach to the study of conflict and its management. More specifically, the present chapter analyses the literature available on certain significant aspects of conflict such as the changing perspective on conflict, antecedents to conflict, conflict outcomes or consequences, desirability of conflict, management of conflict, and the contingency approach to conflict management. At the end of this chapter, certain meaningful conclusions have been drawn regarding such important aspects as the relative efficacy or effectiveness of conflict management styles or methods, the need for a renewed approach to conflict management in the context of growing knowledge and education, abilities and aspirations of industrial employees, the relevance of the contingency approach to conflict management, and so on. It must be mentioned that all these aspects of conflict and conflict management have been dealt with only in a cursorily this chapter as all these aspects will be discussed in an exhaustive manner in the ensuing chapters.

## 3.2 CHANGING PERSPECTIVE OF CONFLICT

The classical approach towards the study of organisational conflict assumed that conflict is inherently bad and is to be avoided at all costs. The classicists believed that conflict indicated a malfunctioning in the organization, being created by troublemakers. Therefore, conflict must be prevented or controlled through the use of legalistic forms of authority. The human relations approach to management posited that conflict is a natural occurrence in all groups and organisations. Therefore, this approach views conflict as inevitable in individual, group or organizational life. It is significant to note, however, that the human relations movement with its focus upon the individual and organisational cost of conflict implied that it was to be avoided or eliminated.[5] This traditional view of conflict was essentially based upon the misconception that conflict is inherently destructive and pathological to the attainment of organizational objectives. Although Kahn *et al.*,[6] viewed that some conflict is necessary for the continued development of competent and mature individuals. They explained that common reactions to conflict and its associated tensions are often dysfunctional for the orgnisation as an ongoing social system and self defeating for the person in the long run. Boudling[7] recognised that an optimum level of conflict along with its associated personal tensions or stress are essential for achieving higher levels of progress and productivity but he portrayed conflict essentially as a social and personal cost. In addition, it may be pointed out that even March and Simon's[8] dispassionate organization theory views conflict as a "breakdown in the standard mechanism of decision making", i.e., as a malfunction of the system.

It may be mentioned that attitudes towards conflict have undergone significant changes with the passage of time. In fact, the current literature on organizational conflict recognizes its cost and benefits, its dangers and promises. Most of the modern management experts have come to recognize that conflict should not be seen as an evil in itself, rather, conflict should be viewed as a phenomenon having positive or negative effects in organizations depending upon its management. As viewed by Robbins,[9] certain degree of conflict must be encouraged by the group leader so as to keep the group viable, self-critical and creative. However, conflict must be controlled and kept within reasonable limits in order to avoid its dysfunctional effects. According to modern organisation theorists, conflict is not always caused by troublemakers; rather, conflict is determined by structural factors and is integral to the nature of change. Thus, it would be inappropriate to classify conflict as being good or bad. The effects or consequences of conflict will depend upon whether such conflict is functional or dysfunctional. While functional conflict encourages the group to achieve its goals and improve performance, dysfunctional conflict is detrimental in nature and obstructs the attainment of group objectives or performance. As stated by Thomas,[10] "with the recognition that conflict can be both useful and destructive, the emphasis has shifted from the elimination of conflict to the management of conflict. Now, it is being increasingly recognized that inter-personal and inter-group conflict, if managed properly, serves many useful functions in the organization.[11]

## 3.3 ANTECEDENTS TO CONFLICT

Conflicts in organisation have been attributed to many factors. The organisational behaviour experts have tried to identify and analyse the sources or determinants of conflicts existing at intra-individual, inter-individual, intra-group and inter-group levels. In the present section, an attempt has been made to analyse or explain the determinants of organisational conflict in a general sense as identified by the behavioural scientists. The underlying assumption is that such an analysis would help the managers in taking necessary steps to prevent or resolve conflicts existing at various organisational levels. The various antecedents to organisational conflict as discussed in the present section, include task interdependence, organisational differentiation, competition for scarce resources, performance criteria and rewards, ambiguities, hierarchical differences in prestige, power and knowledge, identity concerns, barriers to communication, personality attributes, role dissatisfaction, drive for autonomy, and the need for tension release.

**Task interdependence:** Task interdependence refers to a situation in which two functional units or groups operating at the same level are dependent upon each other for information, assistance, compliance or other coordinative acts that are needed for the completion of their respective functions or tasks. Some of the important matters of task dependence are: (1) common use of certain services or facilities; (2) flow of work or information as per the task or hierarchy of authority; and (3) rules of consensus or unanimity about joint activities. Such conflicts occur mostly among individuals or groups engaged in a functional relationship and are also known as the Systems Model of Conflict.[12] As Dutton and Walton[13] have described, mutual task dependence not only facilitates collaboration but also contains considerable scope for conflict and bargaining over issues affecting different departments or groups. As the subunits within an organisation have different sets of active goals or objectives[14] or different preference ordering for the same set of goals or objectives, there is ample scope for inter-unit conflicts or disputes.

### 3.3.1 Organisational Differentiation

Organisational behaviour experts generally agree that standardized or uniform tasks require a bureaucratic organisation structure while non-standardized tasks require a human relations type of organization. In the modern society, most of the organisations have to deal with both uniform and nonuniform tasks and therefore combine these two types of social relations into a professional model. In fact, the inclusion of these two types of contradictory social relations becomes a source of organisational conflict.[15] Lawrence and Lorsch[16] made a comparative study of six organisations operating in the same industrial environment. The subsystems within the organisation such as production, sales, and research performed different types of tasks and coped with different segments of the environment. As a result of this, the subsystem within each organization developed significant internal differences among themselves with regard to four different aspects: (1) formal structure; (2) goal orientation; (3) time orientation; and (4) interpersonal orientation. Lawrence and Lorsch[17] believed that this fourfold differentiation is largely a response to the degree of uncertainty in the relevant environments of different departmental units. Such differentiation between organisational subunits comes in the way of integration or coordinative processes, thus creating ample scope for inter-departmental or inter-unit conflicts. As Lawrence and Lorsch stated, "in complex organisations having different subunits with different goals, norms and orientations, it appeared that inter-group conflict would be an inevitable part of organizational life." Lawrence and Lorsch[18] further suggested that the use of confrontation or problem-solving behaviour as a means of conflict resolution would be an effective integration procedure.

### 3.3.2 Competition for Scarce Resources

A common phenomenon is that conflicts arise among individuals, groups or departments as they compete for limited organisational resources such as personnel, finance, power, authority, etc. In other words, conflicts arise among different interest groups in an organization when there is mismatch or difference between the aggregate demands of such groups and the available resources.[19] Conflicts arise between line and staff managers over their respective jurisdiction or areas of authority; labour and management often compete over their respective shares of profits; departments or groups compete for limited organisational resources such as manpower, capital, equipment, physical space, centralised services, and so on. According to Walton,[20] such conflicts involve both integrative and distributive sub-processes. Each party to the conflict should not only try to maximise the total resource base as much as possible, referred to as expanding the pie"[21] but also secure for itself as large a share of it as possible – a process described as "claiming value".[22] It may be noted, however, that conflict arising due to competition for scarce resources is described as the "bargaining model of conflict" due to the dynamics involved in it.[23] Thus, while the integrative sub-process involves the use of joint problem-solving with a view to maximising outcomes or values, the distributive sub-process is concerned with strategic bargaining over scarce resources.

### 3.3.3 Performance Criteria and Rewards

Inter-departmental or inter-group conflict often arises due to the manner in which performance of subunits or groups is evaluated, and economic and non-economic rewards are distributed. Dutton and Walton[24] noticed that production units often preferred long and economic production runs while the sales units were interested in quick delivery to customers. Similarly, Dalton[25] noted that line units favoured stability while staff units valued change in order to prove their worth. While such inter-departmental differences are inherent in every organisation, the reward system designed by the organization may increase or decrease their divisive effects.[26] If the reward structure promotes the separate performance of each department rather than their combined performance, then conflicts are more likely to arise in the organisation. Similarly, if the reward structure allows only one department or group to maximise its goals or objectives at the cost of other groups, it will ultimately lead to inter-group conflicts and power struggles.[27]

### 3.3.4 Task Ambiguities

It may be mentioned that lack of clarity regarding authority and responsibility relationships among different subunits, groups or individuals leads to conflicts in organisations. Different departments or executives often compete for limited resources and controlling powers in the organisation. This situation often leads to hostilities or clashes between different work groups. Task ambiguities have been attributed to such important factors as the growth and expansion of organisational activities, changes in technology, structure and processes, rapid changes in the external environment, etc. A review of literature has shown that task ambiguities contribute to inter-departmental conflict in several ways. In case there is difficulty in assigning credit or blame between two different departments, it enhances the possibility of conflict between the two units. Dalton[28] observed that although collaboration between line and staff units was required for achieving improvements in efficiency, it became difficult to assess the contribution of each unit, thus giving rise to line-staff conflict. Dutton and Walton[29] noticed that conflicts between production and sales units arose when it could not be ascertained as to which department committed mistakes. It has been found that uncertainty regarding means to achieve goals and low level of routinization increased the potential for inter unit conflict.[30] Similarly, Kahn *et al.*,[31] have noted that ambiguity in criteria used to assess the performance of a unit also causes frustration, tension and conflict.

### 3.3.5 Hierarchical Difference in Prestige, Power and Knowledge

Inter-personal and inter-group conflicts are often caused by hierarchical differences among executives, managers and employees in an organisation. Similarly, inter-departmental or inter-unit conflicts are often caused by differences in the way the units are ranked in terms of status symbols such as power, prestige and knowledge. As found by Seilor,[32] when the flow of direction and influence across departments was based on status ordering, it was accepted by all the departmental units. However, where a higher-status unit received directions from a lower-status unit, the result was a breakdown in inter-unit relationships. Zald[33] made a study of three correctional institutions or units, and explained the effects of relative power. When the three units were studied in terms of their mutual task dependence and divergent views, it was found that conflict occurred between units that were perceived as being in control and those that were unable to control the situation. Similarly, inter-departmental conflicts were bound to occur when inconsistency occurred between the distribution of knowledge among departments and the lateral influence patterns. As observed by Lawrence and Lorsch[34] (1967), consistency between the influence of different departmental units and the key competitive factors leads to more effective resolution of inter-unit issues.

### 3.3.6 Identity Concerns

Mayer and Louw[35] (2009) viewed that identity concerns of individuals in terms of their feelings of being confident, knowledgeable, experienced, etc., have significant effects on conflicts in organisations. Walton[36] made a conceptual analysis of inter-organisational decision-making and favoured the use of problem-solving strategy (as opposed to bargaining) in obtaining high quality decisions. In his views, the identity concerns of organizations play a significant role in the choice of strategies (to be made for joint decision-making) as well as their potential consequences. If the identity needs of two parties are in harmony or consistent (i.e., identity reinforcement), the parties will engage in problem-solving behaviour and exploit their integrative potential in order to maximize their joint gains. However, if the identity needs are in conflict (i.e., identity conflict), the parties are more likely to resort to bargaining behaviour and arrive at sub-optimal decisions.

### 3.3.7 Barriers to Communication

There are many barriers in the formal communication system that obstruct the flow of information and thus create conflicts in an organization. Any such blockade of information or communication creates misunderstanding and mistrust in the minds of organization's members. As the individuals or groups have different information or differing perceptions of certain organizational issues, conflicts are bound to arise among them. Research findings have shown that semantic differential can hamper effective communication as well as cooperation among organisation's members. Straus[37] noticed that differences in the training and development of engineers and purchasing agents created conflicts between them. March and Simon[38] viewed that channeling of information through the formal communication system introduced bias in the minds of participants. In an empirical study of the causes of inter-departmental conflicts, Walton and Dutton[39] (1969) utilized three measures of conflict that existed in the bargaining type of decision-making: (1) over-statement of departmental needs; (2) lack of consideration of another department's needs; and (3) distrust. The underlying assumption was that reducing these three conflict variables would increase problem-solving behaviours. As the findings of the study indicated, communication inhibiting factors and competition incentives were most significantly related to the composite measures of the three conflict variables. The next important causal factors were jurisdictional ambiguity, inter-departmental scarcities, sources of frustration, and salience variables.

### 3.3.8 Personality Attributes

Personality differences among members are bound to exist on account of differences in their upbringing, value systems, family and cultural traditions, etc. These differences often lead to conflicts at various levels. Walton and Mckersie[40] reviewed some experimental studies and found that certain personality attributes such as high dogmaticism, authoritarianism and low self-esteem led to increased conflict behaviour among members. Kahn *et al.*[41] (1964) observed that persons in role conflict who scored lower on neurotic anxiety scales, tended to depart more from cordial, congenial, trusting, respecting and understanding relations." An individual with inadequate behavioural skills is less likely to utilise the integrative potential fully in an inter-unit relationship. He may either engage in bargaining behaviour to the exclusion of collaborative problem-solving or withdraw or become passive.[42] Dalton and Thompson[43] noticed that differences in personality attributes such as education, background, social patterns, values, etc., lowered the chances of interpersonal communication and rapport between the representatives of different departments and thus reduced collaboration between their respective units.

### 3.3.9 Role Dissatisfaction

It has been observed that role dissatisfaction can be a source of interpersonal as well as inter-unit conflict. Conflicts may develop among members due to non-fulfillment of their aspirations or expectations within the organisation. As observed by Dalton,[44] blocking status aspirations in staff members created conflicts with other units. In these cases, the professionals felt dissatisfied due to lack of esteem or recognition from others as well as opportunities for advancement along the organizational hierarchy. Similarly, conflicts were bound to arise in cases where one unit internally reported on the performance or activities of another unit, as has been observed with staff units reporting to management on production irregularities.[45] Argyris and Dalton[46] (1964) and Dalton[47] have viewed that conflict would arise due to role dissatisfaction where one unit with the same or lower status sets standards for another unit.

### 3.3.10 Drive for Autonomy

Conflicts often develop between the seniors and their subordinates because the seniors try to control the behaviour of subordinates which is often resisted by the latter. The subordinate perceives conflict in situations where the superior attempts to exercise control over activities falling outside the latter's jurisdiction (i.e., outside the "zone of indifference") while the superior perceives conflict as his attempts at control are resisted by the subordinate. Generally, the superiors attempt to deal with such subordinate resistance through the imposition of impersonal rules and regulations which define the authority and responsibility relationships more clearly and thereby diminish the subordinate's freedom or autonomy. As a result of this, the subordinate perceives himself to be in conflict with his seniors who are trying to undermine his autonomy.

### 3.3.11 Need for Tension Release

The human need for tension release can be another significant source of organisational conflict.[48] As noted by Agyris,[49] the requirements of formal organisation system often impose inconsistent demands on an individual and therefore violate the basic "givens" of a healthy personality. These inconsistencies between organizational and individual growth often lead to anxieties in the individual. In addition, it has been noted that anxiety may also rise due to identity crisis from extra-organisational pressures. The individuals need to ventilate these anxieties with a view to maintaining their internal equilibrium. In fact, the latent conflicts of different types cause the individuals to display their anxieties against certain suitable targets.

## 3.4 CONFLICT OUTCOMES OR CONSEQUENCES

The traditional notion regarding conflict assumed that conflict is inherently dysfunctional in character and, therefore, is to be avoided at all costs. However, the modern organisational behaviour experts view conflict as a multidimensional conflict being both negative and positive in character.[50] According to Van de Vliert *et al.*[51] conflict can be handled in either a constructive or a destructive way. Despite this modern perspective of conflict, the research studies distinguishing between constructive and destructive conflicts and their respective effects on individual, group or organisation have been a few in number. Robbins[52] viewed that "conflict is constructive when it proves the quality of decisions, stimulates creativity and innovation, encourages interest and curiosity among group members, provides the medium through which problems can be aired and tensions released, and fosters an environment of self-evaluation and change." In fact, there is research to suggest that conflict improves the quality of decision-making as different viewpoints regarding a particular conflict issue or situation are accommodated or weighed in important decisions.[53] Conflict promotes the creation of new ideas as well as reassessment of group goals and activities, and thus enhances the possibility that the group will be sensitive towards organisational changes and respond to them. There is also evidence showing that conflict can be positively related to productivity. It has been demonstrated that performance in groups tended to improve more when conflict existed among members than when the group members had fairly close agreements among themselves.[54] The results of some other studies have shown that groups consisting of members with varied interests tend to produce high quality solutions to a variety of problems as against homogeneous groups.[55] As discussed by Robbins,[56] conflict has certain destructive or dysfunctional consequences in organisations too. In fact, a large body of management literature has explained as to how conflict can reduce group effectiveness. Some of the more undesirable consequences of conflict include breakdown in communication, reduced group cohesiveness, and threat to the very survival of the group.

The findings of some other research studies have shown negative relationship between "disharmony" and the quality of employee relationship, as well as between "disharmony" and product innovation performance. On the other hand, harmonious or cooperative relationship is found to be associated with improved performance levels. Dyer and Song[57] found that constructive conflict led to innovation. Menon *et al.*[58] noticed indirect relationships between dysfunctional (destructive) conflict and market performance in terms of introducing new products. Similarly, Song, Dyer and Thieme[59] noticed that constructive conflict was positively associated with innovation performance while destructive conflict was negatively related to innovation performance.

The functional effects of conflict have been described by Thomas[60]. In the first place, the organisation experts have viewed that a moderate degree of conflict has many functional effects in an organisation. While too little stimulation or tension may lead to individual apathy or stagnation, too much of conflict or stress may have adverse effects on individual as well as group performance and productivity. In conditions of low tension, people may welcome divergent viewpoints, the challenge of competition, and even the possibility of open hostilities. As stated by Deutsch,[61] conflict is part of the process of testing and assessing oneself and as such may be highly enjoyable as one experiences the full and active use of one's capacities.

Research has shown that confrontation of divergent views often produces ideas of superior quality.[62] Divergent views are often based upon different insights, different considerations, and different frames of reference. Disagreements or differences in views may lead an individual to consider factors that were ignored by him previously and thus help him to arrive at more balanced decisions or conclusions.

It has been found that aggressive behaviour in conflict situations is not always illogical or destructive. In fact, the pursuit of conflicting goals in an aggressive manner by two parties may lead to certain positive outcomes. As March and Simon, and Litterer[63] have stated, such conflicts based on aggression often lead to search for ways to reduce the conflict. As one party does not gain at the cost of another party, the conflicting parties may be able to find new arrangements which benefit both of them as well as the organisation.

In addition to the above discussed functions of conflicts, the organisation experts have noted certain other useful effects of conflict too. Litterer[64] observed that conflict in an organisation may call attention to systemic problems requiring change. Hostility between groups also tends to foster internal cohesiveness and unity of purpose in groups.[65] Finally, it should be noted that power struggles often provide the mechanism for determining the balance of power, and thus adjusting the terms of a relationship according to these realities.

Guetzkow and Gir[66] suggested two different aspects of conflict at the work situation. While the first aspect of conflict consisted of disagreements or differences over task related issues, the second one related to emotional or interpersonal issues which led to conflict. These two dimensions of conflict have been described as substantive and affective conflicts,[67] task and relationship conflicts,[68] cognitive and affective conflicts,[69] and task and emotional conflicts.[70] The empirical researches conducted on these two dimensions of conflict have revealed that the distinction between these two conflict dimensions is valid and that they have differential effects in the organisational setting.

It may be mentioned that substantive conflict arises when there is disagreement among members over certain task related issues. Jehn[71] viewed that a moderate level of substantive conflict has beneficial effects as it stimulates group discussion and debates that help group members to achieve higher performance levels. As Jehn[72] observed, "groups with an absence of task conflict may miss new ways to enhance their performance while very high levels of task conflict may interfere with task completion." The findings of research studies have shown that substantive conflict is positively related to individual, group and organizational effectiveness. Groups that report substantive conflict are able to make better decisions than those that do not.[73] In fact, substantive conflict promotes better understanding of issues and leads to better decision-making in organisations. Such conflict encourages open debates and discussions which lead to innovative solutions and tend to reduce possibilities of complacency, status quo and "group think".[74] It has been further noticed that substantive conflict helps to improve group performance through better understanding of different viewpoints and alternative solutions.[75] It must be pointed out, however, that substantive conflict has been found to have beneficial effects on performance only in groups performing non-routine tasks but not in groups performing standardised or routine tasks. Affective conflict refers to inconsistency in interpersonal relationships which arise when the organisation's members develop incompatible feelings and emotions over certain issues. As viewed by Jehn,[76] "summarily stated, relationship conflicts interfere with task-related effort because members focus on reducing threats, increasing power, and attempting to build cohesion rather than working on task ... The conflict causes members to be negative, irritable, suspicious and resentful." Research findings have shown that affective conflict obstructs group performance by limiting information processing ability and cognitive functioning of group members and promoting antagonistic attributions of group members' behaviour.[77] Affective conflicts tend to hamper group performance as decisions are likely to be based on merit and supported by strong commitment for implementation.[78] Such conflicts result in dysfunctional teams and reduced performance and cohesion.[79] In addition, it has been observed that affective conflicts tend to reduce group loyalty or commitment, organizational commitment, and job satisfaction.[80]

## 3.5 MANAGEMENT OF CONFLICT

The preceding discussion has shown that the general views regarding organizational conflict have been changing over the years. The theoretical perspectives as well as the research findings have proved that conflict can have functional or dysfunctional effects in organisations depending upon its management. Although the management aspects of conflict will be discussed more extensively in the subsequent chapters, it is deemed necessary to mention the contributions of leading experts on the desirability or otherwise of conflict from the viewpoint of individual, group, and organizational effectiveness. In this context, it may be mentioned that the available studies on the management of organizational conflict have generally moved in two directions. In the first place, some researchers have attempted to measure the degree or intensity of conflict at various levels of the organisation in terms of tension, stress, anxiety, hostility, etc., and also explore the sources of such conflict. Here, the underlying implication is that a moderate degree of conflict may be maintained by altering these sources of conflict so as to attain optimum organisational effectiveness. Therefore, Brown[81] suggested that "conflict management may require intervention to reduce conflict if there is too much of intervention to promote conflict if there is too little." It must be pointed out, however, that this relationship as suggested by Brown[82] seems to be appropriate for substantive conflict but not for affective conflict. As mentioned earlier, Guetzknow and Gir[83] distinguished between substantive conflict and affective conflict and suggested that substantive conflict (consisting of differences or disagreements between two or more parties over certain organisational issues, tasks or policies) is positively related to certain beneficial outcomes in an organisation. On the other hand, affective conflict consisting of inconsistent relations among organisation members arising due to interpersonal or emotional issues has been found to have adverse effects on group performance and other dimensions of organisational effectiveness. Therefore, Guetzkow and Gir[84] suggested that substantive conflict should be maintained at a moderate level in organisations while affective conflict is to be discouraged as much as possible due to its dysfunctional effects. It is noteworthy that Jehn's [85] conflict instrument can be used to measure affective and substantive conflicts at the interpersonal, intra-group and inter-group levels.

The second approach to conflict management involves attempts made by researchers to examine the efficacy or effectiveness of various conflict handling styles in terms of their effects on organizational objectives. A number of research studies have been conducted on the relationship between conflict handling methods or styles and different aspects or dimensions of individual, group, or organisational effectiveness. At the theoretical level, Blake and Mouton[86] suggested that individuals or organisations utilising problem-solving behaviour would achieve effective interpersonal relations and enhanced organizational effectiveness. Lawrence and Lorsch[87] made an empirical study to examine the utilisation as well as effects of confrontation, smoothing and forcing behaviours in six organisations. The findings of their study indicated that confrontation or problem-solving behaviour was positively related to organisational effectiveness. In addition, it was noted that the presence of forcing as a backup mode to confrontation and the absence of smoothing behaviour were related to effective interpersonal relations and organisational effectiveness. Another empirical study conducted by Burke[88] involved the examination of five different methods or styles of handling conflict (as suggested by Blake and Mouton[89]) in relation to superior-subordinate relations. The findings of the study pointed to the fact that confrontation or problem-solving proved to be the most effective method of resolving conflicts, and it was followed by smoothing behaviour. It was also observed that withdrawing and forcing behaviours were negatively associated with interpersonal effectiveness while compromising was not at all related to effectiveness. In the context of inter-departmental relations, Thomas[90] noticed that managers' satisfaction with inter-departmental negotiations was positively related to confrontation and smoothing behaviours by their colleagues in other departments and negatively related to forcing and withdrawing behaviours by the latter. Aram *et al.*'s[91] study conducted in research and development teams revealed that collaboration had positive relationship with certain measures of members' self-actualisation and well-being. On the other hand, Dutton and Walton[92] found that managers involved in competitive inter-departmental relations experienced too much of frustration and anxiety.

It may be mentioned that the research studies as discussed above on the relationship between conflict management methods or strategies and individual or organisational effectiveness were conducted mostly in the American industrial environment. Since the findings of these foreign studies cannot be generalized to Indian industrial situations or conditions, some research studies have been conducted by Indian researchers too in this context. Sharma and Samantra[93] conducted a study in an Indian computer producing company in order to examine the relative effectiveness of conflict resolution methods in terms of their impact on certain organizational effectiveness dimensions such as productivity, adaptability and flexibility. It was found that confrontation or problem-solving emerged as the most effective method of conflict resolution and it was followed by smoothing behaviour. Compromising and withdrawing behaviours were somewhat positively related to effectiveness although their effects seemed to be relatively marginal. In addition, it was noted that the forcing mode of resolving conflicts was the most ineffective one.

Another research study was conducted by Samantara[94] in an aluminum manufacturing organisation in India with a view to examining such important conflict variables as the issues and sources of conflict, manager's utilization of various conflict management strategies, and the effects of status differences on the management of conflict. Another significant finding of the study was that the manager-respondents as well as their subordinates made predominant use of problem-solving, smoothing, and compromising behaviours along with the relative absence of forcing and withdrawing behaviours in resolving interpersonal conflicts. Similar findings have been obtained even in a study conducted in an Indian computer manufacturing organisation.[95] As discussed earlier, these findings point to the fact that the Indian managers' approach towards the management of conflict is characterized by more of democratic values, emphasis on sound human relations, utilization of creative potential of employees, etc. As Sharma and Samantara[96] stated, the rule of traditional hierarchical control is to be replaced by a democratic approach in which the subordinates are encouraged to express themselves fully and offer creative and innovative solutions to work related problems and issues.

It is significant to note that a highly illuminating research was conducted by Samantara[97] on different conflict management aspects in certain steel and paper manufacturing organisations in Indian industry. The findings of the study indicated that the senior managers made considerable use of problem-solving, smoothing, and compromising behaviours in resolving work-related conflicts with their subordinates while their utilisation of forcing and withdrawing behviours was somewhat insignificant. It was further noted that this pattern of utilization of different conflict management modes was noticed in the case of managers belonging to different hierarchical levels - top management, middle management, and lower-level management. These findings indicate that the Indian managers prefer to adopt a humane approach towards their subordinates and emphasise upon both the production and the human relations aspects of the job equally well. In regard to the relative effectiveness of different conflict management methods or styles, the findings of the investigation clearly revealed that problem-solving is the most effective method of conflict management, and it is followed by smoothing behaviour. The research findings indicated the negative impact of forcing behaviour on different aspects of organisational effectiveness. While the compromising mode seemed to have mixed effects on effectiveness dimensions, the withdrawing behaviour was related to none of the effectiveness aspects.

At this point, it must be mentioned that the relationship between conflict management style or methods and various organisational effectiveness aspects (as investigated in the above-mentioned research studies) has been explored further in some more organisations in the Indian industry. The results of the empirical investigations in these organisations have been reported and discussed in detail in Chapter 7. The research findings obtained are intended to enhance the validity as well as reliability of the research evidence available at present on the relationship between the conflict management styles or methods and various dimensions of organizational effectiveness. These conclusive research evidences are expected to help the Indian managers in making judicious use of different conflict management styles or methods for resolving work related differences or disagreements with their subordinates so as to attain optimum organizational effectiveness.

## 3.6 CONTINGENCY APPROACH TO CONFLICT MANAGEMENT

The normative theories of conflict management[99] argued in favour of the proposition that there is only one style of conflict management. Based on this perspective, a number of empirical research studies were conducted to examine the relationship between conflict handling styles or methods and various dimensions of individual, group and organisational effectiveness.[100] The findings of these studies broadly indicated that problem-solving is the most effective method of conflict management and it tends to be followed by smoothing behaviour. In contrast to these normative viewpoints regarding conflict management, many leading organisation experts have suggested that a particular conflict handling mode may be regarded as functional or dysfunctional depending upon the situational variables. According to these contingency viewpoints, the managers must try to identify and analyse the situational variables before choosing the most appropriate conflict management style to be used in a given situation. At this point, it must be stated that different theorists have identified and analysed different sets of situational variables influencing the choice of conflict management styles or methods. Although the contingency perspectives on conflict management have been discussed in much greater detail in Chapter 8, the present section includes a brief review of literature regarding the contributions of leading management theoreticians on the functionality or otherwise of different conflict management styles or methods in certain given situations.

According to Blake and Mouton,[101] an individual's conflict management styles are determined by forces and pressures arising (1) from within himself such as his personality and value system; (2) from his immediate external surroundings or situation; and (3) from certain organizational characteristics such as established practices and procedures, traditions, customs, etc. As viewed by Blake and Mouton,[102] every individual tends to use a dominant style of managing conflicts and falls back upon a backup style only when the dominant style fails to work in a given situation. The fact that an individual has a dominant style of managing conflicts is influenced by the variables or conditions as described above.

Thomas[103] suggested that although people have a preference for a particular style of resolving conflicts, it has been found that different conflict management styles are effective or useful in different possible situations. The avoiding style is appropriate when the conflict has arisen over certain trivial issues, when victory is impossible, or when someone else is in a better position to solve the problem. The accommodating style of managing conflicts appears to be most appropriate when peace is more valuable than winning one's own position or when the issues involved are more significant to the other party. The compromising approach works best when prolonged deadlock exists over the conflict or when a certain deadline is to be met. The competing style is especially useful in emergency situations in which a fast decision is to be made. The collaborating style is most effective when diverse viewpoints have to be accommodated with a view to getting the best possible solution. It is also quite significant to know that Thomas[104] proposed a structural model of dyadic conflict that explains the pressures and forces influencing the parties involved in a conflict. The conflict management behaviour of each party is influenced by such forces as: (1) behavioural predisposition; (2) social pressure; (3) incentive structure; and (4) rules and procedures.

Derr[105] proposed a contingency perspective on conflict management and suggested three main strategies for resolving conflicts: power-play, bargaining, and collaboration. According to Derr, power-play is intended to achieve a dynamic balance of competing forces and is the only possible means to resolve ideological disputes. Bargaining helps in ensuring power parity between conflicting parties or groups. It is an excellent means of ensuring optimum distribution of scarce resources among the competing parties and helps in achieving a formal agreement to disputes. Collaboration works best when the parties in conflict are willing to openly confront their disagreements or differences and have a sincere desire to solve the dispute.

Pareek[106] viewed that the choice of conflict management style or mode is influenced by two dimensions: (1) integration of the in-group; and (2) criticality of the issue. As there is an increase in these two dimensions from low to high, the approach modes to conflict management such as compromise, arbitration and negotiation become more and more relevant and appropriate. On the other hand, when there is a decrease in these two dimensions, the avoidance modes such as resignation, withdrawal, diffusion, appeasement and flight become predominant. Thus, the underlying implication of Pareek's approach is that a group may choose an appropriate mode of resolving conflicts but then gradually move towards the negotiation mode by strengthening itself on both the dimensions; in group integration and critically of the conflict issue.

Philip and Cheston[107] studied certain incidents of conflict, the methods used to resolve these conflicts, and the effectiveness of these methods. It was found that problem solving and forcing were the most preferred methods used in resolving conflicts. As observed by Philip and Cheston, the problem-solving mode of resolving conflicts was effective in certain conditions such as open-minded attitudes, interdependence, mutual awareness of conflicts, willingness to ignore power issues, and the existing problem-solving procedures. On the contrary, the forcing mode was successful when organisational goals and policies supported a single solution, in-work value conflicts and refusal to co-operate due to old conflicts.

Rahim[108] discussed the effectiveness of five different conflict management styles (integrating, dominating, obliging, compromising, and avoiding) in different possible situations. According to Rahim,[109] integrating or problem-solving style is most suitable for dealing with complex issues which require the use of skills and information to find appropriate solutions. This style is especially useful for dealing with strategic issues related to long-range planning, organisational policies and objectives, etc. The dominating style, also known as the win-lose orientation, may be effective or appropriate when fast decision-making is needed or when trivial issues are involved. The obliging or smoothing style may be appropriate when a party in conflict emphasizes commonalities and even neglects his interests to satisfy the interests of the other party. Compromising may be especially useful when both the conflicting parties are equally powerful or when the goals of both the parties are mutually exclusive. Finally, the avoiding style may be considered useful when the issues of conflict are trivial in nature or when no solutions can be visualised in the immediate future.

Thus, in contrast to the normative theories of conflict management, the contingency viewpoints do not classify any single method of managing conflicts as the best one. Rather, different methods of conflict management are viewed as having functional or dysfunctional effects depending upon the prevailing situational factors or variables. As discussed above, organisational behaviour experts have analysed various situational variables influencing the selection of different conflict management methods and their potential consequences. It must be pointed out, however, that most of the contingency perspectives on conflict management have been offered only theoretically without testing their applicability in organisational situations. Therefore, there is a need to examine the appropriateness or effectiveness of conflict management styles or methods in the light of various organisational and psychological variables.

## 3.7 SUMMARY AND CONCLUSION

It may be stated that the aforesaid review of literature regarding organisational conflict has brought out certain revealing facts. In explaining certain significant aspects of organisational conflict, the contributions of prominent theoreticians and researchers on the subject of organisational conflict have been presented in an integrated manner. The present research may be regarded as highly valuable in that it highlights certain basic issues related to organizational conflict such as the changing views of conflict, antecedents to conflict, conflict outcomes or consequences, management of conflict, and the contingency approach to conflict management. Necessary inferences regarding different aspects of conflict have been drawn on the basis of research evidences obtained through the collection and analysis of the existing literature on the subject. It is expected that the valuable insights gained from this exercise will help the practising managers to view conflicts more objectively or rationally and also attempt to utilise their potential benefits to the organisation in terms of higher levels of performance, organisational innovation and creativity, individual and group development, etc.

Although the above-mentioned aspects of organisational conflict will be dealt with more exhaustively in the ensuing chapters, the present section provides a brief summary of research evidences obtained on these issues through the analysis of the existing literature. As discussed earlier, the traditional notion of conflict as being inherently bad or destructive in nature has undergone significant changes. The modern organisation theorists recognise that conflict can have positive or negative effects in organisations depending upon its management. Therefore, in the modern times, the emphasis has shifted from the elimination of conflicts to the management of conflicts. It was also observed that many antecedents to conflict or causal factors also are responsible for the conflicts at various levels of an organisation. The causal factors or determinants of conflict examined in the present section included task interdependence, organisational differentiation, competition for scarce resources, performance criteria and rewards, ambiguities, hierarchical differences in prestige, power and knowledge, identity concerns, barriers to communication, personality attributes, role dissatisfaction, drive for autonomy, and the need for tension release. The research findings have shown that all these causes or determinants of conflict are inherent in various organisational and environmental factors such as the nature of task being performed, organisation's structure, growth and expansion of organisational activities, changes in technology, structure and processes, availability of limited organisational resources, inter-departmental or inter-group differences in value systems, changes in the external environment, etc. In addition to analysing all these antecedents to conflict, necessary suggestions have also been made as to how the occurrence of such organisational conflicts can be prevented through the use of various organisational measures.

Regarding the consequences or outcomes of conflict, it has been observed that the modern management experts have analysed both the positive and the negative effects of conflict in organisational life. The consensus among organisational experts is that a moderate degree of conflict has many beneficial effects in an organisation. While the existence of too little conflict or tension leads to apathy or indifference in individual beahviour, too much of conflict has serious detrimental effects on individual, group and organisational effectiveness. The management experts have further suggested that conflict can have functional or dysfunctional effects in organisations depending upon its management. The review of literature shows that the management of conflicts has generally moved in two directions. In the first place, some of the researchers have tried to measure the intensity or degree of conflict at various levels of an organisation in terms of stress, anxiety, tension, hostility, etc., and also find out the sources of such conflicts. The purpose is to ensure that a moderate degree of conflict may be maintained by altering the sources of conflict in order to enhance organisational effectiveness. The second approach involves the research attempts made to examine the efficacy or effectiveness of different conflict handling methods or styles in terms of their effects on individual, group and organisational effectiveness. In this context, the findings of a number of research studies have been briefly reported in this chapter.

The findings of the research studies conducted in India regarding the conflict management behaviour of managers have shown that the senior managers made a predominant use of problem-solving, smoothing and compromising modes of managing conflict with their subordinates while their utilization of forcing and withdrawing behaviour was found to be relatively negligible. These findings point to the fact that Indian managers value the human relations aspects of the job and seek to achieve higher productivity only through the voluntary compliance or willing cooperation of their subordinates. Thus, the Indian industrial environment seems to be characterized by a democratic approach to the management of work related conflicts or issues. In addition, it has been broadly observed that confrontation or problem solving is the most effective method of conflict resolution and it is followed by smoothing behaviours. The forcing method of conflict management was found to be the most ineffective one. The effects of other conflict handling styles on individual or organisational effectiveness were generally found to be relatively insignificant or negligible. Therefore, it has been suggested that there is a need to enhance or strengthen the use of problem-solving and smoothing behviours in managing organisational conflict while utilization of forcing behaviour should be discouraged as much as possible. The reliability and validity of these research findings obtained with regards to the relationship between conflict management styles and various aspects or dimensions of organisational effectiveness have been further explored in some more organisations in the Indian industry. The results of these investigations are reported in Chapter 7. It is expected that the conclusive research evidences obtained would help the Indian managers in making a judicious use of different conflict management styles or methods for resolving conflicts with their subordinates.

At the end of this chapter, the contingency approach to conflict management has been examined. While the normative theories of conflict management suggest that there is only one style of conflict management, the contingency perspective on conflict management propagates that a particular conflict handling style or method may be regarded as effective or ineffective depending upon the situational variables. Therefore, the contingency theorists have argued that the managers must identify and analyse various situational factors or variables before choosing the most appropriate style to resolve the conflict. In fact, there are several situational variables such as organisational climate, social norms, employees' education and skills, their economic conditions, etc., which do have a significant impact on the choice of conflict management strategies or methods as well as their effects on several dimensions of organisational effectiveness. Although different contingency theorists have proposed and analysed various sets of situational variables influencing the choice of different conflict management styles or methods as well as their potential outcomes, there is a paramount need to conduct empirical research studies regarding the efficacy or effectiveness of conflict management strategies or methods in the context of various organisational and psychological variables.

## REVIEW QUESTIONS

1. "Conflict is not necessarily an evil". Do you agree?
2. Discuss some of the important antecedents to organisational conflict as described in the literature.

3. Conflicts can have functional or dysfunctional effects in organisations. Discuss with suitable examples.
4. Explain the approaches to management of conflicts in organisations.
5. The research findings have thrown light on the relative effectiveness of conflict management methods or styles. Discuss.

## REFERENCES


1. Dalton, M., *Men who Manage, Fusions of Feeling and Theory in Administration,* John Wiley and Sons, New York, 1959; and McGregor, D., The human side of enterprise, *Management Review*, 1957, pp. 41-49.'
2. Stagner, R., *Psychology of Industrial Conflict,* John Wiley and Sons, Oxford, England, 1956; and Stagner, R. and Rosen, H., Psychology of Union-management Relations, Wadsworth Pub. Co., Inc., Oxford, England, 1965.
3. Burke, R.J., Methods of resolving superior-subordinate conflict: The constructive use of subordinate differences and disagreements, *Organisational Behaviour and Human Performance*, 5(4), 1970, pp. 393-411; Renwick, P.A., Perception and management of superior-subordinate conflict, *Organisational Behaviour and Human Performance* 13(3), 1975, pp. 444-456; Sharma, R.A. and Samantara, R., Conflict management in an Indian firm: A case study, *Decision*, 21(4), 1994, pp. 235-249; Samantara, R., Management of superior-subordinate conflict: An exploration, *Indian Journal of Industrial Relations*, 38(4), New Delhi, April 2003, pp. 444-459; and Samantara, R., Conflict management strategies and organisational effectiveness, *Indian Journal of Industrial Relations*, 39(3), New Delhi, January 2004, pp. 298-323.
4. Lawrence, P.R. and Lorsch, J.W., Differentiation and integration in complex organisations, *Administrative Science Quarterly*, 12, 1967, pp. 1-47.
5. Kelly, J., Make conflict work for you, *Harvard Business Review*, 48(4), 1970, p. 103; and Litterer, J.A. Conflict in organisation: A re-examination, *Academy of Management Journal*, 9(3), 1966, pp. 178-186.
6. Kahn, R.L., Wolfe, D.M., Quinn, R.P., Snoek, J.D. and Rosenthal, R.A., *Organisational Stress: Studies in Role Conflict and Ambiguity*, Wiley, New York, 1964.
7. Boulding, K.E., *Conflict and Defense: A General Theory*, Harper, Oxford, England, 1962.
8. March, J.G. and Simon, H.A., *Organisations,* John Wiley and Sons, Inc., New York, 1958.
9. Robbins, S.P., *Managing Organisational Conflict: A Non-traditional Approach,* Prentice Hall, NJ, 1974.

10. Thomas, K.W., Conflict and conflict management, M.D. Dunettee, *Handbook of Industrial and Organisational Psychology,* Rand McNally, Chicago, 1976, pp. 889-935.
11. Blake, R.R. and Mouton, J.S., *The Managerial Grid*, Gulf Publishing, Houston, 1964; Pondy, L.R., Organisational conflict: Concepts and models, *Administrative Science Quarterly*, 12, 1967, pp. 296-320; and Thompson, J.D., Organisational management of conflict, *Administrative Science Quarterly*, 1960, pp. 389-409.
12. Pondy, L.R., 1962, *op. cit.*
13. Dutton, J. and Walton, R., Inter-departmental conflict and cooperation: Two contrasting studies, *Human Organisation*, 25(3), 1966, pp. 207-220.
14. Simon, H.A., On the concept of organisational goal, *Administrative Science Quarterly*, 9(1), 1964, pp. 1-22.
15. Litwak, E., Models of bureaucracy which permit conflict, *American Journal of Sociology*, 1961, pp. 177-184.
16. Lawrence, P.R. and Lorsch, J.W., 1967, *op. cit.*
17. *Ibid.*
18. *Ibid.*
19. Thibaut, J.W. and Kelley, H.H., *The Social Psychology of Groups*, Wiley, New York, 1959.
20. Walton, R.E., Theory of conflict in lateral organizational relationships, J.R. Lawrence (Ed.), *Operational Research and the Social Science*, Tavistock, London, 1965.
21. Pruitt, D.G., *Negotiation Behaviour*, Academic, New York, 1981.
22. Lax, D.A. and Sebenius, J.K., Interests: The measure of negotiation. *Negotiation Journal*, 2(1), 1986, pp. 73-92; and Olekalns, M., Conflict at work: Defining and resolving organisational conflicts, *Australian Psychologist*, 32, 1997, pp. 56-61.
23. Pondy, L.R., 1967, *op. cit.*
24. Dutton, J. and Walton, R., 1966, *op. cit.*
25. Dalton, M., 1959, *op. cit.*
26. Alper, S., Tjosvold, D. and Law, K.S., Conflict management, efficacy and performance in organisational teams, *Personnel Psychology*, 53(3), 2000, pp. 625-642.
27. Schein, E., *Organisational Psychology*, Prentice Hall, Englewood Cliffs, NJ, 1970.
28. Dalton, M., 1959, *op. cit.*
29. Dutton, J. and Walton, R., 1966, *op. cit.*
30. Zald, M.N., Power balance and staff conflict in correctional institutions, *Administrative Science Quarterly*, 1962, pp. 22-49.

31. Kahn, R.L., Wolfe, D.M., Quinn, R.P., Snoek, J.D., and Rosenthal, R.A., 1964, *op. cit.*

32. Seiler, J.A., Diagnosing interdepartmental conflict, *Harvard Business Review*, 41(5), 1963, pp. 121-132.

33. Zald, M.N., 1962, *op. cit.*

34. Lawrence, P.R. and Lorsch, J.W., 1967, *op. cit.*

35. Mayer, C.H. and Louw, L., Organisational conflict: Reflections on managing conflict, identities and values in a selected South African organisation, *SA Journal of Human Resources Management*, 7(1), 2009, pp. 36-48.

36. Walton, R.E., Inter-organisational decision-making and identity conflict, M.F. Tuite, R. Chisholm, and M. Radner, (Ed.), *Inter-Organisational Decision-making, Aldine Publishing Co.* Chicago, 1972.

37. Straus, M.A., Measuring families, H.T. Christonson, (Ed.), *Handbook of Marriage and the Family*, Rand McNally, Chicago, 1964.

38. March, J.G., and Simon, H.A., *Organisations*, John Wiley and Sons, Inc., New York, 1958.

39. Walton, R.E., and Dutton, J.M., The management of inter-departmental conflict: A model and review, *Administrative Science Quarterly*, 14, 1969, pp. 73-84.

40. Walton, R.E. and Mckersie, R.B., *A Behavoiural Theory of Labour Negotiations*, McGraw Hill, New York, 1965.

41. Kahn, *et al.*, 1964, *op. cit.*

42. Walton, R.E., and McKersie, R.B., Behavioural dilemmas in mixed-motive decision-making, *Behavioural Science*, 11(5), 1966, pp. 370-384.

43. Dalton, M., 1959, *op. cit.*; and Thompson, J.D., 1960, *op. cit.*

44. Ibid.

45. *Ibid.*

46. Argyris, C., *Integrating the Individual and the Organisation*, John Wiley and Sons, New York, 1964.

47. Dalton, M., 1959, *op. cit.*

48. Cosier, L.A., *Continuities in the Study of Social Conflict*, Free Press, New York, 1967; and Pondy, L.R., 1967, *op. cit.*

49. Argyris, C., The individual and organization: Some problems of mutual adjustment, *Administrative Science Quarterly*, 1957, pp. 1-24.

50. Tjosvold, D. and Chia, L.C., Conflict between managers and workers: The role of cooperation and competition. *The Journal of Social Psychology*, 129(2), 1989, pp. 235-247.

51. Van de Vliert, E., Nauta, A., Giebels, E. and Janssen, O., Constructive conflict at work, *Journal of Organisational Behaviour*, 20(4), 1999, pp. 475-491.

52. Robbins, S.P., *Organiastional Behaviour*, Prentice Hall, New Delhi, 2001, p. 393.
53. See, for instance, Cosier, R.A. and Schwenk, C.R., Agreement and thinking alike: Ingredients for poor decisions, *Academy of Management Executive*, February 1990, pp. 69-74; Jehn, K.A., Enhancing effectiveness: An investigation of advantages and disadvantages of value-based intra-group conflict, *International Journal of Conflict Management*, July 1994, pp. 223-238; and Priem, R.L., Harrison, D.A., and Muir, N.K., Structured conflict and consensus outcomes in group decision making, *Journal of Management*, 21(4), 1995, pp. 691-710.
54. Hall, J. and Williams, M.S., A comparison of decision-making performances in established and adhoc groups, *Journal of Personality and Social Psychology*, February 1966, p. 217.
55. Hoffman, R.L., Homogeneity of member personality and its effect on group problem-solving, *Journal of Abnormal and Social Psychology*, January 1959, pp. 27-32; and Hoffman, R.L. and Maier, N.R.F., Quality and acceptance of problem solutions by members of homogeneous and heterogeneous groups, *Journal of Abnormal and Social Psychology*, March 1961, pp. 401-407.
56. Robbins, S.P., 2001, *op. cit.*
57. Dyer, B. and Song, X.M., Innovation strategy and sanctioned conflict: A new edge in innovation, *Journal of Product Innovation Management*, 15(6), 1998, pp. 505-519.
58. Menon, A., Bhardwaj, S.G. and Howell, R., The quality and effectiveness of marketing strategy: Effects of functional and dysfunctional conflict in intra-organisational relationships, *Journal of the Academy of Marketing Science*, 24(4), 1996, pp. 299-313.
59. Song, M., Dyer, B. and Thieme, R.J., Conflict management and innovation performance: An integrated contingency perspective, *Journal of the Academy of Marketing Science*, 34(3), 2006, pp. 241-356.
60. Thomas, K.W., 1976, *op. cit.*
61. Deutsch, M., Towards an understanding of conflict, *International Journal of Group Tensions*, 1971.
62. Pelz, C., Some social factors related to performance in a research organization. *Administrative Science Quarterly*, 1956, pp. 310-325; Hoffman, L.R., 1959, *op. cit.*; Hoffman, L.R. and Maier, N.R., 1961, *op. cit.*; and Hall, J., Decisions, decisions, decisions, *Psychology Today*, 1971, pp. 51-54.
63. March, J.G. and Simon, H.A., 1958, *op. cit*; and Litterer, J.A., 1966, *op. cit.*
64. Litterer, J.A., 1966, *op. cit.*
65. Coser, L.A., *The Functions of Social Conflict*, Vol. 9, Routledge, New York, 1956; and Blake, R.R. and Mouton, J.S., 1964, *op. cit.*
66. Guetzkow, H., and Gyr, J., An analysis of conflict in decision-making groups, *Human Relations*, 1954.

67. *Ibid.*

68. Pinkly, R.L., Dimensions of conflict frame: Disputant interpretations of conflict, *Journal of Applied Psychology*, 75(2), 1990, p. 117; and Jehn, K.A., A qualitative analysis of conflict types and dimensions in organisational groups, *Administrative Science Quarterly*, 1997, pp. 530-557.

69. Amason, A.C., Distinguishing the effects of functional and dysfunctional conflict on strategic decision-making: Resolving a paradox for top management teams, *Academy of Management Journal*, 39(1), 1996, pp. 123-148.

70. Ross, R., Conflict, R. Ross and J. Ross, (Ed.), *Small Groups in Organisational Settings*, Prentice Hall, Englewood Cliffs, NJ, pp. 139-178.

71. Jehn, K.A., A multimethod examination of the benefits and detriments of intragroup conflict, *Administrative Science Quarterly*, 40, 1995, pp. 256-282.

72. Jehn, K.A., 1997, *op. cit.*

73. Amason, A.C., 1996, *op. cit.*; Cosier, R., and Rose, G., Cognitive conflict and goal conflict effects on task performance, *Organisational Behaviour and Human Performance*, 19, 1977, pp. 378-391; Fiol, C.M., Consensus, diversity, and learning in organisations, *Organisation Science*, 5(3), 1994, pp. 403-420; Putnam, L.L., Productive conflict: Negotiation as implicit coordination, *International Journal of Conflict Management*, 5(3), 1994, pp. 284-298; and Schweiger, D.M., Sandberg, W.R., and Raga, J.W., Group approaches for improving strategic decision making: A comparative analysis of dialectical enquiry, devils advocacy and consensus, *Academy of Management Journal*, 29(1), 1986, pp. 51-71.

74. Gero, A., Conflict avoidance in consensual decision processes, *Small Group Research*, 16(4), 1985, pp. 487-499; and Turner, M.E., and Pratkanis, A.R., Mitigating groupthink by stimulating constructive conflict, C.K. De Dreu, and E.Van De Vliert, (Ed.), *Using Conflict in Organisations*, Sage, Thousand Oaks, CA, 1997, pp. 53-71.

75. Bourgeois, L.J., Strategic goals, environmental uncertainty and economic performance in volatile environments, *Academy of Management Journal*, 28, 1985, pp. 548-573; Eisenhardt, K.M., and Schoonhoven, C.B., Organisational growth: Linking founding team, strategy, environmental and growth among US semi-conductor ventures, *Administrative Science Quarterly*, 1990, pp. 504-529; Jehn, K.A., 1995, *op. cit.*; Jehn, K.A., 1997, *op. cit.*; and Jehn, K.A., Northcraft, G.B., and Neale, M.A., Why differences make a difference: A field study of diversity, conflict and performance in work groups, *Administrative Science Quarterly*, 44(4), 1999, pp. 741-763.

76. Jehn, K.A., 1997, *op. cit.*

77. Amason, A.C., 1996, *op. cit.*; Baron, R., Positive effects of conflict: Insights from social cognition, C. De Dreu, and E. Van De Vliert, (Ed.), *Using Conflict in Organisations*, Sage Publications, London, pp. 178-192; Jehn, K.A., 1995, *op. cit.*;

Jehn, K.A., *et al.*, 1999, *op. cit.*; and Wall, V.D., and Nolan, L.L., Perceptions of inequity, satisfaction and conflict in task-oriented groups, *Human Relations*, 39(11), 1986, pp. 1033-1051.

78. DeChurch, L.A., Hamilton, K.L., and Haas, C., Effects of conflict management strategies on perceptions of intragroup conflict, *Group Dynamics: Theory, Research and Practice*, 11(1), 2007, pp. 66-78.
79. Jehn, K.A., and Chatman, J.A., The influence of proportional and perceptual conflict composition in team performance, *International Journal of Conflict Management*, 11, 2000, pp. 56-73; and Sullivan, P.J., and Feltz, D.L., The relationship between intrateam conflict and cohesion within hockey teams, *Small Group Research*, 32(3), 2001, pp. 342-355.
80. Amason, A.C., 1996, *op. cit.*; Jehn, K.A., 1995, *op. cit.*; Jehn, K.A., 1997, *op. cit.*; and Jehn, K.A., *et al.*, 1999.
81. Brown, L.D., Managing conflict at organizational interfaces, *Addision-Wesley*, Reading, MA, 1983.
82. *Ibid.*
83. Guetzkow, H., and Gyr, J., 1954, *op. cit.*
84. *Ibid.*
85. Jehn, K.A., Enhancing effectiveness: An investigation of advantages and disadvantages of value-based intragroup conflict, *International Journal of Conflict Management*, 5(3), 1994, pp. 223-238.
86. Blake, R.R., and Mouton, J.S., 1964, *op. cit.*
87. Lawrence, P.R., and Lorsch, J.W., 1967, *op. cit.*
88. Burke, R.J., Methods of resolving interpersonal conflict, *Personnel Administration*, 32(4), 1969, pp. 48-55.
89. Blake, R.R., and Mouton, J.S., 1964, *op. cit.*
90. Thomas, K.W., *Conflict Handling Modes in Inter-departmental Relations*, Purdue University, 1971.
91. Aram, J.D., Morgan, C.P., and Esbeck, E.B., Relation of collaborative interpersonal relationships to individual satisfaction and organisational performance, *Administrative Science Quarterly*, 16, 1971, pp. 289-296.
92. Dutton, J., and Walton, R., 1966, *op. cit.*
93. Sharma, R.A. and Samantara, R., 1994, *op. cit.*
94. Samantara, R., 2003, *op. cit.*
95. Sharma, R.A., and Samantara, R., 1994, *op. cit.*
96. *Ibid.*
97. Samantara, R., 2004, *op. cit.*
98. Sharma, R.A. and Samantara, R., 1994, *op. cit.*

99. Blake, R.R., and Mouton, J.S., 1964, *op. cit.*; and Likert, R. and Likert, J.G., *New Ways of Managing Conflict,* McGraw Hill, New York, 1976.

100. Lawrence, P.R., and Lorsch, J.W., 1967, *op. cit.*; Burke, R.J., 1969, *op. cit.*; Sharma, R.A., and Samantara, R., 1994, *op. cit.*; and Samantara, R., 2004, *op. cit.*

101. Blake, R.R., and Mouton, J.S., 1964, *op. cit.*

102. *Ibid.*

103. Thomas, K.W., 1976, *op. cit.*

104. *Ibid.*

105. Derr, C.B., Managing organizational conflict: Collaboration, bargaining and power approaches, *California Management Review*, 21(2), 76, 1978.

106. Pareek, U.N., *Managing Conflict and Collaboration,* Oxford & IBH Publishing Company, New Delhi, 1982.

107. Philip, E., and Cheston, R., *Conflict resolution:* What works? California Management Review, 21(4), 1979.

108. Rahim, M.A., A strategy for managing conflict in complex organisations, *Human Relations*, 38(1), 1985, pp. 81-89.

109. *Ibid.*

# 4

# Conflict Management in Organisations

## 4.1 INTRODUCTION

It must be emphasised that the general views regarding conflict and its effects in organisational life have changed quite significantly with the evolution of management thoughts. As mentioned in Chapter 3, the traditional or classical views of conflict assumed that conflict is an undersirable, destructive and unacceptable factor in organisaions.[1] According to the classical viewpoint, conflict is always detrimental to the attainment of organisational objectives and is therefore to be avoided. The classicists believed that conflict indicated manufacturing in an organisation, and it resulted from such factors as inadequate or poor communication, lack of faith or trust among employees and the management's inability or failure to fulfil the employees' needs and expectations, etc. Therefore, the classicists emphasised upon the designing of an organisation's structure including clear-cut definition of authority and responsibility, policies, procedures, etc., so as to prevent the occurrence of conflicts in the organisation.

In contrast to the classical approach to conflict, the neoclassicists or behvarioural scientists viewed conflict as inevitable, and even useful in organisations. The neoclassicists attributed the occurrence of organisational conflicts to the basic incongruence existing between the needs and aspirations of adult, mature employees and the requirements of the modern formal organisation. Therefore, the neoclassicists emphasised upon the existence of sound human relations, informal groups, informal leadership, democratic or participative style of leadership, and so on, in an organisation. As conflict is considered both inevitable and useful in organisations, the neoclassicists stressed upon the amicable solution of conflicts in order to attain sound human relations and higher levels of productivity.

It is significant to note that the interactionist or modern view of conflict has gone further in stating that conflict is not only inevitable in organisational life but also necessary and even desirable under certain specific organisational conditions.[2] While organisations with little or no conflict may stagnate, it is also true that organisational conflict, left uncontrolled, can have serious dysfunctional consequences. Therefore, the modern theorists broadly agree that a moderate degree of conflict is essential for achieving optimum organisational effectiveness. As Brown has suggested, "conflict management can require intervention to reduce conflict if there is too much, or intervention to promote conflict if there is too little."[3]

Research studies on the management of organisational conflict have been conducted in two directions. Some researchers have assumed that a moderate amount of conflict may be maintained for enhancing organisational effectiveness by altering the sources of conflict. Therefore, they have attempted to measure the amount of conflict at various organisational levels in terms of stress, anxiety, hostility, tension, competition, etc., and also explore the sources of such a conflict. Other researchers have attempted to study the relative efficacy or effectiveness of various conflict management strategies or methods in terms of their effects on different aspects or criteria of individual, group or organisational effectiveness. A number of studies have been conducted on the relationship between conflict handling styles and different effectiveness criteria. These studies have not only provided valuable insights into the present conflict handling behaviours of managers but also suggested necessary modifications therein with a view to enhance organisational effectiveness. In the present chapter, an attempt has been made to define conflict management and also analyse various conflict management approaches as suggested by social scientists. These approaches are based upon various methods or styles of handling conflicts in organisations. It is hoped that such an analysis would not only throw light on the evolution of different conflict management approaches but also pinpoint the utility of these approaches in various conflict situations. In addition, the present chapter describes the process of managing conflicts at the macro-organisational level, which is aimed at minimising the dysfunctions of conflict and increasing its functional aspects in order to enhance learning and effectiveness in an organisation. This chapter also explains certain conflict management strategies that may be followed to maintain a desirable level of conflict in the organisation. The adoption of these strategies is also expected to help facilitate a judicious utilisation of various conflict handling styles or methods in conflict situations with a view to enhance organisational effectiveness.

## 4.2 CONFLICT MANAGEMENT

It must be pointed out that the present chapter emphasises upon management of conflict as distinguished from resolution of conflict. Conflict resolution is based upon the assumption of negative character of conflict and therefore implies reduction, elimination or termination of conflict. In fact, most of the studies available on negotiation, bargaining, arbitration, and mediation fall in the category of conflict resolution. Conflict management, on the other hand, is based upon the fundamental premise that conflict has both functional and dysfunctional outcomes in an organisation. It does not necessarily mean avoidance, elimination or reduction of conflict. As viewed by Rahim,[4] conflict management involves designing effectiveness macro-level strategies to minimise the dysfunctions of conflict and enhance the constructive functions of conflict in order to enhance learning and effectiveness in an organisation.

According to Lipsky and Avgar,[5] conflict management "usually refers to the adoption of a proactive approach to handling conflict by managers, supervisors and union representatives (in unionised settings)". Organisations adopting conflict management approaches do not wait till the time work related conflicts occur and then decide about the specific conflict management methods or techniques to be used. Rather, these organisations have certain well-developed policies and procedures that are designed to handle conflicts continuously in keeping with their broad goals and objectives. These organisations have come to recognise that unilateral exercise of authority is not adequate enough to manage workplace conflict effectively and often leads to unnecessary organisational costs. Therefore, the top management teams of these organisations have started emphasising that conflict ought to be proactively managed in the same way as production, marketing, finance and other functional areas. As suggested by Lipsy and Avgar,[6] an integrated conflict management system should have the following characteristics:

1. **Broad scope:** The conflict management system should provide opportunities to the stakeholders such as employees, supervisors, professionals and managers to consider all types of problems;
2. **A culture of toleration and early resolution:** The system should tolerate dissent and encourage early resolution of conflicts through negotiations and bargaining.
3. **Multiple access points:** The employees should be able to identify the individual, department or entity within the organisation that has authority, knowledge or experience and which can offer advice about how to manage the problem in question.
4. **Multiple options:** The system should have rights-based and interest-based options for employees to consider.
5. **Support structures:** The system should include strong support structures that help coordinate and manage multiple access points and multiple options. These structures should introduce conflict management in the organisation's day-to-day operations.

## 4.3 APPROACHES TO MANAGING CONFLICTS

As stated earlier, a number of conflict management approaches have been suggested by social scientists. These approaches are essentially based upon different methods of handling intra-individual, inter-individual or inter-group conflicts in organisations. In other words, these approaches point to the efficacy or effectiveness of different conflict management styles or methods in different conflict situations.

### 4.3.1 Blake and Mouton

In their Managerial Grid, Blake and Mouton[7] provided a theoretical framework for explaining managerial behaviour in terms of two dimensions: concern for production and concern for people. Explaining how these two dimensions of managerial behaviour interact in different possible ways at the work situation, Blake and Mouton proceeded to specify and explain five major theories of managerial behaviour – Task (9, 1), Country Club (1, 9), Impoverished (1, 1), Dampened Pendulum (5, 5), and Team (9, 9). Again, under each of these theories, they enumerated strategies for dealing with conflicts: forcing, smoothing, withdrawing, compromise, and confrontation or problem-solving, as shown in Figure 4.1.

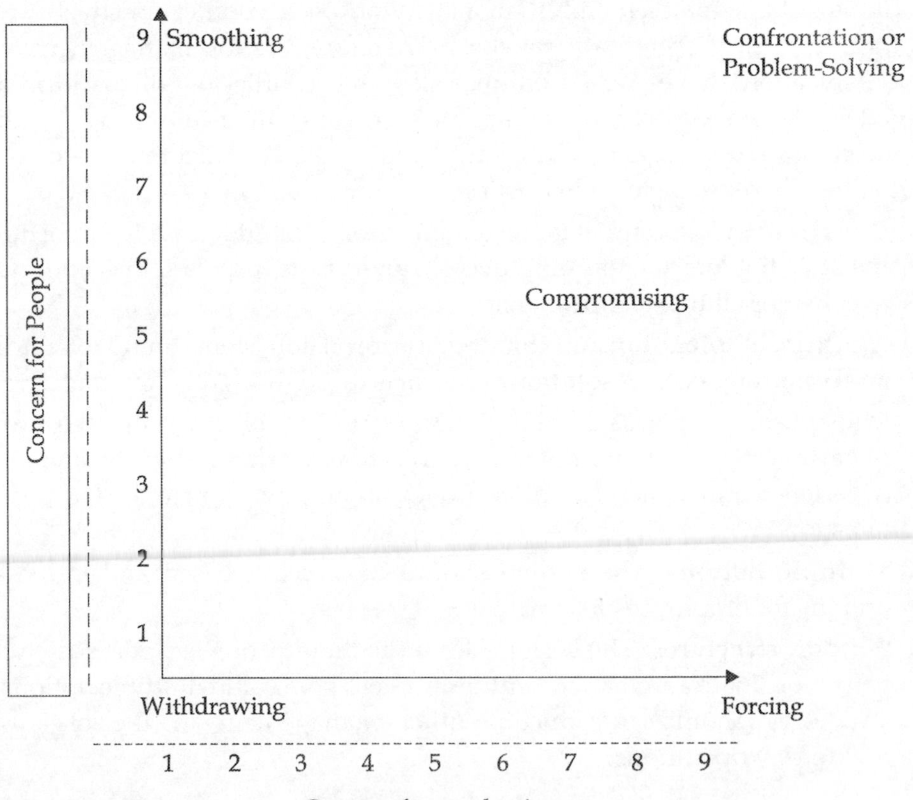


**Figure 4.1:** Blake and Mouton's five styles of conflict management

*Source* : R.R. Blake and J.S. Mouton, *The Managerial Grid,* Houston: Gulf (1964).

A 'task' manager is often guided by negative assumptions about human nature and characteristics. He believes that people dislike work inherently, are not capable of organising their own work activities, and, therefore, must be directed, controlled and often coerced to achieve organisational objectives.[8] As inter-personal or inter-group conflict arises in the organisation, the general rule of conflict management adopted by the manager is suppression or forcing behaviour. In resolving differences or disagreements with his subordinates, peers or even his senior, he uses his power, position or knowledge to force acceptance of his own point of view.

A manager who is primarily relationship-oriented in nature, is very much concerned about his own acceptance by others. Unable to use harsh or stern methods of managing his subordinates, the manger often takes resource to reconciliation through appeasement and other means with a view to maintaining harmonious, accepting relationships with them. In managing conflicts with them, the manager's basic approach remains that of "smoothing over conflict". The manager places high value to avoiding conflict with his boss.

In the face of conflict, the solution for a manager having no concern for both production and people is to avoid it. One way is to withdraw from the conflict situation if it is possible. An alternative is to maintain strict neutrality by not voicing any personal opinion. Such a manager avoids conflict with his subordinates, peers or the seniors by just ignoring disagreeable solutions.

A manager who is concerned about both the production and the human relations aspects on an equal basis is more likely to adopt the method of splitting or separation in managing conflicts. He seeks to manage the conflict by keeping the parties in conflict apart until a solution can be found. An important way of splitting the difference is compromise – finding a middle ground between two divergent points of view. Compromise provides a middle path that people with different positions find better to accept than to retain their own positions and to continue the argument. The compromising method can be used by the manager for resolving conflicts with his subordinates, peers or even with his seniors.

A manager who seeks to integrate high productivity and high morale through concerted team action is likely to use direct confrontation on problem-solving in solving conflicts. According to Blake and Mouton, "Confrontation means facing up to the conflict, getting it out on the table where it can be examined and evaluated by all who are a party to it." In this way, the reasons for conflict can be examined and assessed by the parties involved. And, subsequently, the conditions for its resolution can also be discussed. While resolving conflicts with the subordinates, the manager can use the problem-solving approach to deliberate upon areas of friction that prevent them from working well together. Similarly, he can use this approach to resolve effectively conflicts even with his superior. Instead of withholding his convictions, the manager can try to prevail upon his senior through the process of open dialogue to elicit a positive response from him.

### 4.3.2 Thomas

Thomas[9] developed a two-dimensional model of conflict behaviour on the basis of Blake and Mouton's[10] five category scheme for classifying interpersonal behaviour. The model specifies a party's conflict handling behavioural orientation according to the degree to which he would like to satisfy his own concern (i.e., degree of his assertiveness) and the degree to which he would like to satisfy the concern of the other (i.e., the degree of his cooperativeness). As shown in Figure 4.2, five such conflict handling orientations have been plotted along the two dimensions of assertiveness and cooperativeness: competitive (assertive, uncooperative); collaborative (assertive, cooperative); avoidant (inassertive, uncooperative); and sharing (intermediate in both assertiveness and cooperativeness). In addition, it can be seen that Table 4.1 lists the specific situations in which each of these conflict management styles can be used most effectively.

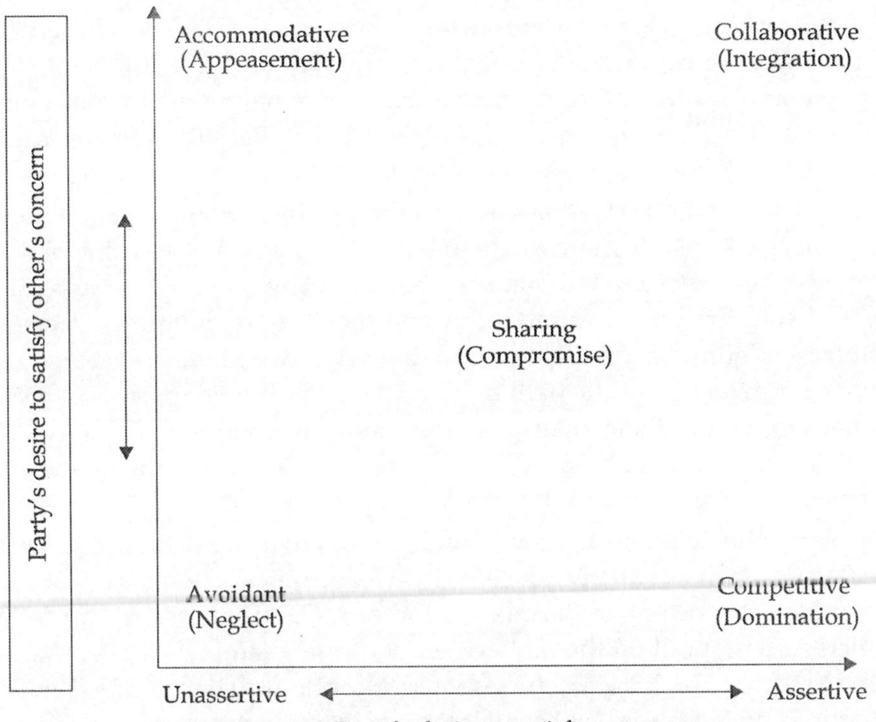


**Figure 4.2:** Five conflict-handling orientations, plotted according to party's desire to satisfy own and other's concern

*Source*: Adapted from K.W. Thomas, "Conflict and Conflict Management", M.D. Dunnettee (Ed.), *Handbook of Industrial and Organisational Psychology*, Chicago: Rand Mc Nally (1976).

**Table 4.1:** Uses of the five conflict handling modes as reported by a group of chief executive officers

| Conflict handling node | Appropriate situations |
|---|---|
| Competing | 1. When quick, decisive action is vital, for example, emergencies.<br>2. On important issues where unpopular actions need implementing, for example, cost cutting, enforcing unpopular rules, discipline.<br>3. On issues vital to company welfare when you know you are right.<br>4. Against people who take advantage of non-competitive behaviour. |
| Collaborating | 1. To find an integrative solution when both sets of concerns are too important to be compromised.<br>2. When objective is to learn.<br>3. To merge insights from people with different perspectives.<br>4. To gain commitment by incorporating concerns into a consensus.<br>5. To work through feelings which have interfered with a relationship |
| Compromising | 1. When goals are important, but not worth the effort or potential disruption of more assertive modes.<br>2. When opponents with equal power are committed to mutually exclusive goals.<br>3. To achieve temporary settlements to complex issues.<br>4. To arrive at expedient solutions under time pressure.<br>5. As a backup when collaboration or competition is unsuccessful. |
| Avoiding | 1. When an issue is trivial or more important issues are pressing.<br>2. When one perceives no chances of satisfying one's concerns.<br>3. When potential disruption outweighs the benefit of resolution.<br>4. To let people cool down and regain perspective.<br>5. When gathering information supersedes immediate decision.<br>6. When others can resolve the conflict more effectively.<br>7. When issues seem tangential or symptomatic of other issues. |
| Accommodating | 1. When one finds one is wrong; to allow a better position to be heard, to learn, and to show one's reasonableness.<br>2. When issues are more important to others; to satisfy others and maintain cooperation.<br>3. To build social credits for later issues.<br>4. To minimise loss when one is outmatched and losing.<br>5. When harmony and stability are especially important.<br>6. To allow subordinates to develop by learning from mistakes. |

*Source*: Adapted from K.W. Thomas, "Toward Multidimensional Values in Teaching: The Example of Conflict Behaviors", *Academy of Management Review*, Vol. 2, 1977, p. 487.

1. **Competing:** The competitive orientation represents a desire to win one's own concern at the other's expense, i.e., to dominate. Blake *et al*[11] refer to such relationship as "win-lose power struggles". This competing or win-lose style of handling conflicts is adopted when the parties have adopted rigid attitude and

are not amenable to reason or appeal. The persons or parties adopting this strategy attempt to find out the issues, test their strengths and weaknesses, and see for themselves the consequences of their actions. The use of competing style demands great emotional or psychological energy as well as great inter-personal skills from the concerned person or parties. In addition to these potentially disruptive consequences, this approach has a great influence on the status and power systems in an organisation. It may be noted, however, that this approach is not willingly or frequently adopted. The use of this approach may be considered appropriate only in emergency situations when some unpopular courses of action may have to be taken for achieving long term organisational effectiveness.

2. **Accommodating:** An accommodative orientation focuses upon appeasement, i.e., satisfying the other's concerns without attending to one's own. A party or person with this orientation becomes generous or self-sacrificing for the sake of maintaining smooth relationships. However, it may be noted that too much reliance upon this approach may frustrate the party concerned because such party is unable to fulfil his own needs and might even lose self-esteem. This style is concerned with the emotional aspects of a conflict rather than its substantive issues. According to Sharma,[12] the accommodative style is often used when (1) smoothing is necessary to defuse a potentially explosive emotional conflict situation; (2) keeping harmony and avoiding disruption are especially important; and (3) the conflict is personality based and so difficult to resolve.
3. **Compromising:** The compromising orientation is intermediate in both assertiveness and cooperativeness. This approach represents a preference for moderate but incomplete satisfaction for both the parties. Each party gives up something and keeps something for himself in order to reach a compromise. In certain situations, the two parties may even engage themselves in bargaining and arrive at a mutually acceptable solution. It may be pointed out that compromising is often used when the time factor is of utmost importance. This style is also an effective backup style when efforts towards collaboration are not successful. It is appropriate when (1) a total win-win agreement is not possible; (2) an agreement on one party's proposal is not possible; and (3) each party does not want to be worse off than it would be if there were no agreement.
4. **Collaborating:** In contrast to compromising, the collaborative approach orientation involves a desire to integrate the concerns of both the parties or to fully satisfy their concerns. Blake *et al.*[13] and Walton McKersie[14] (1965) describe collaborative behaviours as "problem-solving" orientations. The collaborating orientation represents a win-win style that is high on both assertiveness and cooperativeness. The individuals or groups using this style view conflict as natural, useful and even leading to a more creative solution if handled jointly.

This style is appropriate when both the parties have to be committed to an ultimate solution or when different perspectives have to be merged into the final solution. It is a sort of integrative approach which should help establish superordinate goals, separate people from the problem, focus on interests and not on positions, invent options for mutual gain, and use objective criteria for finding a solution.[15]

5. **Avoiding:** The avoidance orientation is low in both assertiveness and cooperativeness, indicating indifference to the concerns of both the parties. This orientation has been described as an instance of withdrawal, isolation, indifference, ignorance or reliance upon fate. It is considered the best approach to use when the parties are in belligerent mood and need time to cool down. It may be most effectively used when (1) the issue involved is minor and not worth the attention; (2) enouh information is not available to deal with the problem; (3) the individual does not have enough power to bring about any improvement in the situation; and (4) others can more effectively resolve the conflict. It must be pointed out, however, that the utilisation of the avoiding style leads to loss of creativity of individuals, and they are not able to put forth their genuine and constructive ideas for bringing about organisational improvements.

### 4.3.3 Rahim

Similar to the conceptualisation of Blake and Mouton[16] and Thomas,[17] Rahim's[18] typology of conflict handling methods or styles was based on two dimensions of human behaviour: (1) concern for self and (2) concern for others. While the first dimension explains the degree to which a person attempts to satisfy his own concern, the second explains the degree to which a person wants to satisfy the concern of others. It may be stated that these two dimensions reflect on the motivational orientations of a particular individual in conflict situations. As it can be seen from Figure 4.3, a combination of these two dimensions results in five specific styles of handling conflicts: integrating, obliging, dominating, avoiding, and compromising.

1. **Integrating style:** This style is also known as problem solving indicating high concern for self and others. The integrating style envisages collaboration between the parties in terms of "openness, exchange of information, and examination of differences to reach a solution acceptable to both parties."[19] The integrating style has two distinguishing aspects: confrontation and problem solving. Confrontation involves open communication between the parties, removing misunderstanding, and analysing the underlying causes of conflict. This should be considered an essential prerequisite for problem solving to occur, which involves the identification of problems and finding solutions thereto with a view to ensuring the optimum satisfaction of the concerns of both the parties.

2. **Obliging style:** The obliging style, also called accommodating, indicates high concern for self as well as for others. This style attempts to play down the differences and emphasising commonalities to satisfy the concern of the other party. In other words, the obliging person sacrifices his own interest with a view to satisfying the interests or concerns of the other party. Such a person has been called a "conflict observer" or a "person, whose reaction to a perceived hostile act on the part of another has hostility or even positive friendliness."[20]
3. **Dominating style:** This style of handling conflicts is also known as competing and indicates high concern for self and low concern for others. This style is very similar to win-lose orientation or to forcing behaviour with a view to establishing the superiority of one's own position or viewpoint. A dominating person always attempts to achieve his objectives, often ignoring the needs and expectations of the other party. A dominating supervisor, for example, is likely to utilise his position or authority to impose his will on his subordinates and thereby command their obedience. A dominating person who does not possess formal authority or positional power may seek to wield power by identifying with seniors through deceit and other unfair means.
4. **Avoiding style:** The avoiding style, also known as suppression, shows low concern for self and others. This style has been associated with withdrawing, buck-passing, seeing no evil and other such situations. An avoiding person may withdraw from the conflict situation or try to postpone the conflict issue until a better time comes. Such a person refuses to acknowledge that a conflict is existing or that it needs to be dealt with. Thus, an avoiding person is unable to fulfil his own concerns as well as the concerns of the other party.
5. **Compromising style:** The compromising style indicates intermediate concern for self and others. It involves mutual concessions made by both the parties with a view to reaching a middle ground position. In other words, the compromising style involves give-and-take in which both the parties give up something to reach a mutually acceptable solution or decision. As Rahim has stated, "a compromising party gives up more than a dominating party but less than obliging party." Similarly, such a party addresses the issue more directly than an avoiding person but does not explore the issue as deeply as an integrating person. Thus, it leads us to conclude that each of the five styles of handling conflict may be appropriate or inappropriate depending upon the prevailing situations. As it has been suggested, integrating and to some extent, compromising styles can be effectively used for handling conflicts involving strategic or complex issues. All other styles such as obliging, dominating, and avoiding can be used to deal with conflicts involving routine or day-to-day problems or issues. Thus, the selection and use of a particular style is considered appropriate or efficacious when it helps in enhancing individual growth and organisational effectiveness.

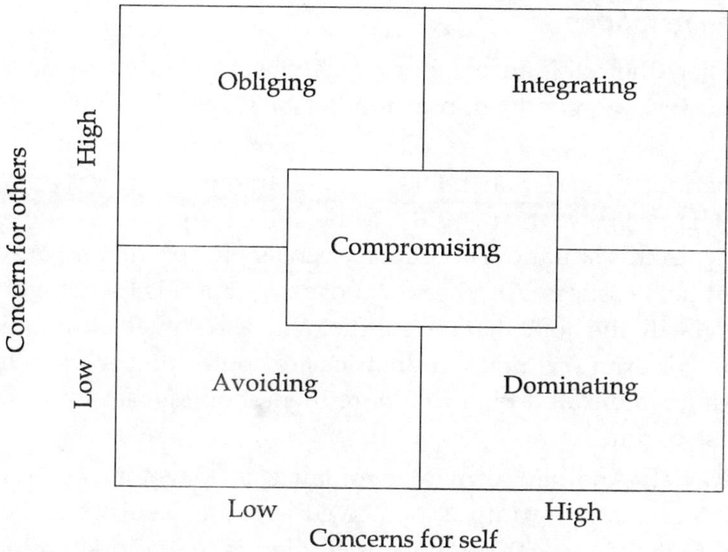


**Figure 4.3:** A two-dimensional model of styles of handling inter-personal conflicts

*Source*: Adapted from M.A. Rahim, "A strategy for managing conflict in complex organisations", *Human Relations*, 38(1), (1985): 81-89.

### 4.3.4 Pareek

Pareek[22] proposed certain conflict management styles or modes in the context of inter-group relations. According to him, a particular conflict management mode is essentially determined by the perception of the conflicting group, i.e., how the out-groups (the other group in conflict) is perceived by the in-group (the group in question). If the out-group is always perceived as belligerent or opposed to the interests of the in-group, then conflict is inevitable. On the other hand, if the out-group is perceived as pursing its own interest but also as being interested in peace, then conflict in this case will be seen as a fact of life, but not inevitable. Similarly, the out-group may be perceived as being unreasonable with the result that there is no hope of any solution, or as being open to reason with the consequent hope of a solution to the problem.

In addition, Pareek[23] stated that a group may generally have an approach orientation or an avoidance orientation. This approach-avoidance dimension plays a significant role in determining the effectiveness of managerial behaviour. Avoidance is characterised by a tendency to deny, rationalise or avoid the problem. Approach, on the other hand, is characterised by making positive effects to find a solution through one's own efforts or with the help of others. A combination of the two aspects, i.e., perception of the out-group and the approach-avoidance dimension gives rise to eight styles or modes of conflict management. The avoidance modes include resignation, withdrawal, appeasement, and diffusion while the approach modes include confrontation, arbitration, compromise, and negotiation.

### 4.3.5 Avoidance modes

As stated earlier, the avoidance modes or styles of conflict management involve avoiding or postponing conflicts in a number of ways. These modes are described below:

1. **Resignation:** Resignation refers to an extreme form of avoidance in which conflict is seen as arising out of the out-group's unreasonable stand and hostility. In this situation, conflict is seen as part of life and is accepted with a sense of helplessness. Another form of resignation is to just ignore the conflict situation with the hope that the conflict will be resolved automatically in course of time. For example, many industries are confronted with recurring conflicts with trade unions and tend to ignore them, hoping that solutions will emerge in course of time.
2. **Withdrawal:** Another form of avoidance is to get away from the conflict situation as the out-group is perceived as being belligerent but still open to reason. One way to get away from conflict is to avoid situations of potential conflict. The second way may be to withdraw from the conflict situation when it actually occurs. Such withdrawal may be from the conflict situation itself or from the relationship with the out-group. The third way of withdrawal may be physical separation. Thus, when two persons in a department fight all the time, the management may transfer one of them to another department with the result that the scope for conflict does not exist anymore. A means of withdrawal is to define the boundaries of interaction with the out-group and make arrangements to limit these boundaries.
3. **Diffusion:** Diffusion involves buying time for dealing with conflict, and it may take several forms. When the emotional issues involved in a conflict situation are running too high, the management may ask the participants to cool down before the actual conflict issues are taken up for resolution. One way to diffuse strong emotions in conflict is to expect that emotions will subsidise with the passage of time, and the group will be prepared to handle the real conflict issues. The second form of diffusion is to appeal to the conflict parties to understand that both of them have common interest, mutuality, interdependence, etc. The third way to diffuse the conflict situation is to make arrangements for mutual interactions through a third party with the result that excessive emotions will gradually settle down.
4. **Appeasement:** Appeasement as an avoidance mode is intended to buy temporary peace. A group in conflict with the out-group may agree to some of the demands of the latter with a view to postponing the conflict. It, therefore, offers some concessions to the out-group in the hope that the out-group will be happy and the conflict will be resolved. It may be noted, however, that appeasement has deleterious effects in that the conflict remains unresolved, the

demands of the out-group keep on increasing, and the situation deteriorates further.

### 4.3.6 Approach Modes

Approach modes or styles involve taking certain concrete steps to confront conflicts and find solutions to them. There are four approach modes or styles as described below:

1. **Confrontation:** When a group in conflict perceives the out-group as being opposed to its interests and unreasonable, it may use confrontation as a means of resolving the conflict. Confrontation means fighting out any issue to get solution in one's favour. Confrontation is often used by management or trade unions to use pressure tactics against the opponent to obtain favourable decisions or solutions. Thus, the confrontation mode involves the use of coercion and is unlikely to lead to any solution. As mentioned by Thibaut and Kelly,[24] there are three problems associated with pressure tactics: (1) the cost of surveillance over the other party's behaviour when threats are employed; (2) the loss of power that sometimes results from the use of threats, punishments and rewards; and (3) the unpleasantness of having to capitulate when the other party is unknown.
2. **Compromise:** If the outgroup is perceived as being interested in peace and reasonable, then efforts may be made to reach a compromise. This is the process of sharing the gains of profits although the conflict still remains unresolved. Compromise is often used in resolving conflicts between management and labour unions. If, for example, the management is interested in fulfilling the demands for certain export orders, it may agree to pay more wages and incentives for a certain period to workers who may decide to work for longer hours during that period.
3. **Arbitration:** If the outgroup is seen as being belligerent and not interested in peace, but not fully unreasonable, arbitration by a third party may be used to assess the situation and offer an award acceptable to both the parties or groups. In this situation, the conflict is usually unresolved and is only postponed for a certain period.
4. **Negotiation:** A satisfactory solution to the problem or conflict becomes possible only when both the groups jointly confront the problem and try to find solutions through the process of negotiation. All the different aspects of negotiation have been described earlier in Chapter 2.

### 4.3.7 Blake, Shepard and Mouton

Blake, Shepard and Mouton[25] have proposed certain conflict management approaches or styles which are relevant especially in the context of inter-group relations. According to them, there are three basic managerial assumptions which are important in regard to conflict management: (1) conflicts are inevitable and agreement is not possible; (2) conflicts are not inevitable and yet agreement is impossible, and (3) although there may be conflict, agreement is possible. In fact, these three managerial assumptions combine with three degrees of active-passive orientation which Thomas[26] calls assertiveness or the extent to which a conflicting party is interested in satisfying his own concerns. These three degrees of "activeness" are: (1) active orientation having high stakes; (2) medium-active orientation having moderate stakes; and (3) passive orientation having low stakes. A combination of the three managerial assumptions about conflict with the three degrees of "activeness" produces nine different conflict resolution modes.

### 4.3.8 Walton

Walton's[27] perspective on conflict management focuses upon two types of lateral relationships: distributive and integrative. Walton's system theory of lateral relationships is based upon these two types of contrasting lateral relationships, and it focuses upon inter-unit relationships in which the parties are required to enter into a joint decision-making process. In this context, there are three components of such relationships: (1) information exchange in the joint decision process; (2) the structure of inter-unit interactions and decision making; and (3) attitudes towards the other unit. Wlaton's[28] theory explains how the modal process used by the conflict parties in joint decision making (i.e., bargaining versus problem-solving) influences, and in turn, is influenced by various aspects of inter-unit structure and inter-unit attitudes. Bargaining type of decision-making occurs in a situation where each party has an interest in an issue so that the gain for one party is at the cost of the other. In fact, this conflict situation has been described as a zero-sum competitive game or a pure conflict game. In bargaining, each party starts with a position favourable to itself and then starts offering concessions to the other party with a view to reaching an agreement on some common ground. The bargaining approach involves withholding information about one's objectives and aspirations while trying to elicit the same information from the other party. On the other hand, the problem-solving type of decision making occurs where the joint gains available to the parties are variable rather than being fixed. In problem solving, the total payoffs vary depending upon the complementarity of the basic interests of the parties and also depending upon their ability to exploit this integrative potential. Although the parties may be having their own alternatives, the best way to resolve this conflict is to ensure a quick and complete sharing of the available information. Such sharing of information is to be followed by a joint search for alternatives that best satisfy the interests of both the parties.

### 4.3.9 Likert and Likert

Likert and Likert[29] propagated the concept of participatory management through his System-4 interaction influence and extended it to the area of conflict management. The authors have shown enough evidence to prove that the participatory management style helps in the effective management of conflicts. While Walton's interactive type of lateral relationship is consistent with the System-4 approach to conflict management, his distributive type of relationship fits the System 1 or 2 pattern of interaction and influence network.

### 4.3.10 Luft and Ingham

Luft and Ingham[30] developed a model of conflict management known as 'the Johari Window' which provides a view of possible conflict situations arising in the context of interpersonal relations. According to this perspective, conflicts arise primarily due to lack of knowledge and information about oneself and others. Therefore, this approach suggests self-disclosure or providing information to the other party and at the same time getting feedback or information from the other party. In other words, this approach suggests a two-way process of information sharing between the two parties so as to help mitigate or resolve the conflict situation. This framework assumes that the self knows certain things about himself and there are certain things that are not known. Similarly, there are certain things one knows about others and there are certain other things which are not known. Thus, the Johari Window is a four-cell matrix shown in Figure 4.4.

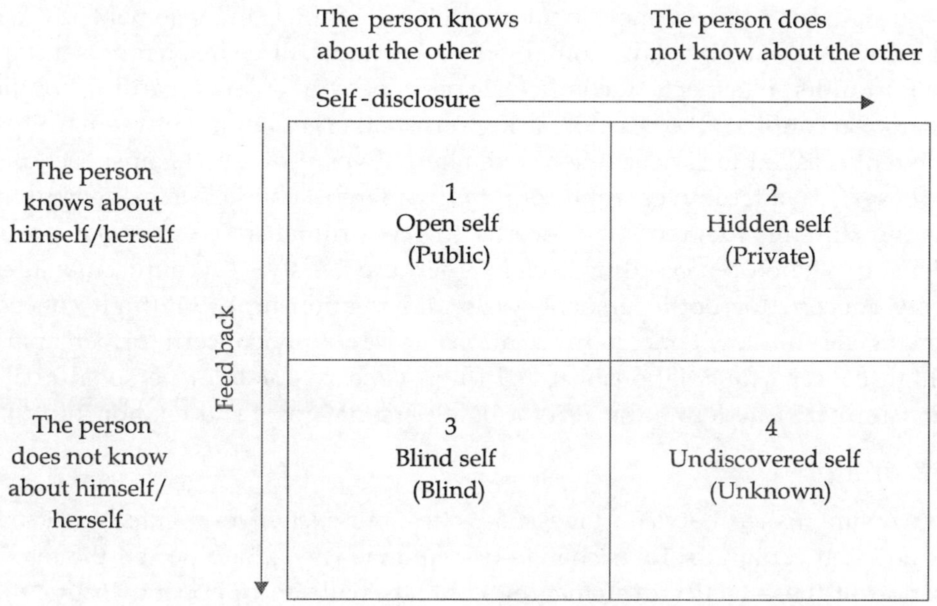


**Figure 4.4:** The Johari window

*Source*: Luft, J. And Ingham, H., "The Johari Window, A graphic model of interpersonal awareness", *Proceedings of the Western Training Laboratory in Group Development*, UCLA, Los Angeles, 1955.

1. **Open self (public)**: This form of interaction includes knowledge about oneself as well as the other person. Therefore, in this situation, there is little scope for misunderstanding and hence interpersonal conflicts.
2. **Hidden self (private):** In this case, the person knows about himself but not about the other. In view of lack of knowledge about the other person, the person concerned keeps himself hidden from the other and does not open up freely. Therefore, there is ample scope for conflict to develop in this case. Here, the remedy lies in trusting others and making a self-disclosure so as to reduce the possibility of interpersonal conflict.
3. **Blind self (blind):** This is a situation where the person does not know about himself but is well informed about the other person. In this situation, the potential for conflict can be mitigated if the person concerned is willing to learn from the framework provided by the other person, if any.
4. **Undiscovered self (unknown):** This is the most explosive situation in which the person does not know about himself and also about the other person. Self disclosure and feedback are the only means through which interpersonal understanding can be improved and the potential for conflict reduced.

### 4.3.11 Hall

Hall[31] proposed a two-dimensional model of conflict management. A conflict instrument developed by Hall[32] contained twelve items, three items representing each of the four different aspects of conflict: (1) one's personal view regarding conflict; (2) interpersonal conflict; (3) conflict in task group; and (4) relations between groups. The respondent is asked to choose one of five alternatives provided against each item. In fact, these five alternatives represent five different conflict management styles, indicating different degrees of concerns for two dimensions: personal goals and relationship. Therefore, according to Hall,[33] there are five styles of conflict management: 1,1 (low concern for both personal goals and relationship); 9,1 (high concern for personal goals and low concern for relationship); 1,9 (low concern for personal goals and high concern for relationship), 9,9 (high concern for both personal goals and relationship); 5,5 (moderate concern for both personal goals and relationship).

### 4.3.12 Pruitt

Pruitt[34] distinguished between pressure tactics and exchange-oriented tactics. Pruitt also suggested certain useful exchange-oriented tactics and advocated the maximum utilisation of these tactics in managing conflicts with an opponent. Pruitt[35] further suggested two major ways of resolving conflicts; bargaining and norm-following. In bargaining "each party endeavours to coerce or lure its adversary into making maximum concessions while conceding as little as possible." In norm following, "both parties attempt to locate and follow rules that are appropriate to the issue in question." Pruitt[36] proposed three types of norm following: content-specific rules, equity rules, and mutual responsiveness.

### 4.3.13 Filley

Filley[37] has made a distinction between power-oriented methods and problem-oriented methods of conflict management. According to him, the problem solving methods evoke intellectual intensity rather than emotional intensity or power. As suggested by Filley,[38] certain significant changes in conditions (perceptual, affective, situational and processual) may be effected so as to facilitate movement from power-oriented methods to problem-solving methods.

The above analysis of various approaches to conflict management points to the fact that Blake and Mouton[39] made a significant contribution in proposing a five-category scheme for classifying and identifying five methods of managing conflicts. Their approach to conflict management is based upon two dimensions of managerial behaviour: concern for production and concern for people. A manager's positioning on these two dimensions reveals his dominant style of managing conflicts with his subordinates, seniors, and peers at the work situation. It must be noted, however, that despite having a dominant style or method of conflict management, every manager tends to fall back upon a backup style when the dominant style of managing conflict fails to work in a particular situation. Similar to the conflict management approach of Blake and Mouton[40] in classifying interpersonal behaviour, subsequent researchers[41] have also classified the methods or styles of managing conflict at the workplace. While these approaches to conflict management are largely applicable to interpersonal conflicts, the approaches of Blake, Shepard and Mouton[42] and Pareek[43] are particularly relevant to the understanding and management of interpersonal relations. Pareek's approach-avoidance dimension is very similar to the active-passive mode suggested by Blake, Shepard and Mouton,[44] and it is very useful in determining the methods or styles of managing interpersonal conflict.

In addition, it may be noted that although various authors have defined the problem-solving approach to conflict management in different ways, most of them agree that this approach is most effective in managing conflicts. A number of empirical studies have shown the efficacy or effectiveness of the problem-solving style of managing conflicts in industrial situations.[45] While the managers have to achieve the production targets set by the organisation, they have also to emphasize upon the welfare of employees, maintain harmonious working relations with them and also involve them in the decision-making process. In the prevailing industrial environment, the personnel profile is changing tremendously in terms of improved education, knowledge, skills, and horizons of understanding of employees. Therefore, the managers need to be sensitive towards the growing needs and aspirations of subordinate employees and also consult them on a number of organisational issues.

## 4.4 MANAGING CONFLICT PROCESS

A common viewpoint accepted by management experts is that a conflict has both functional and dysfunctional consequences in organisations. Therefore, the organisations must manage their conflicts in a constructive way so as to realise the potential benefits of conflicts. As viewed by Rahim,[46] conflict management does not necessarily imply avoidance, reduction or termination of conflict. It involves designing effective macro-level strategies to minimise the dysfunctions of conflict and enhance the constructive functions of conflict in order to increase learning and effectiveness in an organisation. The conflict management process consistent with these macro-organisational approaches is shown in Figure 4.5.

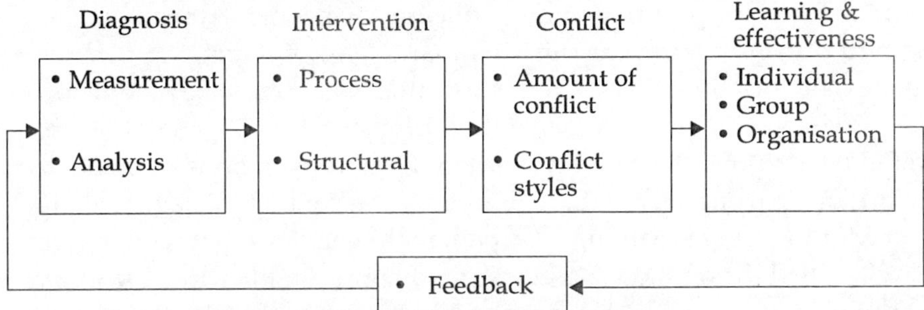


**Figure 4.5:** Process of managing conflict

*Source*: M.A. Rahim, "Toward a theory of managing organisational conflict", *The International Journal of Conflict Management*, 13(3), (2002): 206-235.

**Diagnosis:** The conflict management process begins with the diagnosis of the problem which involves problem finding or recognition. It may be noted, however, that problem finding or recognition has not been adequately investigated in the management literature so far. As a result of this, interventions are often designed or suggested without a proper analysis of the nature of conflicts or problems, which leads to ineffective outcomes. The management experts have specifically suggested the need for diagnosis of problems or conflicts through formal and informal approaches.[47] A correct diagnosis of conflict is necessary as the underlying causes and effects of conflict may be different from what they appear to be. There is also a need to know (a) whether an organisation is having too little, moderate or too much affective and substantive conflict, and (b) whether or not the organisational participants are properly selecting and making a judicious utilisation of conflict management styles in different possible situations. In fact, comprehensive diagnosis should include the measurement of conflict, its sources and effectiveness, and an analysis of relations among them.

**Intervention:** It must be pointed out that a proper diagnosis of conflicts will reveal if there is any need for intervention and also the type of intervention required. An intervention may be needed if there is too much affective conflict or too little or too much substantive conflict, or the organisational members are not handling their conflict effectively. There are two basic approaches to intervention in conflict: process and structural.[48] Beer and Walton[49] described these as human process and techno-structural approaches of intervention for organisation development. As described by Rahim,[50] a process refers to a sequence of events or activities that are undertaken to bring about some desired outcome. Organisational processes include leadership, decision-making, communication, etc., which are required to make the social system work. Structure, on the other hand, refers to stable arrangement of task, technological and other factors so as to ensure that organisational members are able to work together effectively. In fact, both process and structure need to be properly integrated so as to accomplish the goals of an organisation.

It may be mentioned that process intervention attempts to change the intensity of affective and substantive conflicts and the members' styles of handling interpersonal conflict with a view to enhancing organisational effectiveness. Changes in the levels of affective and substantive conflicts will require changes in organisational processes such as culture and leadership, which would help reinforce or strengthen the newly acquired conflict management skills of organisational members. The process approach is, however, mainly intended to help the organisational participants learn how to manage conflicts through proper matching of the styles of handling interpersonal conflict with different situations. In other words, the process intervention enables the organisational members to effectively use the styles of handling interpersonal conflict depending on the nature of situations.

In regard to the utility of structural intervention, it may be mentioned that such intervention attempts to improve organisational effectiveness through changes in the structural design characteristics of an organisation such as differentiation and integration mechanism, hierarchy of authority, procedures, reward system, etc. The structural intervention attempts to manage conflict by altering the perceptions of the intensity of conflict at various levels. As suggested by Rahim,[51] conflicts arising from the organisation's structural design can be managed effectively through appropriate changes in such design.

**Conflict:** As noted by experts, there are two dimensions of conflict: the first one concerning disagreements relating to task issues and the second one concerning emotional and interpersonal issues that lead to conflict. These two aspects of conflict have been labelled as substantive and affective conflicts.[52] The results of studies conducted in recent years indicate that these two types of conflicts have differential effects in the organisation. In addition, the organisation experts have viewed that a moderate amount of conflict is necessary for achieving optimum organisational effectiveness. Organisations with little or no conflict may stagnate whereas organisational conflict, left uncontrolled, may have dysfunctional effects within the organisation. As Brown[53] has suggested, conflict management may require intervention to reduce conflict if it is too much, or to promote conflict if there is too little. Thus, the relation between conflict and organisational effectiveness approximates an inverted U function as shown in Figure 4.6.[54] The studies conducted by Amason[55] and Jehn[56] indicate that the relationship suggested by Brown and Rahim and Bonoma seems to be appropriate for substantive conflict rather than affective conflict that has many detrimental effects at the workplace.

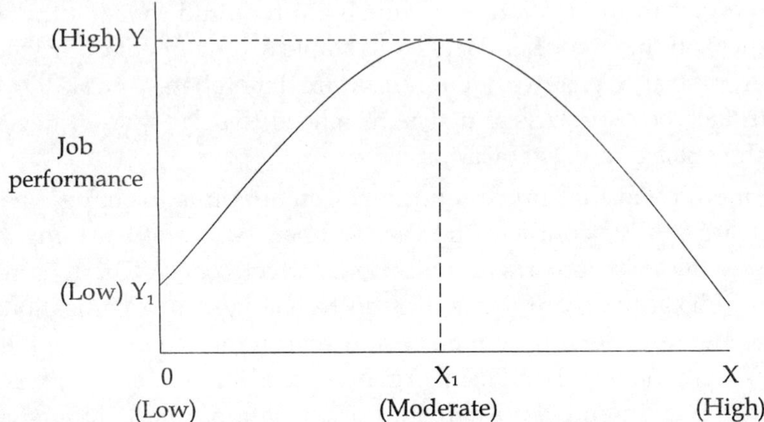


**Figure 4.6:** Relationship between amount of substantive conflict and job performance

*Source*: Adapted from Rahim, A., & Bonoma, T.V. (1979). Managing organisational conflict: A model for diagnosis and intervention. *Psychological Reports*, 44, 1326.

It may be further noted that the Organisational behaviour experts have suggested different approaches to conflict management in terms of differentiating the methods or styles of handling or managing conflicts. Although some experts have suggested that the problem solving or integrating style is most effective in managing conflict,[57] it has been observed by others that one style may be more appropriate than another depending upon the situation.[58] According to Rahim,[59] "In general, integrating and to some extent compromising styles are appropriate for dealing with strategic issues. The remaining styles can be used to deal with practical or day-to-day problems."

**Learning and effectiveness:** Conflict management in organisations is intended to enhance organisational learning that involves acquisition and distribution of knowledge, interpretation of information, and preservation of organisational memory, i.e., preserving information for future access and use. Organisational learning enables the members of the organisation to collectively engage in the process of diagnosis and intervention in problems. It may be noted that individual learning is necessary but not condition for organisational learning. In fact, organisational processes and structures are required for transferring individual learning to the collective entity.

## 4.5 STRATEGIES FOR MANAGING CONFLICTS

As discussed by Rahim (2002), conflict management strategies are effective only when they satisfy certain essential conditions or criteria. According to Rahim, the management literature has generally suggested such essential criteria as: (i) conflict management strategies should be designed to enhance organisational learning; (ii) conflict management strategies should be designed to satisfy the needs and expectations of the strategic constituencies (stakeholders) and to attain a balance among them; (iii) conflicts must be ethically managed through proper consultation and discussion with various stakeholders within the organisation. In addition, it has been suggested that an effective conflict management strategy should incorporate the following important aspects too.

In the first place, it is essential to minimise or reduce affective conflicts at various levels of the organisation. Affective conflicts do occur when the organisational members recognise that their emotions and feelings regarding some organisational issues are incompatible. Such conflicts interfere with the task related efforts of members and also cause the members to be negative, irritable, suspicious and resentlful.[60] It has been empirically shown that affective conflict impacts group performance by limiting information processing ability and cognitive functioning of group members and antagonistic attributions of group members' behaviour.[61] Affective conflicts are often detrimental to team performance as decisions are likely to be made without rationality and objectivity. Affective conflict at also tend to have adverse effects on group loyalty, organisational commitment, and job satisfaction.

As the organisation experts have suggested, it is equally important to attain and maintain a moderate amount of substantive conflict takes place when there is disagreement between two or more members of the organisation over certain tasks or content issues. According to Jehn,[62] a moderate amount of substantive conflict is beneficial in terms of stimulating discussion and debate which help groups to achieve higher performance levels. Substantive conflict promotes better understanding of issues which leads to more effective decision-making within groups. Thus, groups reporting substantive conflict can make more effective decisions and also have higher levels of performance against groups that do not report such conflict. In this context, Robbins[63] has viewed that conflict must be deescalated if it is dysfunctional to the attainment of organisational objectives while it is to be increased if it is existing at a low level within the organisation. Robbins[64] has also suggested certain major conflict resolution and conflict stimulation technique that help members to control conflict levels in organisations, as shown in Table 4.2.

As mentioned earlier, the organisational behaviour experts have differentiated the methods or styles of managing conflicts. Organisational members should be provided with requisite experience so that they would be able to select and utilise appropriate styles of handling interpersonal conflict in different possible situations. Although problem solving or integrative behaviour has often been cited as the best method of conflict management, the managers should adopt flexibility in utilising different conflict management methods or styles as per the demands of specific organisational situations. In other words, the managers should adopt the contingency approach to conflict management at the workplace as far as possible.

**Table 4.2:** Conflict management techniques

| **Conflict resolution techniques** | |
|---|---|
| Problem solving | Face-to-face meeting of the conflicting parties for the purpose of identifying the problem and resolving it through open discussion. |
| Superordinate goals | Creating a shared goal that cannot be attained without the cooperation of each of the conflicting parties. |
| Expansion of resources | When a conflict is caused by the scarcity of a resource, say, money, promotion opportunities, office space expansion of the resource can create a win-win solution. |
| Avoidance | Withdrawal from, or suppression, of the conflict. |
| Smoothing | Playing down differences while emphasizing common interests between the conflicting parties. |
| Compromise | Each part to the conflict gives up something of value. |
| Authoritative command | Management uses its formal authority to resolve the conflict and then communicates its desires to the parties involved. |
| Altering the human variable | Using behavioural change techniques such as human relations training to alter attitudes and behaviours that cause conflict. |
| Altering the structural variables | Changing the formal organisation structure and the interaction patterns of conflicting parties through job redesign, transfers, creation of coordinating positions, and the like. |
| **Conflicts stimulation techniques** | |
| Communication | Using ambiguous or threatening messages to increase conflict levels. |
| Bringing in outsiders | Adding employees to a group whose backgrounds, values, attitudes, or managerial styles differ from those of the present members. |
| Restructuring the organisation | Realigning work groups, altering rules and regulations, increasing inter-dependence, and making similar structural changes to disrupt the status quo. |
| Appointing a devil's advocate | Designating a critic to purposely argue against the majority positions held by the group. |

*Source*: Based on S.P. Robbins, *Managing Organizational Conflict: A Nontraditional Approach* (Upper Saddle River, NJ: Prentice Hall, 1974), pp. 59-89.

## 4.6 SUMMARY AND CONCLUSION

The above analysis of various aspects of organisational conflict and its management leads us to make certain significant observations. Generally, the studies on conflict management have moved in two directions. According to some researchers, a moderate amount of conflict should be maintained in an organisation through the use of various conflict management techniques. Other researchers have tried to examine various styles or methods of handling conflict and their impact on different dimensions or criteria of organisational effectiveness. Although the organisational behaviour experts have generally suggested that a moderate amount of conflict is necessary for attaining optimum organisational effectiveness,[65] subsequent researchers have shown that this relationship holds good for substantive conflicts rather than conflicts that have dysfunctional effects within an organisation. Recent studies have also indicated that a moderate amount of substantive conflict is necessary for attaining an optimum level of job performance in non-routine or standard tasks.[66] Therefore, it is recommended that while a moderate amount of substantive conflict should be attained and maintained, it is also required to minimise affective conflicts at various levels of the organisation.

In addition, it may be noted that there are two types of intervention in conflict: process and structural. Although process intervention is primarily used to help the organisational members to learn how the uses of conflict handling styles are to be matched with different situations, such intervention may also be used for managing the intensity levels of both substantive and affective conflicts through changes in organisational processes such as leadership, communication, culture, etc. Such changes in organisational processes would help in reinforcing or strengthening the members' newly acquired skills of conflict management. Structural interventions, on the other hand, seek to manage conflict by altering the intensity of conflict, at various levels of the organisation through suitable changes in its structural characteristics such as differentiation and integration mechanism, reward system, hierarchy of authority, procedures, etc. Thus, both process and structural intervention must be utilised so as to maintain a moderate amount of substantive conflict while reducing affective conflicts at various levels of the organisation.

The organisational behaviour experts have broadly agreed that although people tend to have preference for a particular style of managing conflicts, they have the freedom to use different conflict handling styles in different possible situations. Thus, while the normative view of conflict management has argued for one best style of managing conflicts, the contingency viewpoint suggests the utilisation of different conflict management styles in different organisational situations. In fact, the management experts favouring the contingency approach to conflict management have analysed various situational variables influencing the choice of conflict management strategies and their attendant consequences. According to Blake and Mouton,[67] a manager's styles of managing conflicts are influenced by forces arising from within himself, from the external situation as well as from the organisational system. In the context of dyadic conflict management, Thomas[68] suggested that the conflict handling behaviour of each party is influenced by four structural variables such as behavioural predispositions, social pressure, incentive structure, and rules and procedures. According to Pareek,[69] two dimensions seem to influence the choice of conflict management mode or method: integration of the in-group and criticality of the conflict issue. Other management experts[70] have also explained the functionality or dysfunctionality of different styles of conflict management in different possible situations. At this point, it must be pointed out that most of these contingency viewpoints have been suggested only theoretically without testing their relevance in the real settings. It is expected that such empirical studies would be conducted by researchers in the future, which may lead to the formulation of certain well-defined contingency theories of conflict management.

## REVIEW QUESTIONS

1. The classical, neoclassical, and modern approaches to organisational conflict represent changing views of conflict and its management aspects. Discuss.
2. What implications does the modern view of organisational conflict have for managers of the present-day organisations? Discuss.
3. Define `conflict management'. Explain the main approaches to conflict management in organisations.
4. What are the five interpersonal conflict-handling methods or styles? Discuss the appropriateness or inappropriateness of these styles in different possible situations.
5. Being a manager, would you promote or avoid conflicts in your department? Give suitable reasons.
6. State the approach and avoidance modes of conflict management.
7. How does our perception of the outgroup determine the approach or avoidance modes being used by us?
8. Explain the processes of managing conflicts.
9. The organisation theorists agree that both too low and too high levels of conflicts can be detrimental to organisational performance. Discuss.
10. How can a manager stimulate conflict in his department? State the techniques to be used by him in this regard.

## REFERENCES


1. Barnard, C., The Functions of the Executive, Cambridge, Masschusettes, 1938; Argyris, C., *Integrating the Individual and the Organisation*, Wiley, New York, 1964; and Likert, R., *New Patterns of Management*, McGraw Hill, New York, 1961.
2. Cyert, R.M. and March, J.G., *A Behavioural Theory of the Firm*, Englewood Cliffs, New Jersey, 1963; and Zaleznick, A., Power and politics in organisational life, *Harvard Business Review*, 1970.
3. Brown, L.D., *Managing Conflict at Organizational Interfaces*, Addison-Wesley, MA, 1983.
4. Rahim, M.A., Towards a theory of managing organisational conflict, *The International Journal of Conflict Management*, 13(3), 2002, pp. 206-235.

5. Lipsky, D.B. and Avgar, A.C., The conflict over conflict management (electronic version), *Dispute Resolution Journal*, 65 (2 – 3), 2010, pp. 38-43.
6. *Ibid.*
7. Blake, R.R. and Mouton, J.S., *The Managerial Grid*, Gulf, Houston, 1964.
8. McGregor, D., Theory X and Theory Y, *Organisational Theory*, 1960, pp. 358-374.
9. Thomas, K.W., Conflict and conflict magement, M.D. Dunnettee (Ed.), Handbook of Industrial and Organisational Psychology, Rand McNally, Chicago, 1976, pp. 889-935.
10. Blake, R.R. and Mouton, J.S., 1964, *op. cit.*
11. *Ibid.*
12. Sharma, R.A., *Organisational Theory and Behaviour*, Tata McGraw Hill, New Delhi, 2000, p. 476.
13. Blake, R.R. and Mouton, J.S., 1964, *op. cit.*
14. Walton, R.E. and Mc. Kersie, R.B., *A Behavioural Theory of Labour Negotiations: An Analysis of Social Interaction System*, McGraw Hill, New York, 1965.
15. Northcraft, G.B. and Neale, M.A., *Organisational Behaviour*, Dryden, Chicago, 1990, pp. 247-248.
16. Blake, R.R. and Mouton, J.S., 1964, *op. cit.*
17. Thomas, K.W., 1976, *op. cit.*
18. Rahim, M.A., A measure of styles of handling inter-personal conflict, *Academy of Management Journal*, 26(2), 1983, pp. 368-376.
19. Rahim, M.A., *Managing Conflict in Organisations*, Quroum Books, London, 2017, p. 28.
20. Boulding, K., *Conflict and Defense: A General Theory*, Harper, New York, 1962.
21. Rahim, M.A., 2017, p. 30, *op. cit.*
22. Pareek, U., *Managing Conflict and Collaboration*, Oxford-IBH, New Delhi, 1982.
23. *Ibid.*
24. Thibaut, J.W. and Kelly, H.H., *The Social Psychology of Groups*, Wiley, New York, 1959.
25. Blake, R.R., Shepard, H.A. and Mouton, J.S., *Managing Inter-group Conflict in Industry*, Gulf, Houston, 1964.
26. Thomas, K.W., 1976, *op. cit.*
27. Walton, R.E., Theory of conflict in lateral organisational relationships, J.R. Lawrence (Ed.), *Operational Research and the Social Science*, Tavistock, London, 1966.
28. *Ibid.*
29. Likert, R. And Lkert, J.G., *New Ways of Managing Conflict*, McGraw Hill, New York, 1976.

30. Luft, J. And Ingham, H., The Johari Window, A graphic model of interpersonal awareness, *Proceedings of the Western Training Laboratory in Group Development*, UCLA, Los Angeles, 1955.
31. Hall, J., *Conflict Management Survey: A Survey of One's Characteristic Reaction to and Handling of Conflict between Himself and Others*, Telemetrics Inc., Houston, 1969.
32. *Ibid.*
33. *Ibid.*
34. Pruitt, D.G., Indirect communication and the search for agreement in negotiation, *Journal of Applied Social Psychology*, 35(2), 1977, pp. 205-329.
35. *Ibid.*
36. *Ibid.*
37. Filley, A.C., Some normative issues in conflict management, *California Management Review*, 21(2), 1978, pp. 61-66.
38. *Ibid.*
39. Blake, R.R. and Mouton, J.S., 1964, *op. cit.*
40. *Ibid.*
41. Hall, J., 1969, *op. cit.*; Thomas, K.W., 1976, *op. cit.*; and Rahim, M.A., 1983, *op. cit.*
42. Blake, R.R., Shepard, H.A. and Mouton, J.S., 1964, *op. cit.*
43. Pareek, U., 1982, *op. cit.*
44. Blake, R.R., Shepard, H.A. and Mouton, J.S., 1964, *op. cit.*
45. Lawrence, P.R. and Lorsch, J.W., *Organisation and Environment: Managing Differentiation and Integration*, Boston: Division of Research, Harvard Business School, Harvard University; Burke, R.J., Methods of resolving inter-personal conflict, *Personnel Administration*, July-August, 1969, pp. 48-55; Thomas, 1976, *op. cit.*; and Sharma, R.A. and Samantara, R., Conflict management in an Indian firm: A case study, *Decision*, 21, October-December, 1994, pp. 235-249.
46. Rahim, M.A., A strategy for managing conflict in complex organisations. *Human Relations*, 38(1), 1985, pp. 81-89.
47. Brown, L.D., Managing conflict among groups, D.A. Kolb, I.M. Rubin and J.M. Mclntyre (Eds.), *Organisational Psychology: A Book of Readings,* Prentice-Hall, Englewood Cliffs, NJ, 1979, pp. 377-389; Du Brin, A.J., *The Practice of Managerial Psychology: Concepts and Methods of Manager and Organisation Department*, Pergamon Press, New York, 1972; Rahim M.A., A structural equations model of leader power, subordinates' styles of handling conflict and job performance, *The International Journal of Conflict Management*, 12(3), 2001.
48. Rahim, M.A. and Bonoma, T.V., Managing organisational conflict: A model for diagnosis and intervention, *Psychological Reports*, 44, 1979, pp. 1323-1344.

49. Beer, M. and Walton, A.E., Organisation change and development, *Annual Review of Psychology*, 1987.
50. Rahim, M.A., 2002, *op. cit.*
51. *Ibid.*
52. Guetzkow, H. and Gir, J., An analysis of conflict in decision-making groups, *Human Relations*, 7, 1954, pp. 367-381.
53. Brown, L.D., 1983, *op. cit.*
54. Rahim, M.A. and Bonoma, T.V., 1979, *op. cit.*
55. Amason, A.C., Distinguishing the effects of functional and dysfunctional conflict on strategic decision-making: Resolving a paradox for top management teams, *Academy of Management Journal*, 39, 1996, pp. 123-148.
56. Jehn, K.A., A qualitative analysis of conflict types and dimensions of organisational groups, *Administrative Science Quarterly*, 42, 1997, pp. 530-557.
57. Blake, R.R. and Mouton, J.S., 1964, *op. cit.*; and Likert, R. and Likert, J.G., 1976, *op. cit.*
58. Rahim, M.A., 2001, *op. cit.*; Rahim, M.A. and Bonoma, T.V., 1979, *op. cit.*; and Thomas, K.W., Towards multi-dimensional value in teaching: The example of conflict behaviour, *Academy of Management Review*, 2, 1977, pp. 484-490.
59. Rahim, M.A., 2002, *op. cit.*
60. Jehn, K.A., 1997, *op. cit.*
61. Amason, A.C. 1996, *op. cit.*; Baron, R.A., Positive effects of conflict: Insights from social cognition, C.K.W. DeDreu and E. Van de Vliert (Eds.), *Using Conflict in Organisations*, Sage, London, 1997, pp. 177-191.
62. Jehn, K.A., A multimethod examination of the benefit and determinants of in-group conflict, *Administrative Science Quarterly*, 40, 1995, pp. 256-282.
63. Robbins, S.P., *Organisational Behaviour*, Prentice Hall, New Delhi, 2001.
64. *Ibid.*
65. Brown, L.D., 1983, *op. cit.*; and Rahim, M.A. and Bonoma, T.V., 1979, *op. cit.*
66. Rahim, M.A., and Bonoma, T.V., 1979, *op. cit.*
67. Blake, R.R. and Mouton, J.S., 1964, *op. cit.*
68. Thomas, K.W., 1976 *op. cit.*
69. Pareek, U., 1982, *op. cit.*
70. Derr, C.B., Managing organisational conflict: Collaboration, bargaining and power approaches, *California Management Review*, 1978; and Rahim, M.A., 1985, *op. cit.*

## CASE STUDIES

**Case 1.** Sandy belonged to a tribal community and was brought up in harsh family conditions due to low income and education levels. At present, he has been placed in a low-paying assembly-line job in a large manufacturing firm. Therefore, Sandy often finds it difficult to support his large family, his wife, four children, and parents. On the payday, he generally spends a lot of money but from the next day onwards, he starts feeling depressed as he knows that his income would not be enough to meet the requirements of his family members. It often so happened that his children had to live without the basic needs of life. At first, Sandy thought of meeting his employer for getting some useful advice and help but refrained from doing so as he did not trust the latter enough to discuss his problems openly with him. Then, he met his Union leader and explained his financial problems and hardships associated with his present job. The Union leader immediately replied that their company was the real source of all problems. The present pay and working conditions within the company were not enough to meet their daily living requirements. Therefore, all the workers have to stay united when their present job contract expires and fight to get adequate justice in terms of more of money and better working conditions.

The above case represents a conflict situation for Sandy as he is supposed to fulfil the expectations arising from his multiple roles at the same time. In this case, Sandy is simultaneously playing the roles of a husband, father, son for elderly parents, provider, worker and Union member. He is hard pressed in an inter-role conflict as he has to fulfil the requirements of multiple roles that must be played at the same time. He has to fulfil his family's needs and expectations, the requirements of his present job, and also respond to the Union leader's organising drive.

**Questions**

1. What kind of conflict is being faced by Sandy in the above case?
2. What type of conflict resolution strategy is being suggested by the Union leader? Explain.
3. What can be done to help Sandy in the above situation? Present your answer as an HR manager.

**Case 2.** The conflict in this case arises from the fact that John and Aman, serving as the heads of Technical Development Department and Product Engineering Department, respectively in the same organisation, are following different styles of managing conflicts. John often complains that Aman is taking staff from his technical development department without obtaining his approval while Aman feels that he is quite justified in taking staff from John's overstaffed department. John feels that there is no overstaffing in his department as there would be enough work in the near future and, therefore, Aman is unnecessarily interfering. Aman, however, views that John's departmental efficiency and output will improve with the reduced workforce. Both of them approach George, the director of the company, exchange their accusations and counter-accusations before him and ask him to resolve the conflict between them.

It may be noted that before this confrontation, John had been deeply involved in his work and he was not bothered by Aman's efforts to take staff from his department. This style of managing conflict is known as withdrawing. In this withdrawing style, the individual concerned tries to avoid or escape from the conflict situation rather than facing it. This style of conflict resolution may be appropriate especially when the rival party attempts aggression or forcing behaviour. Another style of conflict management that is evident in this case is competing or forcing. John was quite sure that he needed every member of his workforce, and Aman was not justified in taking staff from his department. In spite of this stand taken by John, Aman made all-out efforts to obtain staff from John's department. In this case, both John and Aman shared forcing or competing behaviour in order to resolve the conflict. Another possible conflict management style that could have worked in this situation is the win-win approach, also known as collaborating or problem-solving style. This approach involves all parties concerned to discuss their differences or viewpoints and find mutually acceptable solutions to the problems causing conflicts. In this win-win approach, a possible solution would entail letting Aman obtain some staff members of John's department through the legitimate official channels as that would have helped Aman in getting the needed talent in his department while John would have a manageable number of personnel and thereby enhance his work efficiency or productivity.

**Questions**

1. What type of conflict is involved in the above case?
2. Do you think that withdrawing or forcing behaviour shown by John and Aman would have helped in resolving the conflict?
3. Is it that the win-win approach to conflict resolution is the most ideal one in the above conflict situation? Discuss.

**Case 3.** Amar joined X Company in 2019 as a manager in Client Car Services Department. Amar had a bachelor's degree in Psychology and a master's degree in Organisational Behaviour. Before joining X Co., Amar had spent about 15 years in different industries in a variety of managerial roles. Amar found that a major conflict was occurring between two groups of employees in his department. The employees involved were resistant to solving any work related issues. The supervisors and other managerial staff in his department were aware of the ongoing conflicts but did not intervene to solve these conflicts.

After joining X Co., Amar attempted to make his department more cohesive and used the collaborating style of resolving employee conflicts. The collaborating style involved the resolution of conflicts without damaging personal relationships. As a conflict resolution move, Amar tried to improve communication within his department by holding weekly staff meetings and weekly individual meetings. These meetings not only ensured that the entire staff received the same information in a consistent manner but also provided them a sense of togetherness. The individual meetings were equally significant as these meetings gave an opportunity to employees to explain their work objectives and concerns and also enabled Amar to review their work performance and suggest measures to help decrease their problems or conflicts. Another aspect of the conflict was due to the fact that certain tasks had always been performed by a few staff members, which led to a sense of alienation among the other employees. Amar took this opportunity to train all the employees in different job responsibilities and thereby enabled them to perform their duties more effectively in different areas. These significant measures taken by Amar went a long way in resolving inter-group conflicts among employees and in improving their work effectiveness.

**Questions**

1. Do you think that the collaborating style used by Amar in the above situation has been most effective in resolving inter-group conflicts among employees?
2. What styles of conflict management would you use to resolve conflicts among employees if you were placed in the above situation as department manager? Justify your answer with reasons.

# 5
# Management of Senior-Subordinate Conflict: An Empirical Study

## 5.1 INTRODUCTION

The preceding chapters were devoted to a critical analysis of literature relating to several important aspects of organisational conflict and its management. Although these perspectives on conflict led to certain important revelations, it has been noted, however, that empirical research studies of conflict and conflict management are drastically lacking in the management literature. While theoretical knowledge on conflict management in organisations is undoubtedly valuable, it is equally important to empirically examine such knowledge and ideas in the actual organisational settings so that the new insights obtained from empirical research findings lead to further theoretical knowledge and theory building in the area of organisational conflict and its management. In addition, it has been observed that the available literature on organisational conflict has generally focused on certain specialised areas. In fact, some of the well-known empirical studies on organisational conflict and its management have been conducted especially in the context of intergroup relations, e.g., line-staff conflict,[1] labour management disputes[2] and inter-departmental disputes.[3] Although the dynamics of superior-subordinate conflict have been emphasised by leading management theoreticians,[4] it is found that superior-subordinate conflict has not been adequately investigated in the real industrial situations. A few empirical studies have been conducted by researchers on different aspects of superior-subordinate conflict[5] but nevertheless it is felt that there is a need to carry forward such empirical studies across industries and explore the internal dynamics of 'superior-subordinate conflict' which has been used in the management literature to describe the conflict arising between the seniors and their sbordinates at the work situation itself over work-related problems or issues. Therefore, the terms 'superior' and 'senior' have been interchangeably used in the book.

In addition to the above stated general reasons for conducting empirical research studies on senior-subordinate conflict in organisations, there is a need to discuss a few more significant issues in this regard. A review of organisational conflict literature has shown that many issues and sources of senior-subordinate conflict do arise in organisations from time to time. While the issues of conflict relate to different aspects of the job itself, the management style, the overall organisation, etc., the sources of conflict involve certain psychosocial dimensions such as personality differences, differences in value systems, differences in knowledge, skills and expertise, need for tension release, autonomy needs of individuals, etc. Since these issues and sources of interpersonal conflict have important implications for employees' satisfaction and productivity as well as for managerial effectiveness, there is a particular need to investigate into these aspects of senior-subordinate conflict at the workplace. In addition, there is a need to study the conflict management behaviours of Indian managers while dealing with their subordinates. More specifically, it is deemed necessary to investigate the conflict management behaviours of managers in terms of their utilisation of various conflict management methods or styles while dealing with their subordinates. In addition, the author considered it important to explore the effects of status differences on the management of conflicts, if any. Therefore, the conflict management behaviours of both the senior managers and their subordinates were to be analysed with respect to their resolution of conflicts with their counterparts in the course of work itself.

In the light of the above-mentioned facts, the present chapter is intended to examine certain issues of senior-subordinate conflict as well as the underlying sources of such conflict. This chapter also attempts to study the managers' utilisation of various conflict management methods or styles at the workplace while resolving conflicts with their subordinates. In addition, this chapter also makes a comparative analysis of the conflict management behaviour of senior managers and their subordinates in order to find out both similarities and differences in their behavioral orientations and attitudes towards conflict.

## 5.2 RESEARCH METHODOLOGY

### 5.2.1 Sample and Data Collection

An electricity generation and distribution company (Organisation 1) was selected for research analysis purposes as its workforce comprised of managers and employees with diverse educational and professional backgrounds and with different regional affiliations. The managers were contacted at their corporate office in the NCR region of Delhi for data collection purposes through questionnaires. It may be mentioned that the respondent managers had sufficient field experience as they were being transferred from the corporate office at specified intervals to the sites where power generation activities took place and back to the headquarters. Questionnaire data were provided by 52 managers belonging to different departments such as production, engineering, finance, HR, IT, etc. As the Head Office had about 400 managers, the respondents were selected on random basis from different functional areas and across various hierarchical levels. Since collection of data through official administration of questionnaires was often time-consuming due to official procedures, the managers were contacted at their Head Office personally, and data were collected through individual questionnaires. The objective of the study and the method of completing the questionnaires were explained to the respondents. They were assured that the present survey was being conducted for research purposes only, and the data collected from them will be kept confidential. In addition, they were assured that their individual identities as well as the identity of the organisation will also be kept confidential. Although about 80 questionnaires were distributed among the managers, 52 questionnaires were finally collected from the respondents. It was found that those managers who could not complete and return the questionnaires were mainly constrained by the time factor due to their workload.

Regarding the nature of the sample selected for the study, it may be noted that it was heterogeneous in terms of the profile of managers who had varied professional qualifications and experience. Managers working at various levels of the organisation were included in the sample size ranging from junior management to middle management to senior management levels. Therefore, it can be said that the sample of respondent managers for the present study were representative of the management group as a whole. In this context, it must be pointed out that a 'manager' included in the sample size was defined as a person who had the authority to direct and control the work activities of some subordinates. Thus, those managers who had no authority over any subordinates were not considered. In fact, there were about 500 managers in this organisation, who had supervisory authority over one or more subordinates working under them.

### 5.2.2 Research Measures

As mentioned previously, the present chapter includes an examination of certain issues and sources of conflicts arising between the seniors and subordinates at the workplace. Therefore, the questionnaire items relating to various issues and sources of conflict were selected after a careful review of the literature, as it can be seen from Appendix 1. The conflict issues were mainly related to certain aspects of the job itself, the management orientation, and the organisation while the sources of conflict could be attributed to psychosocial dimensions such as personality differences between the parties, differences in their knowledge, skills, expertise, autonomy needs, need for tension release, etc. In regard to the measurement of conflict issues, the manager respondents were asked to rank these issues of conflict in terms of how frequently they had disagreements about them with their subordinates (1 means the most frequent one; 2 the next most frequent one and so on up to 10 which is the least frequent one). The managers were also asked to rank the issues of conflict in terms of how frequently these were perceived as the reasons for disagreement or differences including themselves and their subordinates (1 means the most frequent one; 2 the next most frequent one and so on up to 9 which is the least frequent one).

A significant aspect of the present study is that a Conflict Management Scale developed by the author previously was utilised for measuring the conflict management behaviours of managers in terms of their utilisation of different conflict management methods or styles while resolving conflicts with their subordinates on job related matters. The relevant items of the Conflict Management Scale were duly tested and validated with the help of data collected from the managers of an aluminium manufacturing organisation.[6] In view of the importance of the Conflict Management Scale, the details of its development have been discussed as follows.

In fact, this scale was designed to measure the the conflict management methods or styles as suggested by Blake and Mouton[7] such as problem solving, smoothing, compromising, forcing and withdrawing. It may be noted that the Conflict Management Scale as originally administered to the respondents comprised of 15 different items that were selected after a careful review of the literature. Each method of conflict management was measured by three items that were appropriately designed to obtain responses from managers as precisely as possible. Each manager was asked to indicate on a 5-point scale the extent to which each of the 15 statements described the manner in which he actually resolved conflicts with his subordinates on job related matters. At the same time, he was asked to indicate the extent to which each of the said fifteen items described the manner in which his subordinates resolved job related conflicts with him (Appendix 1). The alternatives on the 5-point scale varied from (1) "describes behaviour which never occurs", to (5) "describes behaviour which usually occurs".

As mentioned above, the Conflict Management Scale as originally administered to the respondent managers consisted of 15 items. An inter-correlation matrix prepared on the basis of managers' responses to these 15 items indicated that 3 of these items appeared to be lacking in their measurement value. Therefore, the managers' responses to these three items were not taken into consideration for data analysis purposes. Thus, the final version of the scale consisted of the remaining 12 items only as shown in Table 5.1. The items that were used to measure each method of conflict management were as follows: item no. 3,6 and 11 - problem-solving; item no. 4 and 10 – smoothing; item no. 2 and 8 – compromise; item no. 1 and 7 – forcing; and item no. 5, 9, and 12– withdrawing. The reliability coefficients were calculated for measuring the internal consistency of the relevant items representing each method of conflict management by using Cronbach's formula.[8] In fact, the reliability coefficients as calculated were quite satisfactory, i.e., 0.62, 0.52, 0.74, 0.48, and 0.50 for problem-solving, smoothing, compromise, forcing and withdrawing, respectively as used by senior managers in resolving conflicts with their subordinates. While the coefficients were 0.62, 0.66, 0.52, 0.58 and 0.50 for problem-solving, smoothing, compromise, forcing and withdrawing as perceived to be used by subordinates in managing conflicts with their seniors. The exact format in which the questionnaire items representing different methods of conflict management were utilised by the author to obtain managers' responses have been given in part A and part B of Appendix 1. An individual manager's score regarding his utilisation of a particular method of conflict management was calculated by averaging his responses to the relevant items so as to obtain a score falling between 1.00 and 5.00. It is significant to note that this Conflict Management Scale has been utilised earlier in research studies conducted by the author in steel and paper industries[9] to determine the relative efficacy or effectiveness of various conflict management methods or styles.

**Table 5.1:** Conflict management scale

| Item no. | Conflict management items |
|---|---|
| 1. | The argument of the most powerful always carries the most weight. |
| 2. | A fair exchange brings no quarrel. |
| 3. | Conflict can be resolved if the conflicting parties understand each other and jointly search for alternate solutions. |
| 4. | While trying to resolve conflicts, each party should ensure that the other's feelings and emotions are not hurt. |
| 5. | In the face of conflict, the best policy is to remain neutral or stay out of it. |
| 6. | When conflict arises, one should try to identify the reasons for it and resolve the underlying issues. |
| 7. | When conflict arises, one should use all possible means (power, position or expertise) to force acceptance of one's point of view. |
| 8. | Whenever conflict occurs, one should try to be fair and firm, and try to get an equitable solution. |
| 9. | A person loses least in a quarrel if he avoids arguments, takes no responsibility and tries not to get involved. |
| 10. | In a conflict situation, one should tone down the differences and emphasise common interests to maintain good relations. |
| 11. | A conflict issue should be resolved through the use of knowledge or reason if we want to have sound, creative decisions. |
| 12. | It is easier to refrain than to retreat from a quarrel. |

## 5.3 DATA ANALYSIS AND RESULTS

It may be mentioned that perceptual data obtained from managers were analysed to determine the comparative importance of various issues and sources of conflict arising between the seniors and their subordinates. The mean values of ranks assigned by managers to each issue or source of conflict were calculated to find out the relative importance of each such issue or source of conflict. These mean values were calculated to determine the extent to which the conflict management methods or styles were utilised by the senior managers in resolving work related conflicts with their subordinates as well as by their subordinates in resolving conflicts with their seniors. Finally, an inter-correlation matrix was prepared including therein the calculated values of inter-correlations among different methods or styles of managing conflicts as used by the senior managers as well as by their subordinates. The purpose was to find out any similarities or dissimilarities in approaches to conflict management as adopted by the senior managers and their subordinates at the workplace.

As it can be seen in Table 5.2, the values of ranks and their respective standard

**Table 5.2:** Mean ranks for conflict issues[a]

| | Conflict issues | Mean | Rank | SD |
|---|---|---|---|---|
| 1. | Conflict over job objectives | 7.54 | (8) | 2.48 |
| 2. | Work standards to be accomplished (volume of work expected, time limits, etc.) | 7.33 | (4) | 2.13 |
| 3. | Planning of activities (what should be done, how it should be done, who should do it, etc.) | 7.35 | (5) | 2.01 |
| 4. | The question as to how equipment and facilities are to be used or other technical issues are to be dealt with | 7.50 | (7) | 2.11 |
| 5. | Amount of time spent on the job (not meeting deadlines, arriving late, leaving early, etc.) | 7.08 | (3) | 2.26 |
| 6. | Errors, misinterpretation of orders, carelessness, etc. | 6.77 | (1) | 2.52 |
| 7. | Supervision, direction and control (too less or too much of freedom, participation in decision-making, etc.) | 7.37 | (6) | 2.13 |
| 8. | Performance appraisal (evaluation of task execution, goal attainment, etc.) | 6.92 | (2) | 2.22 |
| 9. | Administration of wages or salary, promotions, sanction of leave, etc. | 7.96 | (9) | 2.19 |
| 10. | Physical working environment (including noise, space, office temperature, ventilation, etc.) | 8.25 | (10) | 2.10 |

[a]N = 52 for all measures.

deviations for ten different issues of conflict point to certain important inferences. The standard deviations for the rank values of these conflict issues ranged from a minimum of 2.01 to a maximum of 2.52, indicating thereby that the managers have provided somewhat consistent responses regarding various issues of conflict. It can be noticed that the most frequent issue of conflict was "errors, misinterpretation of orders, carelessness, etc.", followed by performance appraisal, amount of time spent on the job, work standards to be accomplished, planning of work activities, supervision, direction, control, etc. In fact, these are some of the individual and managerial issues that required utmost attention in order to improve efficiency at the workplace. There is a need for continuous coordination between the senior managers and their subordinates to find acceptable solutions to such significant issues as time management, adequate care in interpreting official orders and communications, fulfilment of assigned works, planning of work activities, style of supervision, etc. In addition, it may be noted that the least frequent issue of conflict was physical work environment with a lower standard deviation of 2.10. The other insignificant conflict issues included administration of wages, promotions and sanction of leave, conflict over job objectives, utilisation of equipment and facilities, etc. As it has been observed by the author, the physical work environment at the corporate office of the organisation selected for the present study was really excellent with well planned office layout along with the best possible arrangement of office equipment, space and other facilities. The managers and their subordinates had hardly any conflict over issues regarding sanction of wages or salary, promotion, leave, etc., that were governed by certain clear-cut rules and regulations. They had also less of conflict over job objectives that were generally decided by the top management of the organization.

The mean values of ranks and standard deviations for nine different sources of conflict have been presented in Table 5.3. As shown by the relatively smaller values of standard deviations for the rank values of different sources of conflict, there is considerable agreement among the managers regarding various sources of conflicts. The most significant sources of senior-subordinate conflict included differences in knowledge, skills or expertise, differences in basic values, beliefs or opinions, and unreasonable policies, procedures, or rules. Thus, it can be inferred that the senior managers, by virtue of their knowledge, expertise, and value systems, seem to have a broader vision of organisational goals and objectives, which is somewhat lacking with their subordinates. Thus, the subordinates' approach to job related problems may not be as far-sighted or as productive as that of their senior managers. These research findings are somewhat similar to those obtained by the author in a study conducted in an aluminium manufacturing organisation.[10] In addition, it was observed that the most significant sources of conflict were for tension release, drive for autonomy, and personality differences between the senior managers and their subordinates. In fact, these are different intra-individual factors or forces that do not seem to have any significant impact on the interpersonal relations between the seniors and their subordinates.

**Table 5.3:** Mean ranks for sources of conflict[a]

| | Sources of conflict | Mean | Rank | SD |
|---|---|---|---|---|
| 1. | Personality differences (such as family background, education, social pattern, etc.) | 7.56 | (6) | 2.50 |
| 2. | Differences in basic values, beliefs or opinions | 7.25 | (2) | 2.32 |
| 3. | Differences in knowledge, skills or expertise | 6.79 | (1) | 2.18 |
| 4. | Unreasonable policies, procedures or rules | 7.38 | (3) | 2.05 |
| 5. | Barriers to interpersonal communication | 7.50 | (5) | 2.15 |
| 6. | Hierarchical differences in status, power, and rewards | 7.50 | (5) | 2.00 |
| 7. | Competition for a particular position, power or recognition | 7.46 | (4) | 2.06 |
| 8. | Drive for autonomy | 7.71 | (7) | 1.69 |
| 9. | Need for tension release | 7.81 | (8) | 1.94 |

[a]N = 52 for all measures

The inter-correlations among the five conflict management methods used by the senior managers as well as among those five methods perceived by the senior managers to be used by their subordinates have been presented in Table 5.4. As it can be seen in the upper left of the tabulated values, the values of inter-correlations calculated for the five conflict management methods as used by the respondent managers varied from – 0.03 to 0.76 with five values being significantly different from zero. It can be noticed that the seniors utilising problem solving behaviour to a greater extent were also likely to make greater use of smoothing and compromising modes of resolving conflicts. Similarly, the managers who used smoothing behaviour to a greater extent were also likely to engage in more of compromising behaviour with their subordinates. It is interesting to note that these significant correlations among problem-solving, smoothing, and compromising modes were found to be true even with respect to the seniors' perception of how their subordinates managed conflict with them, as shown in the lower right part of the table. These research findings were previously obtained by the author in a study conducted in an aluminium manufacturing organisation.[11] Although the smoothing and compromising modes had significant relationships with withdrawing as indicated in the upper left of the table, these relationships did not hold good with regard to the subordinates' use of those methods in managing conflicts with the senior managers (as shown in the lower right part).

**Table 5.4:** Intercorrelations among the five conflict management strategies

| Conflict management style | 1 | 2 | 3 | 4 | 5 | 6 | 7 | 8 | 9 | 10 |
|---|---|---|---|---|---|---|---|---|---|---|
| Self | | | | | | | | | | |
| 1. Problem-solving | | 074** | 0.69** | -0.01 | 0.10 | 0.73** | 0.67** | 0.57** | -0.01 | 0.17 |
| 2. Smoothing | | | 0.76** | -0.03 | 0.32* | 0.66** | 0.79** | 0.63** | -0.03 | 0.23 |
| 3. Compromise | | | | -0.02 | 0.29* | 0.66** | 0.72** | 0.82** | -0.04 | 0.30* |
| 4. Forcing | | | | | 0.23 | 0.00 | -0.08 | -0.04 | 0.74** | 0.28* |
| 5. Withdrawing | | | | | | 0.16 | 0.21 | 0.27 | 0.28* | 0.70** |
| **Subordinate** | | | | | | | | | | |
| 6. Problem-solving | | | | | | | 0.80** | 0.73** | -0.03 | 0.21 |
| 7. Smoothing | | | | | | | | 0.73** | -0.05 | 0.22 |
| 8. Compromise | | | | | | | | | -0.08 | 0.27 |
| 9. Forcing | | | | | | | | | | 0.25 |
| 10. Withdrawing | | | | | | | | | | |

[a]N = 52 for all measures *p < 0.05 **p < 0.01

It can be further noticed in Table 5.4 that the senior managers' use of problem solving or smoothing or compromising mode is positively related to the subordinates' use of problem solving, compromising and smoothing behaviours. While the subordinates' utilisation of withdrawing behaviour is positively related to the seniors' use of compromise and forcing behaviours, it was also noted that the subordinates' use of forcing behaviour had positive and significant relationship with the seniors' use of withdrawing behaviour. Another noticeable finding is that the correlation between the respondent managers' utilisation of any particular conflict management method is both positively and significantly related to his perception of the subordinates' utilisation of that method. These findings have been more or less consistent with those of a research study conducted by the author earlier.[12]

Table 5.5 indicates the relative importance of different methods of conflict management as used by the senior managers in resolving conflicts with their subordinates. It can be noticed that the managers perceived problem-solving as the most preferred strategy for managing conflicts with their subordinates, and it was followed by smoothing, compromise, withdrawing, and forcing. The predominant use of the problem solving mode of resolving conflicts has been shown in the findings of various research studies.[13] In addition, it can be noted that while the managers made considerable use of problem solving, smoothing and compromising in resolving work-related conflicts with their subordinates, their utilisation of forcing and withdrawing behaviours has been somewhat negligible. It must be pointed out that this pattern of conflict management behaviour was shown by managers falling within each hierarchical level–top management, middle management, and lower level management. These findings point to the fact that the managers prefer to confront conflicts and resolve these in the best possible manner rather than avoiding or withdrawing from the conflict situations. The fact that the forcing mode of resolving conflicts is least used by managers indicates that their approach to conflict management is based on democratic values and attitudes.

**Table 5.5:** Managers' and their subordinates' utilisation of various conflict management styles[a]

| Conflict management styles | Mean value | Rank | SD |
|---|---|---|---|
| **Perception of self** | | | |
| 1. Problem-solving | 3.90 | (1) | 0.84 |
| 2. Smoothing | 3.58 | (2) | 0.97 |
| 3. Compromise | 3.58 | (2) | 1.06 |
| 4. Forcing | 2.70 | (4) | 0.96 |
| 5. Withdrawing | 2.91 | (3) | 0.73 |
| **Perception of subordinate behaviour** | | | |
| 1. Problem-solving | 3.76 | (1) | 1.02 |
| 2. Smoothing | 3.59 | (3) | 0.89 |
| 3. Compromise | 3.65 | (2) | 1.04 |
| 4. Forcing | 2.62 | (5) | 0.91 |
| 5. Withdrawing | 2.93 | (4) | 0.76 |

[a]N = 52 for all measures.

As shown in Table 5.5, perceptual data were also provided by the senior managers about the manner in which the subordinates utilised different conflict management methods in resolving conflicts with their seniors. The mean values of conflict management methods used by subordinates indicate that the subordinates made considerable use of problem solving, compromise, and smoothing modes of resolving conflicts as against their occasional use of forcing and withdrawing behaviours. In this context, it is noteworthy that both the managers and their subordinates tended to make maximum use of the problem solving mode of resolving conflicts. This fact indicates that the subordinates too demonstrated their ability and willingness to resolve work related conflicts with their seniors on an equal basis. In fact, the subordinate managers do possess requisite task related knowledge and competence and have the ability to understand the intricacies of various job related issues and problems that do occur from time to time. While the seniors utilised smoothing and compromising modes almost equally, the subordinates tended to make greater use of compromising than smoothing behaviours. This may be attributed to the fact that the subordinates have lower hierarchical authority, position, and status and, therefore, often feel compelled to engage in compromising behaviour with their seniors while resolving work related conflicts. Another interesting research finding is that the subordinates too made considerably lesser use of forcing and withdrawing behaviours as did their senior managers. Thus, the subordinates too did not wish to avoid the conflict situations as a normal practice and also restrained themselves from engaging in forcing behaviours that went against the democratic principles of management of work related conflicts and issues. These broad research findings indicate that both the senior managers and their subordinates engaged in rational problem solving and valued both the production and human relations aspects of the job on an equal basis with a view to finding amicable solutions to conflicts at the work situation.

## 5.4 DISCUSSION AND CONCLUSION

The present study has thrown up certain interesting findings regarding different aspects of senior-subordinate conflict at the workplace. In every organisational setup, the senior managers have to sit down with their subordinates and resolve various work related conflicts that do occur from time to time. On account of the need for continuous interactions between the seniors and subordinates and the need for managerial direction and control, the subject of senior-subordinate conflict formed the central focus of attention in the present study. In this context, it was noted that different issues of senior-subordinate conflict related to the job itself, the style of management, the overall organisation, etc., while the sources of such conflict were more psychosocial in nature and could be attributed to personality factors, differences in background and value systems, differences in knowledge or expertise, autonomy needs of individuals, etc. The mean values of ranks assigned by the respondent managers to ten different sources of conflict with their subordinates indicated the relative importance of these conflict issues. The lower values of standard deviations calculated for the rank values of these conflict issues indicated that the managers' responses regarding the relative weightage attached to ten different conflict issues were somewhat consistent or reliable. In general, it was observed that the most significant conflict issue was "errors, misinterpretation of orders, carelessness, etc., followed by performance appraisal, time spent on the job, achievement of prescribed work standards, planning of work activities, supervision, direction and control, etc. It may be pointed out that these are certain individual and managerial issues or factors that required the urgent attention of senior managers to coordinate with their subordinates and find productive solutions to work related conflicts. In fact, there is a need to focus managerial attention on certain critical areas such as time management, accurate interpretation of official orders and communications, achievement of assigned work targets, planning of work, style of supervision, etc. In addition, it was found that the least frequent issue of senior-subordinate conflict was physical work environment followed by issues relating to wage or salary administration, promotion, leave, etc., conflict over job objectives, and use of equipment and facilities. In general, it was observed by the author that the physical surrounding of the work situation in the selected organisation was quite satisfactory with an excellent office layout. The job objectives for each manager or position holder were generally decided through an efficient administrative system while the managers and their subordinates were generally happy with the promotion and leave rules of the organisation as well as with the salary structure and other monetary incentives provided by the organisation.

Regarding the sources of senior-subordinate conflict examined in the present study, the senior managers provided reasonably consistent responses as shown by the relatively smaller values of standard deviations calculated for the rank values of nine different sources of conflict. The most significant sources of conflict included differences in knowledge, skills or expertise, differences in basic value systems and beliefs, and unreasonable policies, procedures or rules. The least significant source of conflict was individual need for tension release followed by autonomy needs of individuals, and personality differences between the seniors and their subordinates. Thus, it can be inferred that individual differences between seniors and subordinates in terms of job knowledge or expertise, and managerial philosophy and orientations were cited as the most predominant factors or sources of conflict. Similarly, hierarchical differences in status, power and rewards were also not perceived to be a major source of senior-subordinate conflict as against our expectations. These findings indicate that both the senior managers and their subordinates seem to be satisfied with the status differentials, positional power, and monetary rewards provided by the organisation to each one of them according to their position in the organisational hierarchy. As a result of this, competition between the seniors and their subordinates for a particular position, power or recognition was also not regarded as a major source of conflict. In the end, it may be noted that personality differences, individual needs for tension release, and drive for autonomy were purely personal factors that did not have any significant impact on senior-subordinate interactions at the workplace. Therefore, the sources of senior-subordinate conflict were found to be relatively less significant in the present study.

The inter-correlations among different conflict management methods or styles used by the senior managers and their subordinates revealed certain important facts. It was found that the inter-correlations among problem-solving, smoothing and compromising modes used by the seniors in resolving conflicts with their subordinates were both positive and significant. These positive inter-correlations among the three methods were found to hold good also when these methods or styles were used by the subordinates in managing conflicts with their seniors. These findings indicate that problem-solving, smoothing, and compromising methods or styles of conflict management tend to move together in the same direction as these methods or styles reflect the management orientation of individual managers occupying various positions in the organisational hierarchy. All these three methods are based on democratic attitudes and ideas of managers who are expected to recognise the abilities and job expertise of their subordinates and take them into confidence in resolving various job related issues and problems. In fact, the present-day managers can no longer afford to rely upon forcing and withdrawing behaviours in resolving work-related conflicts especially when the industrial situation is changing significantly in terms of enhanced employee education and knowledge, growing consciousness of employee needs and aspirations as well as the desire and ability of both the managers and the employees to participate in organisational decision-making.

In regard to the correlations between different conflict management methods used by the senior managers and those used by their subordinates, it was observed that the problem-solving or smoothing or compromising mode used by the senior managers correlated significantly with problem solving, smoothing and compromising modes utilised by their subordinates in resolving interpersonal conflicts. Again, this finding indicates that these three methods of conflict management are democratic in character and tend to move together in the same direction. As would be seen later, the managers have been generally utilising these three methods or styles of conflict management to a considerable extent as against their relatively insignificant use of forcing and withdrawing behaviours. The fact that the respondent managers' utilisation of any particular conflict management method had positive and significant relationship with their perception of their subordinates' utilisation of that particular method implies that status differences among managers did not play a major role in the choice of appropriate conflict management strategies or methods at the work situation.

The mean values and standard deviations of conflict management methods as utilised by the senior managers and their subordinates revealed certain important facts. While both the seniors and their subordinates made considerable use of problem-solving, smoothing, and compromising modes in resolving work related conflicts, their use of forcing and withdrawing behaviours was somewhat negligible. This pattern of conflict management behaviour was exhibited by managers belonging to different hierarchical levels - top management, middle management, and junior management. This finding indicates that the managers, irrespective of their organisational position and status, tended to place high values on the human relations aspects of the job. Their conflict management approaches are based on the premise that production targets are to be achieved but only through the willing and meaningful cooperation of their subordinates or seniors as the case may be. The fact that both the seniors and their subordinates are using problem-solving to the maximum possible extent means that they often engage in the rational process of identifying the alternative courses of action, evaluating the alternatives, and finally choosing the best alternative out of the whole lot in order to find amicable and acceptable solutions to work related problems and issues. As it was expected, the analysis of data revealed that the forcing and withdrawing modes of managing conflicts are being rarely used by the senior managers and their subordinates. This finding shows that the managers are willing to confront or face conflicts and find productive solutions thereto rather than avoiding the situations. In addition, they are somewhat reluctant to use the forcing method of resolving conflicts, which is highly undemocratic in nature. In fact, the forcing method is based on the assumption that one should try to win one's position through the imposition of one's views on others through the use of all possible means such as power, position, expertise, etc. It was further noted that while the senior managers made maximum use of problem-solving followed by their utilisation of smoothing and compromising on equal basis, the subordinates too used problem-solving to the maximum possible extent, followed by compromise and smoothing, respectively. Thus, it can be stated that the subordinates, by virtue of their hierarchical position, often feel compelled to make compromises with their seniors in order to find amicable solutions to job related conflicts.

The research findings of the present study obtained regarding management of senior-subordinate conflict at the workplace lead us to some important conclusions. The managers' maximum possible utilisation of problem-solving, smoothing, and compromising modes indicates that their approaches towards the management of work related conflicts are based on democratic ideas and value systems. This particular development in the area of management of organisational conflicts can be attributed to certain important factors. In the first place, the present-day managers have started recognising the fact that it is possible to enhance organisational productivity and also establish sound human relations within an organisation only through the use of creative potentialities of employees who have greater understanding of the intricacies of the work situations. The development of important management concepts such as participative decision-making, industrial democracy, industrial relations, collective bargaining, etc., have made the employees more and more conscious of their basic rights, needs and aspirations at the workplace. Therefore, the traditional norms of managerial control are to be replaced by democratic approaches to conflict management in which the subordinates get ample opportunities to express their talent and capabilities fully and thereby offer constructive suggestions on a variety of organisational issues and problems.

The increasing use of problem-solving, smoothing, and compromising behaviours in resolving work related conflicts can also be attributed to changes in employee profile in terms of enhanced employee education, knowledge and income levels. Employees possessing technical knowledge and skills along with high level of maturity cannot be expected to work under traditional authority and control systems or under monotonous job conditions. In fact, the present-day industry managers and employees have already attained a certain level of fulfilment of their basic needs including social and economic security, which do not serve as motivators for them any longer. Therefore, they can be motivated only through the provision of opportunities for challenging or satisfying work, recognition, advancement, and a sense of fulfilment at the workplace. There is a paramount need to involve them in the decision making process, and their viewpoints, suggestions and ideas have to be duly considered by their senior managers on a number of organisational issues and problems.

In the end, it must be mentioned that the growing knowledge and appreciation of behavioural science research findings also lead to the increased use of problem solving and smoothing modes of resolving conflicts along with a reduction in forcing behaviour. In fact, a number of research studies have indicated the positive effects of problem-solving and smoothing behaviours on organisational effectiveness while at the same time demonstrating the negative impact of forcing behaviours on effectiveness dimensions. The new insights and knowledge gained from research studies have led to appropriate modifications in the conflict management behaviours of both the managers and the employees in the industrial situations.

## REVIEW QUESTIONS

1. What are some of the common issues of senior-subordinate conflict? Explain.
2. Explain some of the major sources of senior-subordinate conflict. Which ones are most relevant in today's organisations?
3. Explain the conflict management behaviours of Indian managers in terms of their utilisation of various conflict management methods or styles. Cite necessary research evidences in this regard.
4. Are there any differences between the conflict management behaviours of senior managers and their subordinates? Discuss.
5. What are the driving forces behind the managers' maximum use of problem-solving, smoothing, and compromising modes of managing conflicts? Discuss.

## REFERENCES


1. Dalton, M., Conflicts between staff and line managerial officers, *American Sociological Review*, 15, 1950, pp. 342-351; and McGreger, D., *The Human Side of Enterprise*, McGraw Hill, New York, 1960.
2. Stagner, R., *The Psychology of Industrial Conflict*, Wiley, New York, 1956; and Stagner, R., and Rosen, H., *Psychology of Union Management Relations*, Belmont, Wordsworth, California, 1956.
3. Lawrence, P.R., and Lorsch, J.W., *Organisation and Environment: Managing Differentiation and Integration, Divsiion of Research*, Harvard Business School, Harvard University, Boston, 1967.
4. Simon, H.A., *The New Science of Management Decisions*, Harper and Row, New York, 1960; and Pondy, L.R., Organisational conflict: Concept and models, *Administrative Science Quarterly*, 12, 1967, pp. 296-320.
5. Renwick, P.A., Perception and management of superior-subordinate conflicts, *Organisational Behaviour and Human Performance*, 13, 1975, pp. 444-456; Sharma, R.A., and Samantara, R., Conflict management in an Indian firm: A case study, *Decision*, 21, October-Decmber, 1994, pp. 235-249; and Samantara, R., Management of superior-subordinate conflict: An exploration , *Indian Journal of Industrial Relations*, 38(4), 2003, pp. 444-459.
6. Samantara, R., 2003, *op. cit.*
7. Blake, R.R., and Mouton, J.S., *The Management Grid*, Gulf, Houston, 1964.
8. Cronbach, L.J., Coefficeint alpha and the internal structure of tests, *Psychometrica*, 16(3), September, 1951, pp. 297-334.
9. Samantara, R., Conflict management strategies and organisational effectiveness, *Indian Journal of Industrial Relations*, 39(3), January, 2004, pp. 298-323.
10. Samantara, R., 2003, *op. cit.*
11. *Ibid.*
12. *Ibid.*
13. Lawrence, P.R., and Lorsch, J.W., 1967, *op. cit*; Burke, R.J., Methods of resolving interpersonal conflict, *Personnel Administration*, July-August, 1969, pp. 48-55; Mital, P., Role stress with its actual and desired modes of conflict resolution, *Indian Journal of Industrial Relations*, January, 1995; Samantara, R., 2003, *op. cit.*; and Samantara, R., 2004. *op. cit.*

# 6

# Organisational Effectiveness: Concepts, Models and Issues in Measurement/Assessment

## 6.1 OBJECTIVES OF THE STUDY

The research study conducted in a electricity generating and distributing company provided some illuminating results concerning the managers' utilisation of various conflict management strategies, effects of status differences on the management of conflicts, etc. These issues are to be explored further across industries with a view to obtaining some generalisable findings. However, at the same time, there is a need for making a broad-based research study that would examine the relative efficacy or effectiveness of conflict management strategies. More significantly, there is a need to examine the conflict management strategies in the context of certain well-defined, comprehensive measures of organisational effectiveness. Since the construct of organisational effectiveness is a pivotal one in this analysis, there is a need for focus on certain conceptual issues related to the effectiveness construct - its meaning and definitions, the problem of criteria identification associated with it, the models of effectiveness, and, finally, some of the significant issues related to the measurement or assessment of organisational effectiveness. The insights gained from this conceptual analysis are expected to facilitate the desired investigations in certain selected organisations in the Indian industry.

Organisational effectiveness as a subject of study has motivated the writings of economists, organisation theorists, management philosophers, consultants and practitioners ever since Adam Smith[1] published his treatise "Wealth of Nations", arguing that efficiency results from specialisation and division of labour. The modern era of research on management theory with an emphasis on effectiveness dates back to the Scientific Management movement and the publication by Taylor of "Principles of Scientific Management". In fact, the subject of effectiveness received considerable attention during the early eighties which witnessed a plethora of popular writing in the form of explanations of what makes some firms excellent, productive, efficient, healthy, or possessing vitality – all proxies for the concept of organisational effectiveness as used in the literature. Innovations, closeness to customers, participative leadership, etc., have been singled out as the most important predictors of effectiveness of organisations.

## 6.2 CONCEPT OF ORGANISATIONAL EFFECTIVENESS

As stated by Goodman and Pennings,[2] effectiveness is a central theme in almost all studies of formal organisations, and it is difficult to conceive of a theory of organisation that does not include the effectiveness construct. While effectiveness is clearly a concept of central importance, the literature available on this subject is plagued with problems of definition, circumspection and criteria identification. One major problem pertains to the elusiveness of a well-meaning, comprehensive definition of effectiveness. At the most, the concept of effectiveness remains a vague one. It means different things to different people, depending upon one's frame of reference; it means profit or return on investment to an economist or financial analyst, quantity or quality of output to a production manager, new products or inventions to a research scientist, quality of working life to a social scientist, and so on. The diversity of opinion regarding the conceptual meaning of effectiveness can be well gauged from the wide variety of definitions offered by some researchers.

Etzioni[3] views effectiveness as the degree of goal achievement. According to Argyris,[4] organisational effectiveness represents a condition where the organisation increases output with constant or decreasing inputs or has constant output with decreasing inputs. Katz and Kahn[5] define effectiveness in terms of "maximisation of return to the organisation by all means. Such maximisation by economic and technical means has to do with efficiency; maximisation by non-economic or political means increases effectiveness without adding to efficiency." As viewed by Jackson, Morgan and Paollilo,[6] "effectiveness is commonly referred to as the degree to which predetermined goals are achieved." Kondalkar[7] viewed that an organisation will achieve a higher degree of effectiveness when individual and organisational goals are integrated. Mohr[8] views effectiveness as "a measure of how well or to what extent something is accomplished". Drucker[9] distinguished efficiency or effectiveness by associating efficiency to "doing things right" and effectiveness to "doing right things". As viewed by Asmild *et al.*,[10] effectiveness is the extent to which the policy objectives of an organisation are achieved. According to Reddin,[11] effectiveness is the extent to which the manager achieves the output requirements of the job, by what he achieves rather than what he does. Effectiveness depends on judging observable actions or behaviours leading to the accomplishment of organisational goals.[12]

Georgopoulos and Tennenbaum[13] define organisational effectiveness as "the extent to which an organisation as a social system, given certain resources and means, fulfils its objectives without incapacitating its means and resources and without placing undue strain upon its members." This conception of organisational effectiveness includes the following criteria: (1) organisational productivity; (2) organisational flexibility or the ability to adjust to both internal organisational changes and external changes imposed by the general outside environment; and (3) absence of intra-organisational strain or tension or conflict. In fact, these three criteria of effectiveness are applicable to all types of organisations.

Organisational effectiveness is often described as an organisation's ability to acquire resources from the broader environment and utilise those resources to achieve specified goals. In carrying out these processes, the organisation has to engage itself in such tasks as resource acquisition, production of goods and services, rational coordination of its activities, organisational adaptation and renewal, satisfaction of the claims of multiple constituency stakeholders, etc., through a system of social norms, laws, rules and regulations, and so on. In this context, it is worthwhile to consider Cameron's[14] four proposed primary criteria that can be used to assess the degree to which an organisation is effective. These four criteria of organisational effectiveness as shown in Figure 6.1 are as follows:

1. accomplishment of goals ;
2. success in resource acquisition ;
3. health of internal organisational processes ; and
4. satisfaction of strategic constituencies.

**Figure 6.1:** Four interrelated approaches to organisational effectiveness

*Source*: Adapted from K. Cameron, "Effectiveness as Paradox: Consensus and Conflict in Conceptions of Organizational Effectiveness", *Management Science*, May 1986, pp. 539-553. In R.A. Sharma, *Organisational Theory and Behaviour*, Tata McGraw Hill, New Delhi, 2000, p. 577.

It may be noted that the organisation theorists have recently shifted their emphasis from goalistic criteria to systems level criteria of effectiveness. Schein[15] has stated some reasons that have indeed undermined the importance of goalistic criteria of effectiveness as viable ones. The reasons may be stated as follows:

1. It is observed that the rational organisations tend to behave inefficiently if the sole criterion of effectiveness is regarded as profit maximization or providing a quality service to customers.
2. It is noted that organisations often perform multiple functions and have multiple goals which may be conflicting with one another. The performance of these organisations may be highly satisfactory with regard to some goals while it may not be so in regard to others.
3. In addition, an organisation should not be regarded as effective or ineffective by simply comparing its current level of performance to that of the previous year. Rather, the effectiveness of an organisation should be judged through its comparison with similar organisations at a particular point of time.

In order to resolve this dilemma, the modern organisation theorists have attempted to understand organisational effectiveness in terms of systems level criteria of effectiveness. A number of organisation theorists have emphasized upon systems level effectiveness that includes an organisation's capacity to survive, grow, and maintain itself irrespective of the particular functions performed by it. Seashore and Yuchtman,[16] working from the systems perspective, defined effectiveness in terms of the organisation's ability to exploit its environment in the acquisition of scarce and valued resources to sustain its functioning. The highest level of effectiveness is reached when the organisation maximizes its bargaining position with the environment and optimizes procurement of its resources. Another significant systems level perspective of effectiveness has been proposed by Bennis[17] : the systems level criteria of organisational effectiveness include the following:

1. Adaptability – the ability to solve problems and to react with flexibility to changing environmental conditions.
2. A sense of identity–knowledge and insight on the part of members of the organisation regarding its goals, objectives, missions, activities, etc.
3. Capacity to test reality–the ability to perceive and interpret the real properties of the environment.

## 6.3 EFFECTIVENESS VERSUS EFFICIENCY

It is commonly observed that there are some organisations which are highly effective but inefficient. Similarly, there are organisations which are highly efficient but ineffective. Therefore, it is necessary to draw a proper distinction between the terms 'effectiveness' and 'efficiency'. Effectiveness is a broad concept, and it refers to the degree to which an organisation is able to realize its goals. On the other hand, efficiency has a limited perspective that refers to the productivity or productive capacity of an organisation. Efficiency refers to the amount of resources required or utilised to produce a particular unit of output. To put it differently, efficiency can be said to refer to the maximum possible output that can be produced with a certain level of resource inputs used. Efficiency is generally measured as the ratio of input to output. A decline in cost per unit of output indicates an improvement in the efficiency of an organisation but it must be remembered that this improvement in efficiency will not necessarily lead to increased profits. Although an organisation's efficiency is improving, it may be incurring losses due to a declining market. Similarly, it is also possible that an inefficient organisation may be able to reap high profits due to the existence of a rising market for its products. Thus, efficiency is primarily concerned with the technical and economic aspects of the organisation whereas effectiveness relates to the attainment of organisational goals and objectives. Thus, the survival prospects of an organisation are not solely dependent upon the consideration of efficiency in its internal working.

As mentioned earlier, an efficient organisation may not necessarily be effective just as an effective organisation is not always the efficient one. Efficiency may help an organisation to become effective and it may facilitate the long-term growth and survival of the organisation. It must be clearly understood, however, that efficiency is merely an aspect of organisational effectiveness. As Drucker[18] has observed, effectiveness is the foundation of success-efficiency is a minimum condition for survival after success has been achieved. Efficiency is concerned with doing things right. Effectiveness is doing the right things.

### 6.3.1 Perspectives on Effectiveness

Lawless[19] has highlighted the significance of three different perspectives of organisational effectiveness: individual, group, and organisational effectiveness. The concept of individual effectiveness focuses on the task performance of individual members of an organisation. Such individual performance of members is assessed through performance evaluation techniques that are used as the basis for pay revision, promotions and other positive incentives within the organisation. When individuals are considered collectively, they form a group and are engaged in the performance of certain assigned group tasks. Individuals in an organisation seldom work alone or work in isolation from one another. Therefore, it is significant to consider another perspective of effectiveness, i.e., group effectiveness. Since organisations consist of both individuals and groups, it can be stated that organisational effectiveness comprises both individual and group effectiveness. In this context, it may be noted, however, that organisational effectiveness may be more than the sum of individual and group effectiveness. Through synergic efforts, organisations are able to achieve higher levels of performance than the sum total of their parts.

According to Lawless,[20] the relationships among these three perspectives of effectiveness vary depending upon the task being performed, the level of technology used and the type of organisation being considered. In fact, these three different perspectives of effectiveness are in a state of mutual dependence among themselves. Individual effectiveness is caused by such factors as personality traits, physical attributes, motivation and morale, etc., whereas group effectiveness is caused by communication, socialisation, leadership, etc. The causes of organisational effectiveness include technology, environmental conditions, competence of individual employees, the innovative abilities of managers, etc.

## 6.4 DETERMINANTS OF ORGANISATIONAL EFFECTIVENESS

As will be seen later, the organisation theorists have attempted to delineate the construct space of effectiveness or to identify all possible determinants of effectiveness. Unfortunately, however, the attempts made by authors in this regard have met with only limited success. Even then, it would be worthwhile to discuss the notable contributions made by some theorists to identify the indicators of organisational effectiveness. Likert[21] developed a model of organisational effectiveness that explains the relationship between three types of variables such as causal, intervening, and output. These three taken together determine the effectiveness of an organisation over time. Although Likert's[22] model of effectiveness has been discussed at length later on, it would be important to briefly discuss here the role and importance of these three variables in determining organisational effectiveness.

**Causal variables** refer to those factors that influence the attainment of organisational goals or objectives. These independent variables can be controlled by the organisation or its management and include such variables as leadership behaviour and skills, management's decision, organisation structure and policies, and so on.

**Intervening variables** represent the current condition of the internal state of an organisation. It must be mentioned that the causal variables as discussed above have an influence on the intervening variables in an organisation. Intervening variables include such internal organisational factors as motivation and morale of organisation's members, leadership skills, decision making, problem-solving, communication, etc.

**Output or end-result variables** reflect the actual achievement of the organisation. These variables include production, costs, sales, earnings, employee turnover, union-management relations, etc. It is noteworthy that more than 90% of managers consider output measures alone in assessing the effectiveness of organisations.

It is equally significant to note that a number of leading organisational behaviour researchers have discussed organisational effectiveness by focusing specially on output variables. Fiddler[23] in his leadership studies, evaluated leadership effectiveness in terms of group performance on the group's primary assigned task. As stated by Reddin,[24] the effectiveness of a manager should be measured "objectively by his profit centre performance—maximum output, market share, or other similar criteria". Kaplan and Norton[25] suggested that businesses should consider four important perspectives in deciding about performance measures: (1) the customers perspective; (2) the internal operations perspective; (3) the change perspective; and (4) the financial perspective.

In the words of Hersey, Blanchard and Johnson,[26] the causal variables largely produce the level or condition of the intervening variables which, in turn, influence the end result variables. Attempts to improve the intervening variables directly will usually be much less effective than attempts to improve them by changing the causal variables. The end result variables, also, can be improved most effectively by modifying the causal variables rather than the intervening variables."

**Long-term versus short-term goals:** In addition to highlighting the role and importance of causal, intervening, and output variables in influencing organisational effectiveness, Hersey, Blanchard and Johnson[27] further suggested that the effectiveness of organisations is primarily determined by both long-term and short-term goals of an organisation. It may be pointed out that intervening variables represent the long-term goals of an organisation as these variables are concerned with organisational development and renewal. As there is a constant need for effective managers in industry, the middle level managers or executives are frequently promoted on the basis of short-term output variables such as increased production and increased earnings without due regard for the long-term potential of an organisation and its development. Therefore, the managers attempt to pressurise employees to produce higher levels of output which has an adverse effect on the morale and motivation of employees and on their leadership, decision-making, and problem-solving skills. The findings of Behavioural Science research have shown that this condition of low employee morale and high productivity cannot be sustained for long. The obvious outcomes of these deteriorating intervening variables at the work situation are reflected in the form of increased employee turnover, increased absenteeism, and numerous grievances.

## 6.5 THE CONSTRUCT SPACE OF EFFECTIVENESS IS NOT KNOWN

It must be emphasised that organisational effectiveness is not a concept, but a construct. While concepts can be defined and exactly specified by observing objective events, constructs cannot be so specified. Constructs are mental abstractions that have no objective reality, they cannot be pinpointed, counted or observed. Constructs are intended to give meaning to ideas or interpretations. This highly abstract nature of the effectiveness construct and the lack of agreement as to its structure accounts for a major portion of the confusion in the effectiveness literature.

Authors have attempted both theoretically and empirically, to identify the boundaries of the construct space of effectiveness, i.e., to determine all possible indicators of effectiveness. Although a number of theoretical perspectives have been offered to explain effectiveness, it can be stated that none of these captures the total construct space or the total meaning of effectiveness. Price[28] attempted to develop a comprehensive model or theory of effectiveness by reviewing and integrating 50 studies. His model of effectiveness comprises the dependent variable called 'effectiveness' and five intervening independent variables such as productivity, conformity, morale, adaptiveness, and institutionalisation. Price adhered to the goal-oriented approach and provided an inventory of 34 propositions linking the above-stated predictor variables to effectiveness. In his effectiveness model, there are five systems: economic system, political system, control system, population system, and ecology system or environmental system (Figure 6.2). These five different systems tend to influence the intervening independent variables and thereby determine organisational effectiveness.

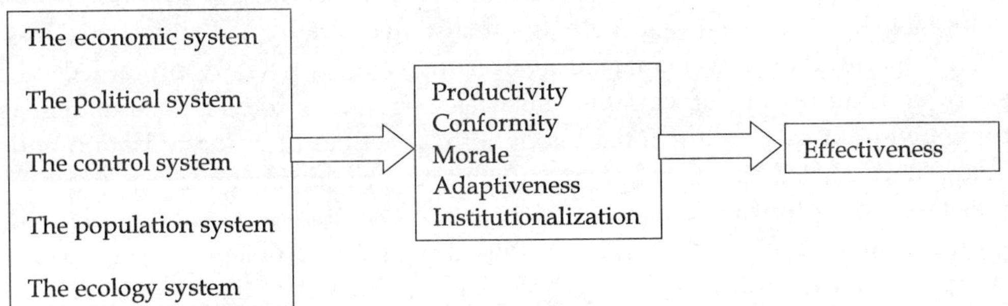


**Figure 6.2:** Price's model of organisational effectiveness

*Source:* Adapted and abridged from James I. Price, *Organizational Effectiveness*, Homewood, III, Irwin, 1968. In V.S.P.Rao, and P.S. Narayana, *Organization Theory and Behaviour*, Vani Educational Books, New Delhi, 1986, p. 705.

Steers[29] reviewed 17 organisational effectiveness studies and summarised the 14 evaluation criteria mentioned in two or more cases (as shown in Table 6.1). Of these, adaptability/flexibility was mentioned in more than half of the studies reviewed. This was followed by productivity and satisfaction which were mentioned in about a third of the studies. All other criteria were mentioned in less than a quarter of the studies reviewed. Steers attributed this general lack of agreement on evaluative criteria to such problems as: (1) existing evaluation criteria are often unstable; (2) different criteria may be relevant for different time perspectives (short-term versus long-term); (3) multiple criteria are often in conflict with one another; (4) some criteria are not applicable to certain types of organisations; and (5) some criteria may be difficult to measure accurately.

**Table 6.1:** Frequency of occurrence of evaluation criteria in 17 models of organisational effectiveness

| Evaluation criteria | Number of times mentioned (N = 17) |
|---|---|
| Adaptability-Flexibility | 10 |
| Productivity | 6 |
| Satisfaction | 5 |
| Profitability | 3 |
| Resource acquisition | 3 |
| Absence of strain | 2 |
| Control over environment | 2 |
| Development | 2 |
| Efficiency | 2 |
| Employee retention | 2 |
| Growth | 2 |
| Integration | 2 |
| Open communications | 2 |
| Survival | 2 |
| All other criteria | 1 |

*Source*: R.M. Steers, "Problems in the Measurement of Organisational Effectiveness", *Administrative Science Quarterly*, 1975, 20. pp. 546-548.

Campbell[30] reviewed the organisational effectiveness literature, and presented a taxonomy of various criteria that, he believed, accounted for "all variables that have been proposed seriously as indices of organisational effectiveness" (Table 6.2). Campbell, however, went on to suggest a relative lack of value in such "objective" enquiry, arguing that the development of organisation-specific models based on clear, explicit assumptions would be generally more promising.

Thus, it appears that theoretical attempts to discover the boundaries of the effectiveness construct have not met with any meaningful success. On account of this, subsequent authors have been hesitant to propose a general theory of organisational effectiveness. As a way out to this dilemma, they have resorted to the adoption of empirical approaches to delineating the boundaries of effectiveness. Some of the important empirical approaches taken in this regard may be discussed as follows.

Georgopoulos and Tannenbaum[31] studied effectiveness criteria in an industrial service organisation specialising in the transportation and delivery of retail merchandise. The three criteria of organisational effectiveness studied by them were as follows:

(i) organisational productivity;

(ii) organisational flexibility or the ability to adapt to both internal changes within the organisation and externally induced changes; and

**Table 6.2:** Campbell's list of effectiveness criteria

| | |
|---|---|
| Overall effectiveness | Productivity |
| Efficiency | Profit |
| Quality | Accidents |
| Growth | Absenteeism |
| Turnover | Job satisfaction |
| Motivation | Morale |
| Control | Conflict/cohesion |
| Flexibility/adaptation | Planning & goal setting |
| Goal consensus | Internalisation of organisational goals |
| Role and norm congruence | Managerial interpersonal skills |
| Managerial task skills | Readiness |
| Information management & communication | Utilization of environment |
| Evaluations by external entities | Stability |
| Participation and shared influence | Value of human resource |
| Achievement emphasis | Training & development emphasis |

*Source*: J.P. Campbell, "On the Nature of Organisational Effectiveness", P.S. Goodman and J.M. Pennings (Eds.), *New Perspective on Organisational Effectiveness*, San Francisco: Jossey-Bass (1977).

(iii) Absence of intra-organisational strain or tension or conflict between organisational sub-groups.

It may be noted that each of the three criteria of effectiveness was found to be related to an independent assessment of effectiveness by experts, thereby lending support to the validity of these criteria. Thus, Georgopoulos and Tannenbaum produced research evidence for certain valid and generalisable measures or criteria of organisational effectiveness. In their effectiveness model, the organisation's structure included certain sub-systems known as 'stations'. They obtained some valid research findings and concluded that "effective stations were more productive, lower in inter-group strain and conflicts, and somewhat flexible than non-effective stations."[32]

Seashore and Yuchtman[33] identified ten effectiveness criteria in their study of 75 insurance agencies by factor analysing 76 objective measures of performance. The 10 resulting factors or dimensions were integrated into the system resource model of effectiveness developed by the researchers. These effectiveness dimensions included business volume, production cost, new member productivity, youthfulness of members, business mix, work force growth, devotion to management, maintenance cost, productivity, and market penetration.[34] They assumed that the mutual interdependence between an organisation and its environment assumes the form of input/output transactions involving scarce resources. According to them, the resources available in the environment are limited in supply, and any attempt to acquire these resources leads to competition among organisations. Therefore, they defined organisational effectiveness in terms of the bargaining position that is achieved by the competing organisations. The boundaries of the effectiveness construct were drawn by them so that only criteria relating to an organisation's bargaining position in acquiring scarce and valued resources were included.

Quinn and Rohrbaugh[35] used Campbell's "comprehensive" list of effectiveness criteria, and tried to reduce and combine these criteria through the use of cluster analysis techniques. They found that the resulting clustered criteria closely matched four major theoretical perspectives on organisations: rational goal models, open system models, decision process models, and human relations models. Certain fundamental value dimensions were empirically identified that underpinned these major theoretical perspectives, and that individuals use in judging organisational effectiveness. The construct space for effectiveness was defined by three major value dimensions: organisation concerns versus individual concerns, flexibility versus control, and means versus ends. A more detailed explanation of Quinn and Rohrbaugh's spatial model of organisational effectiveness is presented in the next section.

From the above analysis, it appears equally well that the empirical approaches too have failed to bound the construct of organisational effectiveness. Each group of authors has approached the problem with a different methodology and thereby derived a different set of indicators. The boundaries and meaning of the construct are not the same for any of them. Several reasons for this discrepancy have been pinpointed by Cameron and Whetton.[36] One reason is because in empirical approaches the results are based on limited types of organisations with unique characteristics. Another reason is that the number of constituencies from whose point of view effectiveness is judged may be limited. The general tendency is to use obtainable data, and ignore some of the important constituencies holding different performance criteria for the organisation. The third reason is that the level of analysis and the focus of activity often differ among the criteria selected for different studies (e.g., subunit goal attainment was used in one study while organisational resource acquisition was used in another). Finally, the conceptualisation of organisations accepted by the researchers may restrict relevant criteria of effectiveness to be used.

Thus, it has become amply clear that with the divergence of criteria used in relation to organisational effectiveness, no single, unambiguous meaning of the construct is available. However, this lack of specificity of the construct space of effectiveness should not be interpreted negatively. As has been advocated by some authors, defining the construct space of organisational effectiveness may be dysfunctional because it restricts organisational possibilities. An unprescribed construct of effectiveness allows for a wide variety of organisations to be simultaneously judged as effective, even with contradictory characteristics. Similarly, it allows for criteria to be included that are not considered significant by the organisation's major constituencies, but that may become crucial to the survival of the organisation in the future.

## 6.6 MODELS OF ORGANISATIONAL EFFECTIVENESS

A wide variety of models has been proposed to explain the effectiveness construct. Although considerable debate has been made over which of these models should be viewed as the best one, the utility of each individual model cannot be undermined. In fact, each model represents a unique way of looking at the effectiveness construct with different assumptions, different sets of relationships among the variables studied, and different dimensions of effectiveness. As Cameron and Whetton[37] have pointed out, "the utility of any particular model may depend upon the environment, the constituency under investigation, and the life-cycle stage."

Although several models have been proposed by organisation theorists for explaining or measuring the effectiveness construct, two early models that gained prominence in effectiveness research were: (1) the rational goal model, and (2) the systems model. However, as discussed later, these two models had certain limitations as well. Therefore, the organisation experts have proposed some other effectiveness models too - the process model,[38] the internal process or maintenance model,[39] the strategic constituencies model,[40] and the legitimacy model.[41] It is also heartening to note that some empirical models of effectiveness have been developed with immense practical relevance. As mentioned earlier, some of the important empirical models are the system resource model,[42] the Mahoney and Weitzel model[43] and the Spatial model.[44] A brief description of some of the important models of organisational effectiveness is presented below along with a critical analysis of their relative strengths and weaknesses.

### 6.6.1 The Rational Goal Model

An organisation is primarily created to achieve certain goals. Therefore, goal achievement has been the most widely used criterion of organisational effectiveness. It must be mentioned that the rational goal perspective of effectiveness reflects a Weberian point of view. This model places a great deal of emphasis on the planned, rational and mechanical aspects of organisational functioning. It assumes that goals of formal organisations can be neatly established, and that material and human resources can be systematically manipulated towards the fulfilment of goals. The effectiveness of an organisation, then, can be represented by the attainment of or progress towards the stated goals. As stated by Barnard,[45] "what we mean by effectiveness ..... is the accomplishment of recognised objectives of cooperative effort. The degree of accomplishment indicates the degree of effectiveness".

Robbins[46] suggests that the rational goal approach can be made really useful only when the following assumptions are made:

1. Organisations must have some ultimate goals.
2. The goals must be well-defined and properly understood by all the members of the organisation.

3. There must be general consensus on these goals.
4. The goals must be few enough so that they are manageable.
5. The progress towards the attainment of these goals must be measurable.

The goal model appears to be an objective, reliable and analytical tool for the assessment of organisational performance. However, some authors believe that the goal model has methodological as well as practical shortcomings. First of all, the rational goal model seems to be inapplicable to those organisations that do not produce tangible output. In addition, Etzioni[47] argues that goals as ideal states do not offer the possibility of realistic assessment of organisational effectiveness. Goals, as norms or target states, are cultural entities whereas organisations, as systems of coordinated activities, are social systems. Thus, it seems more logical to make a comparison of organisations with each other rather than with an objective standard. Another shortcoming of the goal model concerns the way goals of an organisation are stated. The yardstick for measuring organisational effectiveness may be based on the goals an organisation claims to be pursuing (public or official goals), or it may be based on the goals the organisation actually follows (private or operational goals). The public or official goals often fail to be realised because they are, in many cases, not intended to be realised. Another problem relates to the fact that organisations are generally known to be serving multiple goals. These multiple goals often compete with one another and are sometimes even incompatible. Finally, it must be noted that the rational goal approach presupposes the existence of some commonly agreed goals of the organisation. In view of diverse interest groups existing with their multiple and varied goals, however, the consensus regarding some common organisation goals may not always be possible. Therefore, to reach some consensus regarding the goals, organisations are sometimes forced to "state goals in such ambiguous terms as to allow the varying interest groups to interpret them in a way favourable to their self-interests."[48]

In spite of the problems as discussed above, it must be mentioned that the rational goal model continues to be the most dominating one in the field of organisational effectiveness. The rational goal approach exerts tremendous influence on the practising managers of corporate entities and also has a commonsense appeal to researchers and evaluators engaged in the task of assessment of organisational effectiveness.

### 6.6.2 The Systems Model of Effectiveness

The systems model of organisational effectiveness implies that organisations are composed of interrelated parts. The effectiveness of an organisational system depends upon the performance of its individual sub-parts. The systems approach emphasises upon the interrelationship between different parts of an organisation and its environment as they work together to influence effectiveness. In other words, the systems model focuses on the functional complementarity of parts of the organisation and the nature of the organisation's relationship to the environment. The organisation is viewed as an open system receiving inputs from the environment, transforming these inputs and providing new outputs to the environment. The task of the organisation is to survive. At any particular time, the effectiveness of an organisation as a whole is ascertained by analysing the manner in which the parts and the whole maintain each other in a network of interdependent, reciprocal relationship. The focus is on an optimum or balanced distribution of resources among the various organisational needs rather than satisfaction of any one activity at the expense of others.

The systems approach to effectiveness emphasises upon the fact that the managers have a responsibility to understand the organisation's environment and set realistic goals in keeping with the needs or demands of the environment. The systems viewpoint highlights the importance of such factors as the organisation's flexibility of responses to the changing needs of the environment, efficiency in the transformation of inputs into outputs, employees' job satisfaction, clarity of organisational communication, etc. Thus, it can be said that the more effective organisations are those that successfully adapt their structure, technologies, policies, work methods, etc., to the changing environment to facilitate the attainment of their goals.

The systems model is, however, not without criticisms. Although the systems theorists focus on the idea of "optimisation" as an important component of effectiveness, they have shown little concern for trying to measure optimisation. In addition, it is argued that the systems theorists have expressed the need for general measures of effectiveness, but none have developed these measures that they claim to be so necessary. Finally, it is believed that the frame of reference used in the systems analysis is somewhat confusing. The confusion centres around the multi-dimensional approach to effectiveness with multiple measures of a series of different analytical concepts.

Another theoretical problem with the systems approach is its separation from the goal model. It is to be expected that those who rely on the goal model would advocate the use of goals as criteria of effectiveness while those who rely on the systems model would advocate systemic criteria of effectiveness. However, two of the most ardent advocates of the systems model, Parsons and Etzioni, insist upon relating effectiveness incongruously with goal attainment.[49]

The positions of Parsons and Etzioni as stated above make sense, if one takes into account the system-within-system logic of the structural-functional theorists. Initially, the organisation is viewed as a sub-system of a larger social system or society. Organisational goals, therefore, are synonymous with the primary societal mission or functions performed by the organisation which give it its legitimacy and uniqueness. Considering this approach from the external frame of reference, organisation's goals emerge as outputs provided by the organisation for the system which contains it. Judgements of organisational effectiveness are made in terms of the quality and relevance of the organisation's output towards assuring the survival, stability and growth of some other system. Viewed again from the organisation's frame of reference, organisational goals or outputs emerge as one of the functional requirements which the organisation has to meet in order to ensure its own survival, stability and growth. Thus, the goal model which appears to be an outright contradiction to the systems model, may, in fact, be a logical extension of the systems model.

### 6.6.3 Strategic Constituencies Model

The strategic constituencies model is based upon the fundamental premise that effectiveness refers to the minimal satisfaction of all the strategic constituencies of the organisation. In fact, the organisation is perceived as a set of internal and external constituencies that negotiate a complex set of constraints, goals and referents.[50] An effective organisation is one that satisfies the demands of those constituencies in its environment from whom it requires support for its continued existence.[51] These constituencies involve people connected to the organisation and assuming different roles such as the consumers of the organisation's products and services, the resource providers, the facilitators of the organisation's output, the main supporters and dependents of the organisation.[52] This model assumes the comprehensive nature of effectiveness and evaluates the factors existing in the organisation and also in the broader environment. Thus, the strategic constituencies model emphasises upon the concept of social responsibility (CSR) that was not adequately considered in the traditional approaches to the study of organisational effectiveness. This model is particularly useful in evaluating how far an organisation has been effective or successful in fulfilling the needs and expectations of various interest groups or stakeholders with a view to ensuring its continued survival and growth in the society.

To ensure that the adoption of the strategic constituencies approach leads to organisational effectiveness, the following steps must be followed:

1. First of all, the management must identify all the relevant constituencies in the environment upon which the organisation depends for its survival.
2. The relative power of each of constituency must be judged on the basis of the degree to which the organisation depends upon it.
3. It is also important to identify the expectations of different constituencies from the organisation.
4. All these constituencies should then be arranged by the management in order of their power and expectations.
5. The effectiveness of an organisation can then be assessed in terms of its ability to satisfy these constituencies that have been arranged or ranked.

It must be pointed out, however, that the strategic constituencies model is not devoid of limitations. In the first place, it is difficult to separate the strategic constituencies from the broader environment. It is difficult because these critical constituencies keep on changing with changes in the environment. The second problem is that it is not easy to assign weightage to the critical constituencies according to the degree of dependence of the organisation on them. Finally, it is also extremely difficult to identify and measure the varied expectations of the strategic constituencies from the organisation.

### 6.6.4 Behavioural Approach to Organisational Effectiveness

The behavioural approach to organisational effectiveness emphasizes upon the role and importance of individual behaviour that significantly influences organisational success or failure. When the individual objectives of employees are compatible with those of the organisation, we can say that there is perfect integration of individual and organisational goals. This situation leads to high degree of organisational effectiveness as in this case, the individuals make maximum possible efforts towards the attainment of organisational objectives. It must be noted, however, that this situation of perfect integration of individual and organisational goals can aptly be described as a myth as it represents an ideal situation. When there is high degree of integration of individual and organisational goals, the obvious result would be high degree of organisational effectiveness. When there is lower integration of individual and organisational goals, the lesser will be the degree of effectiveness.

The empirical research studies on organisational effectiveness have revealed the following important aspects of effectiveness criteria:

1. Although different organisations have different criteria of effectiveness, productivity has been cited as the most frequently used criterion of effectiveness as the review of management literature suggests.
2. A number of effectiveness criteria have been revealed by the research studies. While the external criteria of effectiveness include adaptiveness, profitability, resource acquisition, etc., the internal criteria include employee morale, stability, low stress, etc.
3. An organisation is not required to be fully effective in all the areas; rather, it would be enough if the organisation is able to optimise its effectiveness especially with regard to its technical, economic, and social aspects.
4. Irrespective of the criteria of effectiveness applicable to a particular organisation, it must be ensured that these effectiveness criteria are measurable.

### 6.6.5 Competing Values Model

Another important model of organisational effectiveness is the competing values model that draws upon past attempts made by organisation experts to formalise effectiveness criteria.[53] This model of effectiveness has been utilised in several research studies including effectiveness of management information systems, organisational transformation, organisational culture and strategy. Quinn and Rohrbaugh[54] utilised multidimensional scaling and developed a spatial model of organisational effectiveness on the basis of three value dimensions: internal-external, flexibility-control, and means-ends. At a later stage, it was, however, demonstrated that out of these three value dimensions, only two (i.e., internal-external and flexibility-control) were adequate enough to explain the effectiveness construct. These value dimensions, when combined, gave rise to four quadrants representing: (1) rational goal model; (2) open system model; (3) internal process model; and (4) human relations model, as shown in Figure 6.3.

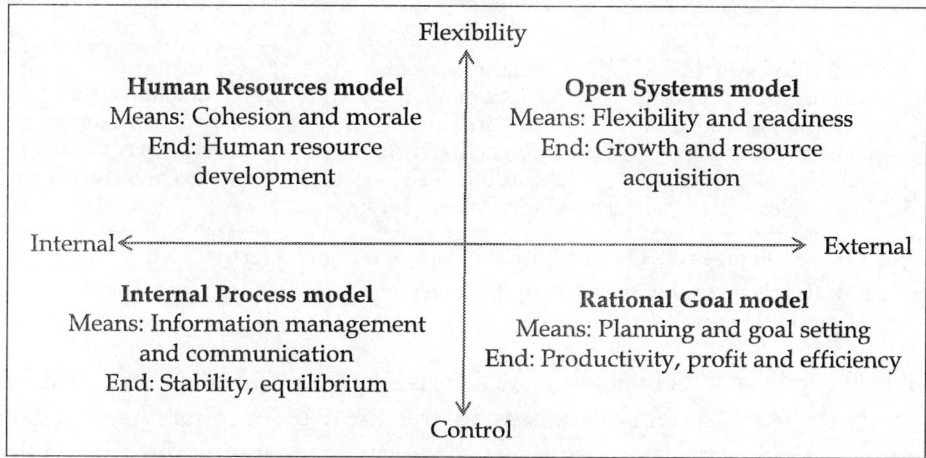


**Figure 6.3:** Quinn and Rohrbaugh's competing values framework

*Source*: Quinn, R.E. and Rohrbaugh, J., "A competing values approach to organisational effectiveness", *Public Productivity Review*, 5, 1981, pp. 122-140.

The rational goal model seeks to maximise profit and productivity through direction and goals. The open system model relates insight, innovation and adaptation as a path towards external recognition, support, acquisition and growth. The internal process model views internal processes including measurement, documentation and information management as means or methods to achieve control, stability and continuity. The human relations model visualises participation, discussion and openness as means to enhance employee morale and commitment. It is significant to note that Quinn and Spreitzer[55] tested and established the validity of these four quadrants or value dimensions on a sample of 796 executives belonging to 86 public utility firms in US. The validity of the spatial model of effectiveness has also been tested by Kallaith, Bluedorn and Gillespic[56] through the use of a Structural Equation Modelling (SEM) approach on a sample of 300 managers and supervisors employed by a multi-hospital system in the United States.

### 6.6.6 Likert's Model of Organisational Effectiveness

According to Likert,[57] organisational effectiveness depends quite significantly upon the strategies or means adopted by an organisation to ensure the development of its employees. Effectiveness is thus related to the personal growth of employees who display high level of motivation, morale, and commitment to work objectives. As shown in Figure 6.2, Likert identified three types of variables in his effectiveness model – causal variables, intervening variables and output variables that together determine the effectiveness of an organisation.

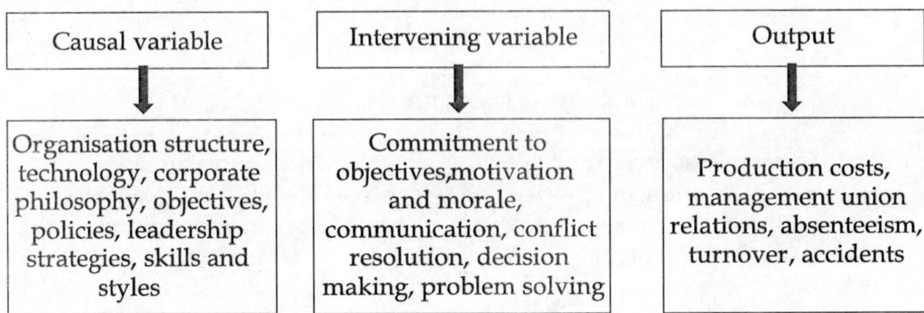


**Figure 6.4:** Likert's model of organisational effectiveness

*Source*: Likert, R., *The Human Organisation: Its Management and Values*, McGraw Hill, New York, 1967.

In Likert's model of effectiveness, causal variables act as stimuli upon the intervening variables that create certain responses in the form of outputs. As noted earlier, intervening variables can be improved successfully by changing the causal variables. Similarly, the output or end result variables can be improved by changing the causal variables rather than by modifying the intervening variables. According to Likert, the effectiveness of an organisation depends upon the extent to which individual employees participate in decision-making in the organisational system. Likert viewed that "System 4" approach to management is a true indicator of a healthy and effective organisation. In describing the nature of an effective organisation, Likert considered perceptual measures of certain organisational processes or characteristics such as leadership, motivation, communication, interaction-influence, decision-making, goal setting or ordering control, performance goals and training.

### 6.6.7 Schein's Approach to Organisational Effectiveness

Schein,[58] a famous social scientist, suggested that organisations are able to maintain their effectiveness through the adaptive coping cycle. This cycle implies that organisations try to adapt themselves with a view to coping with environmental changes. According to Schein, the adaptive coping cycle has the following six stages :

1. sensing a change in some part of the internal or external environment;
2. bringing the relevant information about the change to those parts of the organisation that can act upon it;
3. changing production or conversion process in the organisation as per the information obtained;
4. stabilizing internal changes so that the equilibrium of the organisational system is restored;

5. exporting new products or services that are in line with the originally perceived changes in the environment; and
6. obtaining feedback or information regarding how the new products or services are performing.

It must be emphasized that the adaptive coping cycle goes on and on, and continuous reappraisals and readjustments pave the way for redefining goals so as to provide stability and survival to the organisation. At each stage of the adaptive coping cycle, there are problems and challenges which need to be overcome in order to have effective coping with the environmental changes. In this process of coping, organisations must develop the ability to receive and communicate valid and reliable information, have adequate internal flexibility to adopt necessary changes as demanded by the environment, and ensure the integration of individual and organisational goals and thereby promote employees' commitment and an internal organisation's climate of support and trust based relationships.

### 6.6.8 Cunningham's Approach to Organisational Effectiveness

Since the construct space of organisational effectiveness is unbounded with the existence of multitude of effectiveness criteria, Cunningham[59] proposed seven different conceptual frameworks for assessing or measuring organisational effectiveness in different possible situations. Each of these alternative frameworks or approaches focuses upon certain relevant criteria of effectiveness, depending upon the organisational situations pertaining to the organisational structure, the performance of the organisation's human resources, and the impact of the organisation's activities. As shown in Table 6.3, the seven models of organisational effectiveness are: rational goal model, system resource model, managerial process model, organisational development model, bargaining model, structural functional model, and functional model. In addition, the table also indicates that organisational effectiveness includes a variety of evaluation possibilities. In other words, the particular evaluation situations require the assessment of appropriate effectiveness criteria such as accomplishments and achievements, efficiency in allocation and utilisation of resources, capability or productivity of managers, team work within the organisation, resource utilisation, ability to develop organisational structures, and functionality.

The rational goal approach emphasises upon the organisation's ability to attain its goals. An organisation is assessed on the basis of effectiveness criteria derived from the organisation's goals as specified in its manuals, charters and other documents. Assessment or evaluation criteria may also be derived from the organisation's informal and operative goals, and societal missions or functions. The organisation is evaluated by comparing the actual activities performed with the planned ones. In the system resource model, an organisation is viewed or defined as a network of interconnected parts or subsystems. The organisational system functions effectively to the extent that its subsystems are well coordinated and function in harmony with one another.

**Table 6.3:** Cunningham's organisational effectiveness approaches

| Organisational effectiveness model | Organisational situation | Central focus or purpose | Assumption | Limitations |
|---|---|---|---|---|
| Rational goal | Evaluation of performance of organisational structures | Determine degree to which organisations are able to achieve their goals | An organisation is rational if its activities are organised to achieve its goals | The model frequently shows that organisations do not reach their goals. There is also a difficulty in identifying and defining these goals. |
| Systems resource | Evaluation of performance of organisational structures | Determine decision-maker's efficiency in allocating and utilising resources for fulfilling various system needs. | An organisation in order to survive, must satisfy some basic needs:<br>1. Acquiring resources,<br>2. Interpreting the real properties of the external environment<br>3. Production of outputs<br>4. Maintenance of day-to-day internal activities<br>5. Coordinating relationships among the various subsystems<br>6. Responding to feedback<br>7. Evaluating the effect of its decisions<br>8. Accomplishing goals | Measures of all systems needs are difficult to develop. |
| Managerial process | Evaluation of performance of organisation's human resources | Determine capability or productivity of managers or managerial processes | An organisation can be considered rational when its various managerial processes and patterns enhance the individual's productivity or capability to obtain objectives | Measures of productivity and capabilities pinpoint personal problems and limitations. |

| | | | | |
|---|---|---|---|---|
| Organisational development | Evaluation of performance of organisation's human resources | Determine organisation's ability to work as a team and fulfil the needs of its individual members | Work which is organised to meet people's needs as well as organisational requirements tends to produce the highest productivity | Emphasis on the informal organisation takes precedence over the formal. Individuals may be reluctant to accept interpersonal feedback supplied by the model. |
| Bargaining | Evaluation of impact of decisions | Determine use or users which various decision-makers make of their resources in achieving organisational goals | An organisation is a cooperative, sometimes competitive, resource distributing system. | The model deals with a very specific part of the organisation's activities. |
| Structural functional | Evaluation of impact of organisation's structure on performance. | Determine organisation's ability to develop structures to maintain and strengthen performance | A system's survival is equated to satisfy five basic needs: 1. Security of organisation in relation to environment 2. Stability of lines of authority and communication 3. Stability of informal relations in organisation 4. Continuity of policy-making 5. Homogeneity of outlook | The model deals with a very specific part of the organisation's activities. |
| Functional | Evaluation of impact of organisational activities | Provide information on social consequences of organisational activities and on organisation's ability to meet needs of key client groups in its environment | Every system must define its purpose for being (goal attainment), determine resources to achieve its goals (adaptation), establish means for coordinating its efforts (integration), and reduce strains and tensions in its environment (pattern maintenance) | The model deals with a very specific part of the organisation's activities. |

*Source*: Cunningham, J.B., "Approaches to the Evaluation of Organisational Effectiveness", *Academy of Management Review*, 2(3), 1977, 463-474.

In ensuring such coordinated functioning, the organisation must provide for optimum or balanced distribution of resources among the subsystems' needs rather than maximum satisfaction of these needs. The managerial process model evaluates an organisation's effectiveness on the basis of its ability to perform effectively such managerial functions as planning, organising, staffing, directing, controlling, etc. Thus, the model seeks to measure the productivity or capability of the managerial processes for achieving the organisation's goals. The organisation development (OD) model visualises effectiveness in terms of the organisation's problem-solving and renewal capabilities. The model focuses upon promoting sympathetic supervisory behaviour, team work, cooperation between management and workers, and employees' freedom to decide upon their own work objectives. Thus, it would be apt to say that the OD model seeks to integrate organisational objectives or goals with the needs and aspirations of employees for their growth and development. The bargaining model assumes that decision-making in an organisation is firmly rooted in exchanges and transactions between individuals and groups pursuing a variety of goals. Thus, organisational achievements are the result of a complex process of adjustment and accommodation between different parts of the organisation. The bargaining model focuses upon the question as to how the decision-makers in the organisation utilise their resources and capabilities for achieving their objectives. In fact, a high degree of cooperation takes place if the decision-makers bargain among themselves and pool their resources so as to achieve the stated objectives. According to the structural-functional model, every organisation must develop certain structures for maintaining itself and defining its relationships with the environment. This model presumes that an organisation's effectiveness is enhanced by its ability to develop such structures consisting of contracts, doctrines, commitments, traditions, mechanisms, or means of participation. These structural patterns are intended to ensure security of the organisational stability of authority and responsibility relationship as well as informal relations, continuity of policy-making and homogeneity of outlook among organisational members. The functional model assumes that an organisation's effectiveness is determined by the social consequences of its activities. According to this model, every organisation must define its goals and objectives, determine the resources to be utilised for achieving its goals, identify means for coordinating its activities, and reduce the strains and tensions in its environment. An organisation will be considered effective if such activities help in serving the needs of its client groups.

Cameron and Whetton[60] have provided certain plausible reasons for the multiplicity of effectiveness models as existing in the effectiveness literature. In the first place, authors have conceptualised organisations in many ways. Organisations have been called rational entities in pursuit of goals, coalitions of powerful constituencies, individual need meeting cooperatives, meaning producing systems, information processing units, open systems, social contracts and so on. Research conducted under these different conceptualisations focuses on different phenomena, proposes different relationships among variables, and judges effectiveness differently. For example, if one conceives of organisations as deliberate, rational, goal seeking activity systems, then it is natural to argue that successful goal accomplishment is an appropriate measure of effectiveness.

Similarly, if one views organisations as political arenas wherein competing interest groups vie for control over resources, then it logically follows that effectiveness should reflect the extent to which critical constituencies are satisfied with their involvement in the resource allocation process.[61] Thus, multiple models of organisational effectiveness have come into existence because of the fact that there is no universally accepted theory of organisation.

In addition, several authors argue that so far as the construct of effectiveness is a product of personal values, preferences, and needs, there will always be great divergence in its meaning and use among researchers and practitioners. Managers use judgements of organisational effectiveness to justify their actions, to manage conflicts, to motivate change, to displace or assign responsibility, and so on. Researchers are more keen to focus on circumscribing effectiveness so that measurable indicators can be identified and reliable judgments made. Theorists prefer not to circumscribe effectiveness but to develop propositions and relationships that have generalised applicability in organisations. This divergence of usage of the construct has come in the way of development of a single, consensual model of effectiveness.

## 6.7 INTEGRATION OF MODELS

As it was discussed earlier, different models of effectiveness should not be viewed as competing ones for each model explains certain unique aspects of the total effectiveness construct. The ideal approach is not to choose among different models but to treat them as complementary to one another. The focus should be on finding out how various models of effectiveness relate to one another. In this connection, it may be mentioned that Scott, Seashore and Cameron[62] have attempted to integrate the effectiveness literature to some extent.

As suggested by Scott,[63] the numerous criteria of effectiveness can be reduced to three basic models: the rational system model, natural system model and open system model. According to Scott, the rational system model with its mechanistic and instrumental bias, focuses on productivity and efficiency. The natural system model considers not only the production function, but also the human activities required for the unit to maintain itself. In this organic perspective, attention is focused on such characteristics as morale, satisfaction and cohesion. The open system model includes system-elaborating as well as system-maintaining functions. This model emphasises upon such activities or functions as adaptability and resource acquisition.

Seashore[64] also has suggested a three-model integration of the effectiveness literature. His goal model is very similar to Scott's rational model while his natural system model covers both the natural and open system approaches described by Scott. In his third model, i.e., the decision-process model, an effective organisation has been described as the one which "optimised the process for getting, storing, retrieving, allocating, manipulating and discarding information". Here, the focus is essentially on the acquisition and management of information.

Cameron[65] has proposed a four-model framework consisting of goal, system resource, internal processes, and participant satisfaction models. His goal model resembles Scott's rational model and Seashore's goal model; his system resource-model resembles Scott's open system model; and his internal process model is similar to Seashore's decision-process model. His last model, i.e., the participant satisfaction model or the strategic constituency model, is an elaboration of the natural system model mentioned by both Scott and Seashore. In his last model, the organisation is viewed as a dynamic coalition entity in which attempts are made to satisfy each constituency for the sake of the organisation's continued survival and growth.

The aforesaid three attempts to integrate the effectiveness literature reflect both consensus and disagreement. Many well-defined themes seem to be existing in the effectiveness literature but each theorist has offered an integration that differs somewhat from each other. While their agreement is considerable, the effectiveness construct as it has been used in the literature is certainly ambiguous and has generated the apparent divergencies as to which concepts fall in the construct, how they relate to each other, and what particular clusters of concepts should be known as.

## 6.8 MEASUREMENT OF ORGANISATIONAL EFFECTIVENESS

Broadly speaking, the approaches to the measurement of effectiveness in organisations have taken two different forms. Some approaches view the effectiveness construct in a unidimensional framework, focusing on only one evaluation criterion. These approaches are known as univariate measures of effectiveness. In contrast, the multivariate effectiveness measures employ several different criteria treated simultaneously.

In the initial stages, the attempts made by industrial psychologists and sociologists to measure organisational effectiveness typically viewed the concept in terms of the attainment of some ultimate criterion, e.g., productivity, satisfaction, profit, etc. Such univariate attempts employ one of these variables as the dependent variable and compare this variable with other independent or predictor variables to study the relationship between them. At this point, it would be pertinent to note that the use of univariate measures of effectiveness is constrained by several problems.[66] In the first place, none of these measures, by itself, can be considered fully or even adequately representing the construct of effectiveness. Second, several variables employed to measure effectiveness appear to represent value judgements by researchers or managers of what "ought to be" instead of objective or realistic measures of effectiveness. Third, even though the research literature has been fairly rigorous in defining and measuring specific dependent variables, it has been much less specific as to how such variables contribute to a meaningful understanding of the organisational effectiveness construct.

A more meaningful approach to the measurement of organisational effectiveness involves model building attempts in which hypotheses are generated and tested concerning the relationship between major variables that can affect organisational success. These models have a distinct advantage over univariate techniques in that they generally represent attempts to study more comprehensively the major sets of variables involved in the effectiveness construct and to demonstrate how such variables fit together. Thus, while it is suggested that multivariate measures should be preferred over univariate ones in the assessment of organisations, it cannot be said that multivariate models are completely devoid of any problems. As discussed earlier, a comparison of various models points to the fact that there is lack of consensus as to what constitutes a useful set of measures of organisational effectiveness. Although each model has set forth its three or four defining characteristics (or determinants) of success, there is surprisingly little overlap among the approaches. Another major problem with multidimensional models relates to their ability to generalise their evaluation criteria. This problem relates to the question of external validity, i.e., the extent to which the models are valid or applicable in other organisational settings.

In view of the obvious uses and limitations of multivariate effectiveness measures, the assessment approach should be to concentrate on limited domains of the effectiveness construct (as has been successfully done in the case of measurement of other constructs like motivation, intelligence, leadership, etc.). This requires making informed choices about what criteria to include and what aspect of the organisational effectiveness construct space to focus on, especially in the context of given organisational settings.

## 6.9 PROBLEMS AND ISSUES CONCERNING MEASUREMENT OR ASSESSMENT OF EFFECTIVENESS

The organisational behaviour experts broadly agree that there is a need to measure the effectiveness of individuals, groups, and subunits within organisations on a continuous or regular basis. Through the measurement of the actual performance of various parties and its comparison with some pre-determined standards, the top management would be able to take necessary corrective steps and thus ensure that the organisation is moving in the desired direction of achieving its overall objectives or gaols. In this context, it may be pointed out that organisational effectiveness is quite a broad and multidimensional concept that has been subjected to varied interpretations by different authors. Therefore, the process of measurement of effectiveness in organisations has been beset with several problems as discussed below.

In the first place, it is difficult to say whether an organisation should be regarded as effective or not if it is found to be effective on some criterion but not on others. For instance, an organisation may be highly effective in terms of its production efficiency and revenue generation but at the same time it may be faced with acute labour problems such as labour unrest, absenteeism, job satisfaction, and so on. Similarly, it is also possible that an organisation may be producing a poor quality product but it is able to sell it at a high price and thereby make huge profits due to favourable market conditions. Therefore, there is a serious problem of developing some commonly accepted criteria of effectiveness on the basis of which an organisation can be described as effective or ineffective.

In the second place, it must be noted that some goals are tangible or measurable while others may not be. For example, it may be simple to say whether an organisation has been successful or not in terms of quantifiable measures of sales turnover or net profits or return on investment, etc. However, it is not possible to make such judgement if effectiveness is considered in terms of such qualitative criteria as the organisation's goodwill, customer satisfaction, corporate social responsibility, and so on.

The third problem relates to the frame of reference being used for the measurement of effectiveness. Members of an organisation often use different performance criteria from what the individuals and groups outside the organisation do. Public agencies often point out the relevance of such social goals as community services, consumers' safety, ethical standards and so on whereas the corporate executives emphasize upon production efficiency, quality of products or services provided, etc. Therefore, the selection and use of effectiveness criteria depends on whether the evaluators of effectiveness are inside or outside a particular organisation.

Another problem is that the criteria of effectiveness being used to assess an organisation may change over time. In times of fast changing price levels, for example, comparison of a firm's profits earned during one year with those of another year may not have much of relevance. Instability of effectiveness criteria prevents the possibility of developing and utilising certain long lasting sets of performance indicators upon which the evaluators can rely.

Still another problem relates to the fact that most of the organisations are continuing entities, and their goals are generally ambiguous or vague. In the first place, it must be stated that no organisation can be said to have achieved its goals fully. Second, the measurable aspects of goals are often overemphasized by the evaluators. In this process, the not-so-measurable aspects are likely to be ignored or neglected thereby leading to distortion of goals. Therefore, an organisation has to strike a proper balance between the measurable and the non-measureable aspects of goals.

Cameron and Whetton[67] have discussed several important issues relating to the assessment of effectiveness (in the form of guidelines), following the works of Cameron,[68] Goodman and Pennings,[69] and Steers.[70] All these issues must be properly resolved in an evaluation exercise so that they can help circumscribe the construct boundaries of effectiveness, and also help identify the indicators of effectiveness being considered. According to Cameron and Whetton,[71] these guidelines, if widely used, "can help develop a cumulative literature on organisational effectiveness by providing a general framework against which research can be compared".

At the outset, it is very important for an evaluator to be clear as to from whose perspective effectiveness is to be judged. That is, effectiveness must be defined and assessed from someone's viewpoint, and it is required that the viewpoint be made explicit. The criteria used by different constituencies to define effectiveness often differ markedly, and debates about which constituency's criteria are most valuable continue in the literature. Organisations never satisfy all their constituencies, and, in fact, what appears to be high effectiveness from one point of view may be interpreted as being mediocre or low effectiveness from another point of view. The specific point of view being considered, therefore, must be made explicit.

The domain of activity to be focused upon in the judgement of effectiveness is also an important issue. Organisational domains are circumscribed by the constituencies served, the technologies employed, and the services or outputs provided. Domains arise from the primary tasks that are emphasised in the organisation, from the competence of the organisation, and from the demands placed upon the organisation by external forces.[72] A variety of domains can be identified for almost all organisations, but no organisation can be maximally effective in all its domains. While analysing organisational effectiveness, it is, therefore, important that the domains being assessed are properly specified.

The level of analysis to be used in the assessment programme is another relevant consideration. Judgements of effectiveness can be made at the individual level, subunit level, organisational level, industry level or even at the societal level. The fact remains, however, that effectiveness judged on these levels of analysis is often not compatible, and effectiveness in one level may run counter to effectiveness on another level. In fact, the selection of the appropriate level of analysis is critical because data on effectiveness at one level are often rendered irrelevant when viewed from another level. Without attention being paid to which level of analysis is most appropriate, meaningful appropriateness judgements cannot be made.

In any attempt to judge organisational effectiveness, the purposes of judgement or evaluation must be clearly identified as they invariably affect the judgement itself. It has been pointed out that changing the objectives of evaluation creates different consequences for the evaluator as well as for the unit being evaluated. The purposes of the evaluation are significant in that they help determine appropriate constituencies, domains, levels of analysis and so on; hence, a clear conception of purposes is necessary for judging effectiveness.

An appropriate time frame must be selected for the assessment programme. This is necessary because long-term effectiveness may be incompatible with short-term effectiveness. In addition, some organisations may sacrifice short-term effectiveness in favour of long-term effectiveness or vice versa. Also, organisational outcomes and effects sometimes cannot be detected if the wrong time frame is selected because they may occur incrementally over a long period of time, or they may occur suddenly in the short term. Judgements of effectiveness are always made with some time frame in mind and, therefore, it is important that the time frame is made explicit.

Adequate attention must be given also to the type of data to be utilised in judgements of effectiveness. In other words, a choice must be made between objective data (organisational records) or subjective, perceptual data obtained from the members of various constituencies (interviews or questionnaire responses). Objective data have the advantage of being quantifiable, possibly less biased than individual perceptions, and representative of the official organisational position. However, objective data are frequently gathered only on "official" effectiveness criteria or on criteria that are used only for public image purposes. On the other hand, the major benefit of subjective or perceptual data is that a broader set of criteria of effectiveness can be assessed from a wider variety of perspectives. In addition, operative data can more easily be tapped. The disadvantage, however, is that bias, dishonesty or lack of information on the part of respondents may hinder the reliability and validity of the data. Adequate caution should be exercised in the selection of data for assessment purposes because an organisation may be judged effective (or ineffective) on the basis of subjective perceptions while objective data may indicate that the organisation is ineffective (or effective).

Finally, due consideration must be given to the question as to which type of referent to use, against which effectiveness may be judged. There are a variety of referents or standards against which organisational effectiveness could be judged. One alternative is to compare the performance of two different organisations against the same set of indicators. The second alternative is to select a standard or an ideal performance level, and then compare the organisation's performance against the standard. The third alternative is to compare organisational performance on the indicators against the stated goals of the organisation. The fourth alternative is to compare the organisation's performance on the indicators against its own past performance on the same indicators. The fifth alternative is to evaluate an organisation on the basis of the extent to which it possesses certain desired characteristics, independent of its performance on certain indicators. Since judgements of effectiveness can differ tremendously depending on which referent is used, it is important to be clear about the referent that serves as the basis for those judgements.

## 6.10 HOW TO STUDY ORGANISATIONAL EFFECTIVENESS?

Ghorpade[73] has laid down certain steps for the assessment of organisational effectiveness. According to Ghorpade, these steps will help the organisation experts in designing an appropriate methodology for the assessment programme to be undertaken:

1. **Formulation of a conceptual scheme:** First of all, a researcher should identify the composition of an organisation's internal structure, its relationship with other organisations as well as with the broader environment and so on.
2. **Choosing meaningful criteria of effectiveness:** As effectiveness is a multidimensional concept, the choice of effectiveness criteria for assessment purposes will ultimately depend upon the needs and values of the parties involved in the assessment program. Therefore, the researcher should be clear about the short-term and long-term goals of the organisation and also decide upon the frame of reference to be used, i.e., from whose angle effectiveness is to be judged. It may be the owners, investors, employees, consumers, government or the society at large. It is important to find a clear-cut answer to this question as the effectiveness criteria would be different for different frames of reference.
3. **Underlying dynamics of organisational functioning:** This means an adequate understanding of organisational processes such as parts of the organisational system, the nature of relationships existing among themselves as well as with the overall system, functional or dysfunctional parts, and so on.
4. **Designing of a methodology:** When the researcher has taken important decisions regarding the above-mentioned three points, he should be able to identify suitable data techniques or methods to be used in the assessment of effectiveness.

An assessment of organisational effectiveness on the basis of the above steps is expected to reveal the organisational situations as they are. A study of organisational effectiveness conducted on the basis of the systems approach requires considerable time, efforts, and resources of the researcher. However, it must be remembered that this systems approach is the only way out if an organisation is to be realistically evaluated from a long-term perspective. As stated by Sharma,[74] "an organisation which is able to adapt itself to internal and external changes and is able to survive and grow is regarded as effective even if it is not one hundred per cent effective".

## 6.11 SUMMARY AND CONCLUSION

So far we have seen that the organisational effectiveness construct lies at the very centre of all organisational theories and all organisational studies. All conceptualisations of the nature of organisations have embedded in them notions of the nature of effective organisations, and the differences that exist between effective and ineffective organisations. In addition, the construct of effectiveness is the ultimate dependent variable in organisational research. Evidence for effectiveness is required in most investigations of organisational phenomena. The need to demonstrate that one structure, reward system, leadership style or information system is better in some way than another makes the notion of effectiveness a pivotal empirical issue. In view of the significance of the effectiveness construct in studies of formal organisations, the present chapter seeks to explore some of the critical issues related to organisational effectiveness. It examines both theoretical and empirical research efforts made by researchers to delienate the construct space of effectiveness. This chapter discusses certain important models of organisational effectiveness as existing in the management literature, and also some of the integration efforts made by authors in this regard. Finally, this chapter attempts to examine some significant issues regarding the assessment or measurement of organisational effectiveness.

It may be mentioned that certain pioneering theoretical research works have been done by management theoreticians to define or limit the construct space of effectiveness. These theoretical works include the scholarly contributions of such famous researchers as Price, Steers, and Campbell. Similarly, empirical research works have also been done in this regard by such leading scholars as Georgopoulos and Tannenbraum, Seashore and Yuchtman, Mahoney et al., and Quinn and Rohrbaugh. A critical analysis of both theoretical and empirical research works revealed that these efforts have failed to limit the construct space of effectiveness. In addition, a critical examination of certain important models of effectiveness was made so as to analyse different sets of meaningful relationships among the variables studied. The models of effectiveness examined included rational goal model, systems model, strategic constituencies model, competing values model, Likert's model, and Cunningham's model. In this context, Cameron and Whetton have provided certain convincing reasons for the multiplicity of effectiveness models existing in the management literature. The reasons include different conceptualisations of organisations being used by researchers, limited number of constituencies or stakeholders being studied by researchers, differences in personal preferences, needs and values, differences in the levels of analysis or activities being studied, etc. It was also noted that some of the well-known researchers including Scott, Seashore, and Yuchtman have made some efforts to integrate the effectiveness literature. Their integration efforts emphasise upon the fact that different models of effectiveness should be viewed as complementary ones (rather than as competing ones), as each model explains some of the unique aspects of the total effectiveness construct. In the end, certain important issues regarding the measurement or assessment of organisational effectiveness have been discussed.

Despite the importance of the effectiveness construct, it would be quite pertinent to note, however, that no theories of organisational effectiveness have been developed, the criteria for assessing the construct are both divergent and difficult to identify, and prescriptions for improving organisational effectiveness are not founded on systematic research. In organisational studies, different attempts to map the effectiveness construct have been made with not much of consideration given to how they relate to one another. Isolated assessments have been the norm, and theoretical works have generally attempted to replace rather than to add to one another. Some research works are too general to provide much insight into the characteristics of the effectiveness construct, and some have focused too narrowly on univariate ratings on limited viewpoints. The resulting confusion has led some authors to propose that the construct of effectiveness should be abandoned altogether in scholarly activity.[75] Nevertheless, it has been pointed out by some authors that these confusions or problems existing in effectiveness studies should not be viewed negatively as they have stimulated meaningful studies of various organisational possibilities and complexities. Thus, it can be stated that studies on organisational effectiveness will continue to occupy a pivotal place in the realm of organisational behaviour.

## REVIEW QUESTIONS

1. Explain the concept of organisational effectiveness.
2. Do you agree that the construct space of effectiveness is still not known? Discuss.
3. Explain the term 'effectiveness' and distinguish it from 'efficiency'.
4. Explain different perspectives of organisational effectiveness.
5. What are the determinants of organisational effectiveness? Discuss.
6. The organisational behaviour experts have proposed different models to explain the effectiveness construct. Explain.
7. Explain the rational goal approach to organisational effectiveness and also point out its limitations.
8. Critically examine the systems approach to organisational effectiveness.
9. Do you think that the adaptive-coping cycle has immense significance in explaining the effectiveness construct? Comment.
10. The strategic constituencies approach to effectiveness emphasises upon the concept of social responsibilities of an organisation. Discuss.
11. Explain, with suitable arguments, whether the single-purpose or multi-purpose organisations should be considered more effective.
12. What difficulties are generally encountered in the measurement of organisational effectiveness? Discuss.

## REFERENCES

1. Smith, A., *The Wealth of Nations*, Strahan and Cadell, London, 1776.
2. Goodman, P.S. and Pennings, J.S. (Eds.), *New Perspective on Organisational Effectiveness*, Jossey-Bass, San Francisco, 1977; Critical issues in assessing organisational effectiveness, Lawler, E.E., Nadler, D.A., and Common, C. (Eds.), *Organisational Assessment: Perspectives on the Measurement of Organisational Behaviour and the Quality of Work Life*, Wiley, New York, 1980, pp. 185-215.

3. Etzioni, A., *Modern Organisations*, Prentice Hall, New Delhi, 1964.
4. Argyris, C., *Integrating the Individual and the Organisation*, Wiley, New York, 1964.
5. Katz, D. And Kahn, R.L., *The Social Psychology of Organisations*, John Wiley, New York, 1978.
6. Jackson, J.H., Morgan, C.P., and Paollilio, J.G.P., "Organisation theory – A macro perspective for management", *Academy of Management Review*, 12(2), 1987, 395-401.
7. Kondalker, V.G., *Organisational Effectiveness and Change Management*, PHI Learning, New Delhi, 2009.
8. Mohr, L.B., The concept of organisational goal, *American Political Science Review*, 67(2), 1973, pp. 470-481.
9. Drucker, P.F., *An Introductory View of Management: Instructor's Manual*, Harper and Row, New York, 1977.
10. Asmild, M., Paradi, J.C., Reese, D.N. and Tam, F., Measuring overall efficiency and effectiveness using DEA, *European Journal of Operational Research*, 178(1), 2007, pp. 305-321.
11. Reddin, W.J., Managerial Effectiveness, McGraw Hill, New York, 1970.
12. Morse, J.J. and Wagner, F.R., Measuring the process of managerial effectiveness, *Academy of Management Journal*, 21(1), 1978, pp. 23-35; Willcocks, S.G., Managerial effectiveness and the public sector: A health service example, *International Journal of Public Sector Management*, 5(5), 1992.
13. Georgopoulos, B.S. and Tannenbaum, A.S., A study of organisational effectiveness, *American Sociological Review*, 22(5), 1957, 534-540.
14. Cameron, K., Effectiveness as paradox: Consensus and conflict in conceptions of organisational effectiveness, *Management Science*, May 1986, pp. 539-553.
15. Schein, E.H., *Organisational Psychology*, Prentice Hall of India, New Delhi, 1973.
16. Seashore, S.E., and Yuchtman, E., Factorial analysis of organisational performance, *Administrative Science Quarterly*, 12, 1967, pp. 377-395.
17. Bennis, W.G., Towards a truly scientific management: The concept of organisational health, *General Systems Yearbook*, 7, 1962.
18. Drucker, P.F., *Management: Tasks, Responsibilities, Practices*, Harper and Row, New York, 1973, p. 45.
19. Lawless, D., *Effective Management: Social and Psychological Approach*, Prentice Hall, Englewood Cliffs, NJ, 1972, pp. 391-399.
20. *Ibid.*
21. Likert, R., *The Human Organisation: Its Management and Values*, McGraw Hill, New York, 1967.

22. *Ibid.*
23. Feidler, F.E., *A Theory of Leadership Effectiveness*, McGraw Hill, New York, 1967, p. 9.
24. Reddin, W.J., 3-D Management style theory-typology based on task and relationships orientations, *Training and Development Journal*, 1967.
25. Kaplan, R.S., and Norton, D.P., Putting the balanced scorecard to work, *Harvard Business Review*, September-October 1993, p. 134.
26. Hersey, P., Blanchard, K.H., and Johnson, D.E., *Management of Organisational Behaviour: Utilising Human Resources*, Prentice Hall of India, New Delhi, 1998.
27. *Ibid.*
28. Price, J.L. *Organisational Effectiveness: An Inventory of Propositions*, Irwin, Homewood, Ill., 1968.
29. Steers, R.M., Problems in the measurement of organisational effectiveness, *Administrative Science Quarterly*, 20, 1975, pp. 546-548.
30. Campbell, J.P., On the nature of organisational effectiveness, Goodman, P.S. and Pennings, J.M. (Eds.), *New Perspective on Organisational Effectiveness*, Jossey-Bass, San Francisco, 1977.
31. Georgopoulos, B.S. and Tannenbaum, A.S., 1957, *op. cit.*
32. *Ibid.*
33. Seashore, S.E. and Yuchtman, E., 1967, *op. cit.*
34. *Ibid.*
35. Quinn, R.E. and Rohrbaugh, J., A competing values approach to organisational effectiveness, *Public Productivity Review*, 1981, pp. 122-140.
36. Cameron, K.S. and Whetton, D.A., *Organisational Effectiveness: A Comparison of Multiple Models*, Academic Press, New York, 1983.
37. Cameron, K.S. and Whetton, D.A., Perceptions of organisational effectiveness over organisational life cycle, *Administrative Science Quarterly*, 26, 1981, pp. 525-544.
38. Steers, R.M., 1975, *op. cit.*
39. Bennis, W., *op. cit.*; Nadler, D.A. and Tushman, M.L., A model for diagnosing organisational behaviour, *Organisational Dynamics*, 9(2), 1980, pp. 51.
40. Keeley, M., A social-justice approach to organisational evaluation, *Administrative Science Quarterly*, 1978, pp. 272-292.
41. Zammuto, R.F., *Assessing Organisational Effectiveness: Systems Change, Adaptation and Strategy*, Surry Press, 1982.
42. Seashore, S.E. and Yuchtman, E., 1967, *op. cit.*
43. Mahoney, T.A. and Weitzel, W., 1969, *op. cit.*
44. Quinn, R.E. and Rohrbaugh, J., 1981, *op cit.*

45. Barnard, C.I. *Functions of the Executive*, Harvard University Press, Cambridge, Mass., 1938, pp. 19-20.
46. Robbins, S.P., *Organisational Theory: The Structure and Design of Organisations*, Prentice Hall, Englewood Cliffs, 1983.
47. Etzioni, A., Two approaches to organisational analysis: A critique and a suggestion, *Administrative Science Quarterly*, 5, 1960, pp. 257-278.
48. Robbins, S.P., *op. cit.*, p. 26.
49. Ghorepade, J., *Assessment of Organisational Effectiveness: Issues, Analysis and Readings*, Goodyear, Pacific Palisades, Calif, 1971.
50. Goodman, P.S. and Pennings, J.S. (Eds.), 1977, *op. cit.*
51. Pfeffer, J., and Salancik, G., *The External Control of Organisations*, Harper and Row, New York, 1978.
52. Cameron, K., Construct space and subjectivity problems in organisational effectiveness, *Public Productivity Review*, 5, 1981, pp. 105-121.
53. Quinn, R.E. and Rohrbaugh, J., A spatial model of effectiveness criteria: Towards a competing values approach to organisational effectiveness, *Management Science*, 29, 1983, pp. 363-377.
54. *Ibid.*
55. Quinn, R.E. and Spreitzer, G.M., *The Psychometrics of the Competing Values Culture Instruments and an Analysis of the Impact of Organisational Culture on Quality of Life, Emerald*, 1991.
56. Kalliath, T.J. Bluedorn, A.C. and Gillespie, D.F., A confirmatory factor analysis of the competing values instrument, *Educational and Psychological Measurement*, 59(1), 1999, 143-158.
57. Likert, R., 1967, *op. cit.*
58. *Ibid.*
59. Cunningham, J.B., Approaches to the evaluation of organisational effectiveness, *Academy of Management Review*, 2(3), 1977, pp. 463-474.
60. Cameron, K.S. and Whetton, D.A., 1983, *op. cit.*
61. Pfeffer, J., The micropolitics of organisations, *Environments and Organisations*, 1978, pp. 29-50.
62. Scott, W.R., Effectiveness of organisational effectiveness studies, Goodman, P.S. and Pennings, J.M. (Eds.), *New Perspectives on Organisational Effectiveness*, Jossey-Bass, San Francisco, 1977; Seashore, S.E., Assessing organisational effectiveness with reference to member needs, paper presented at the 1979 meetings of the Academy of Management; Cameron, K., Evaluating organisational effectiveness in organised anarchies, presented at the 1979 meetings of the Academy of Management.

63. Scott, W.R., 1977, *op. cit.*
64. Seashore, S.E., 1979, *op. cit.*
65. Cameron, K., 1979, *op. cit.*
66. Steers, R.M., 1975, *op. cit.*
67. Cameron, K.S. and Whetton, D.A., 1983, *op. cit.*
68. Cameron, K., Critical questions in assessing organisational effectiveness, *Organisational Dynamics*, 9(2), 1980, pp. 66-80.
69. Goodman, P.S. and Pennings, J.S., 1980, *op. cit.*
70. Steers, R.M., 1975, *op. cit.*
71. Cameron, K.S. and Whetton, D.A., 1983, *op. cit.*
72. Cameron, K., 1981, *op. cit.*
73. Ghorpade, J., 1971, *op. cit.*
74. Sharma, R.A., *Organisational Theory and Behaviour*, Tata McGraw Hill, New Delhi, 2000, p. 580.
75. Hannan, M.T. and Freeman, J., Obstacles to comparative studies, Goodman, P.S. and Pennings, J.S., 1977, *op. cit.*

# 7

# Conflict Management Strategies and Organisational Effectiveness: Some Empirical Research Evidences

## 7.1 INTRODUCTION

It would be pertinent to re-emphasize that the organisational behaviour experts have proposed different approaches towards conflict management in organisations. Although they have suggested different methods or styles of managing interpersonal and inter-group conflicts, the fact remains that very few systematic research studies have been made to determine the comparative efficacy or effectiveness of different conflict management methods or styles. In view of this, the present research attempts to study the current conflict management practices or behaviours of Indian managers and then examine the relative efficacy of these behaviours in terms of their impact on certain well-defined measures of organisational effectiveness. Thus, in nutshell, the present chapter intends to evaluate the impact of each conflict management strategy or method on organisational performance in the Indian industrial situations and thereby fill a serious gap in the management literature. Subsequently, attempts have been made to suggest necessary changes or modifications in the conflict management behaviours of managers in order to enhance organisational effectiveness. In this context, it may be pointed out that a comprehensive research study was conducted by the author within two steel manufacturing and two paper manufacturing units[1] to determine the relative effectiveness of conflict management methods or styles. Although this study provided certain substantive research findings, the present chapter makes further investigation of the above stated research questions in cement manufacturing organisations in the private sector. It is hoped that the research findings obtained will provide additional evidences regarding the present conflict management behaviour of Indian managers and also help them to bring about necessary improvements in their conflict management behaviour with a view to enhancing organisational effectiveness.

In the light of the above-mentioned objectives of the proposed study, the present chapter is divided in four parts. The first part of the chapter includes a review of relevant literature regarding the efficacy or effectiveness of different conflict management methods or styles. This part also includes some critical observations regarding the research studies conducted on the subject and points out their limitations. The second part describes the research methodology and the scope of the present study. The third part analyses statistical data relating to the impact of different conflict management strategies or methods on various dimensions of organisational effectiveness in two cement manufacturing units. The last part of the chapter summarises the broad conclusions of this research and draws meaningful inferences in the light of the research findings of the existing studies.

## 7.2 REVIEW OF LITERATURE

As discussed earlier, most of the modern organisation theorists agree that conflict is an inherent part of organisational life and it can serve many useful functions. Therefore, many leading management theoreticians have proposed different strategies or methods for managing conflicts and explain their effects on individuals, inter-departmental or organisational effectiveness.[2] A closer examination of these viewpoints reveals that Blake and Mouton[3] were the pioneers in proposing, in their Managerial Grid, five different methods of conflict management: problem solving, smoothing, compromise, forcing and withdrawing. It may be noted that subsequent researches in the area of conflict management are, by and large, based upon Blake and Mouton's five-category classification scheme. Regarding the effectiveness of conflict management methods, Blake and Mouton[4] suggested that individuals and organisations using problem solving behaviours would achieve both effective interpersonal relations and increased organisational effectiveness.

Lawrence and Lorsch[5] conducted an empirical study to examine the effects of confrontation, smoothing, and forcing behaviours in six organisations. As noticed by them, managers in the two highest performing organisations were using confrontation to a significantly greater extent than those in the other four organisations. Similarly, managers in the two medium performing organisations were using confrontation to a much greater extent than those in the two low performing organisations. Thus, the researchers concluded that confrontation or problem solving behaviour in resolving work related conflicts was positively related to organisational effectiveness. The findings of the study further suggested that the presence of forcing as a back-up mode (to confrontation) and the absence of smoothing were related to effective interpersonal relations and organisational functioning.

Burke[6] conducted an empirical study to examine the five methods of conflict management as suggested by Blake and Mouton[7] in the context of superior-subordinate relationships in two important areas: (1) constructive use of differences and disagreements; and (2) planning job targets and evaluating accomplishments. The research findings showed that confrontation or problem solving was positively related to these dependent variables. While smoothing was somewhat positively related to these variables (but not consistently), compromise showed no relationships with these variables at all. In addition, it was noted that forcing and withdrawing behaviours were negatively related to these variables. Thomas[8] examined the effectiveness of certain conflict management methods in the context of inter-departmental relations. As observed by him, managers' satisfaction with inter-departmental negotiations was positively related to confrontation and smoothing behaviours by their counterparts in other departments and negatively to the latter's forcing and withdrawing behaviours. Aram[9] conducted a study in research and development teams and found that collaboration or problem solving had positive relationships with members' self-actualization and well-being. On the other hand, Dutton and Walton[10] found that managers involved in competitive inter-departmental relations experienced frustration and anxiety.

In the Indian context, Sharma and Samantara[11] attempted to examine the relative efficacy or effectiveness of conflict management methods in terms of their effects on certain organisational effectiveness dimensions such as productivity, adaptability and flexibility. As shown by the findings of this study, confrontation or problem solving emerged as the most effective method of conflict management and it was followed by smoothing behaviour. Although the compromising and the withdrawing modes were positively related to organisational effectiveness, their effects appeared to be somewhat negligible. It was further noted that the forcing mode of resolving conflicts was the most ineffective one.

As mentioned earlier, a comprehensive research study was conducted by Samantara[12] on various aspects of conflict management in the steel and the paper industries located in the eastern and southern parts of India. More specifically, the study focused on such significant aspects as the management of superior-subordinate conflict, the effects of the utilisation of conflict management strategies or methods on various effectiveness dimensions such as productivity, adaptability and flexibility. In this study, it was broadly observed that the senior managers made predominant use of problem-solving, smoothing, and compromising modes of resolving conflicts with their subordinates together with the relative absence of forcing and withdrawing behaviours. This pattern of utilisation of conflict management styles or methods was noticed in the case of managers belonging to the top, middle, and lower levels of the organisational hierarchy. These findings indicate that the Indian managers seek to achieve the production objective of the organisation but only through the voluntary and willing cooperation of their subordinates. They tend to emphasize upon harmonious and useful relations with their subordinates and thus adopt a humane approach towards the latter at the workplace.

When the conflict management methods were examined in terms of their impact on various effectiveness dimensions such as productivity, adaptability and flexibility, the findings of the study indicated that problem solving is the most effective method of conflict resolution and it is followed by smoothing behaviour. The results of the study revealed the negative effects of forcing behaviours on several effectiveness aspects. While compromising had mixed effects with regard to the effectiveness aspects, the withdrawing behaviour seemed to have no impact on organisational effectiveness. The fact that the Indian managers are making a predominant use of problem solving and smoothing modes in resolving work related conflicts with their subordinates is to be welcomed and needs to be enhanced further. In fact, the compromising mode has been found to have adverse effects on organisational performance, innovation or creativity. Therefore, the managers' excessive use of this method in resolving conflicts with their subordinates needs to be discouraged as much as possible. The present research has thrown up sufficient evidence regarding the negative effects of forcing behaviour in the management of organisational conflict. It is quite heartening to note that the managers have shown sagacity in their sparing use of this conflict handling mode or strategy. The fact that the Indian managers are hardly utilising withdrawing behaviours in resolving conflicts is quite consistent with the finding that withdrawing behaviours are scarcely related to the effectiveness dimensions.

In the light of the valuable findings of empirical research studies conducted on the relationships between conflict management strategies or methods and individual or organisational effectiveness as described above, a few critical observations seem to be necessary. In the first place, the above-mentioned research studies are not completely free from methodological inconsistencies or limitations. It may be pointed out that Lawrence and Lorsch[13] examined empirical research data at the organisation level and stated that forcing was an effective method of conflict management and could be used as an effective back-up mode to confrontation or problem solving behaviour. However, Burke[14] examined data collected at the individual level and noticed that the forcing mode of resolving conflicts was highly dysfunctional from an individual's viewpoint. In fact, Bruke's analysis of data suggested that smoothing was an effective backup mode to confrontation or problem-solving whereas forcing was not. There is a need to examine these inconsistencies in research findings and offer appropriate suggestions in relation thereto.

In the second place, it must be stated that Lawrence and Lorsch's[15] study suffers from some serious methodological limitations. Lawrence and Lorsch[16] attempted to examine the effectiveness of conflict management methods in three different types of organisations varying in their levels of effectiveness, i.e., high-performing, medium-performing, and low-performing organisations. The basic assumption of their study was that a particular method of conflict management will be regarded as effective or ineffective depending upon whether it was used to a higher or lower degree in the more effective organisation than in the less effective one. However, it is generally agreed that the relative efficacy or effectiveness of conflict management methods could be assessed more realistically only when these methods are explicitly related to certain well-defined measures of organisational effectiveness.

In addition, it may be noted that a large majority of the existing research studies seeking to explore the relationships between conflict management methods or styles and various aspects of organisational effectiveness have been conducted in the American organisational settings. These studies may not have much of relevance to the organisational or industrial situations prevalent in India on account of differences in socio-economic conditions, cultural factors, educational and income levels and personal profiles of Indian managers and employees. As discussed in detail beforehand, a few research studies have been conducted by Indian researchers[17] to examine the important questions of determining the present conflict management behaviours of Indian managers in terms of their utilisation of conflict management modes, examining the relative effectiveness of these modes in terms of their impact on organisational performance, and suggesting necessary behavioural modifications that may be required of managers so as to enhance organisational effectiveness. Although the findings of these research studies have been highly illuminating, it is felt that still there is a need to explore all these important research questions relating to organisational conflict and its management across a wide spectrum of Indian industries so that the research findings obtained will have more of validity and will be regarded as generally applicable to industrial situations.

## 7.3 RESEARCH METHODOLOGY USED

Keeping in view the major research consideration as discussed above, the author proceeded to examine various aspects of the conflict management behaviour of Indian managers in two cement manufacturing units. More specifically, the research study attempted to explore the relationship between the conflict management methods as proposed by Blake and Mouton[17] and certain perceptual measures of organisational effectiveness. The five methods of conflict management examined in the present study included: (1) problem solving, (2) smoothing, (3) compromise, (4) forcing, and (5) withdrawing. A detailed explanation of the conceptual meaning and definitions of these five different methods has been presented in Chapter 5. In spite of both theoretical and empirical research attempts made by experts to delineate the construct space of organisational effectiveness, it has been found that the boundaries of the effectiveness construct are still undefined or unbounded. Therefore, in the present study, the scope of the investigation has been limited to the study of certain selected measures of organisational effectiveness: (1) productivity, (2) adaptability, and (3) flexibility. A review of organisational effectiveness literature of Steers[19] has shown that these three measures have been most frequently utilised in various effectiveness models.

A Conflict Management Scale developed by Samantara[20] was used to collect perceptual data from managers regarding their utilisation of different methods of managing work related conflicts with their subordinates. The Conflict Management Scale has been mentioned as a part of the questionnaire described in Appendix 2. The details of development of the scale were presented in Chapter 5. This scale was used to measure Blake and Mouton's[21] methods of conflict management such as problem solving, smoothing, compromising, forcing, and withdrawing. As mentioned before, each of these methods was represented by certain relevant items and, accordingly, the conflict management scale comprised 12 different items presented in the form of statements. It may be stated that the questionnaire items related to each particular conflict management method were decided after a careful review of the literature and also statistically tested for their reliability. The respondent managers were asked to respond to each specific item or statement and indicate on a 5-point Likert type scale the extent to which it described the manner in which they resolved conflicts with subordinates on job related matters. In calculating an individual manager's score for each method of conflict management, his scores on the related items or statements were averaged so as to obtain a score falling between 1.00 and 5.00.

It may be mentioned that the organisational effectiveness scale developed by Mott[22] was utilised to measure three major aspects of organisational effectiveness: productivity, adaptability, and flexibility. The details of the questionnaire items related to this scale have been mentioned in Appendix 2. The first three items of this scale deal with three important components of organisational productivity such as quantity of output, quality of output, and efficiency in production while the next two items represent two different aspects of organisational adaptability, i.e., promptness of adjustment and prevalence of adjustment. While promptness of adjustment refers to the pace with which the members of an organisation accept and adjust to changes in work routines, equipment, etc., prevalence of adjustment indicates the proportion of organisation's members who readily accept and adjust to the above-mentioned changes. The last item of the scale represented organisational flexibility, i.e., the organisation's ability to handle emergency situations. All the six items of the scale were measured on a Likert type scale. The individual scores for each respondent with regard to productivity, adaptability, and flexibility were obtained by averaging his responses to the related items. Similarly, the overall effectiveness score for each respondent manager was calculated by averaging his scores for productivity, adaptability, and flexibility. In calculating the overall effectiveness score for each respondent, equal weightage was assigned to each of the three major components of organisational effectiveness such as productivity, adaptability, and flexibility. In this regard, it may be noted that the present study utilised only 6 out of 8 items originally proposed in Mott's organisational effectiveness scale.[23] The remaining two items of the scale that were not considered relevant for purposes of the present study dealt with symbolic adaptation to organisational changes. In addition, it may be noted that flexibility has been regarded as a separate and independent dimension of organisational effectiveness as distinguished from organisational adaptability. As described by Mott,[24] "flexibility is conceptually different from adaptability because the organisational changes that result from meeting emergencies are usually temporary, usually the organisation returns to its pre-emergency structure. Adaptive changes are more likely to be permanent."

As stated above, two cement manufacturing firms were selected for investigation purposes in the present study. Since these two organisations shared certain similar characteristics in terms of nature of production, industry affiliation, ownership, cultural characteristics, etc., it was assumed that a comparative study of these two with respect to their conflict management strategies and effectiveness dimensions will provide certain revealing research information. Since some research studies have been conducted by Indian researchers on these significant aspects as discussed earlier,[25] the basic purpose of the present study is to produce additional evidences regarding the conflict management strategies or methods adopted by Indian managers and their impact on various dimensions of organisational effectiveness. The research findings obtained are expected to be more valid and can be regarded as applicable to various industrial situations. In the process of collecting data from managers, it was assured to them that their identities and the identity of their respective organisations would be kept confidential. In addition, the respondent managers were assured that the research data obtained from them would be utilised for research purposes only. Therefore, the two cement manufacturing organisations selected for the study have been labelled as Organisation 1 and Organisation 2, respectively. It may be mentioned that questionnaire data were provided by 60 managers of Organisation 1 and by 57 managers of Organisation 2, respectively. The respondent managers were selected on random basis and belonged to diverse functional areas such as finance, production, marketing, HR, etc. At the same time, the managers represented various levels of the organisational hierarchy - top management, middle management, and lower level management. Thus, it can be said that the managers selected for data collection purposes represented their respective organisations quite well.

## 7.4 DATA ANALYSIS AND RESULTS

An analysis of perceptual data provided by managers was made to determine the weightages assigned to different conflict management strategies or methods and various dimensions of organisational effectiveness. Mean values of scores assigned by managers to each conflict management method and each specific dimension of organisational effectiveness were calculated along with their respective ranks. At the same time, standard deviations were calculated for each method of conflict management and each effectiveness dimension with a view to determining the consistencies in managers' responses regarding these organisational variables. Intercorrelations among the conflict management methods and various effectiveness dimensions were also computed to find out the direction of the movement of these variables when any two of these variables were considered. These inter-correlations were calculated to indicate the relationships among the conflict management methods as well as between each method of conflict management and each effectiveness dimension. Finally, multiple regression analysis was done to determine the proportions of variance explained by the five conflict management methods with respect to various organisational effectiveness aspects.

It can be seen that the mean values and ranks of different conflict management methods and organisational effectiveness dimensions for Organisation 1 have been shown in Table 7.1. These results indicate that the managers utilised withdrawing behaviour to the maximum possible extent in resolving job related conflicts with their subordinates, and it was followed by problem solving, compromise, smoothing, and forcing behaviours. While the managers' use of problem-solving, compromising, and smoothing has been on the higher side, their utilisation of forcing behaviour is somewhat negligible, falling just above the "seldom occurs" category. In addition, it can be observed that the managers' reliance upon compromising behaviour has been greater than their utilisation of smoothing behaviour. This situation indicates that the subordinates have grown up to a certain level so as to maintain valued relationships with their superiors by virtue of their increasing education and income levels, growing needs and aspirations, and their heightened consciousness regarding their rights and obligations at the workplace. While adopting the compromising mode of resolving conflicts with their subordinates, the superior managers tend to value both the production and the human relations aspects of the organisation equally but to a medium extent. As expected, the managers utilised problem-solving to a sufficiently greater extent while their use of forcing behaviour was somewhat insignificant. The

**Table 7.1:** Conflict management styles and organisational effectiveness dimensions in organisation 1[a] (Cement Industry)

| Conflict management styles | Mean | S.D. | Organisational effectiveness dimensions | Mean | S.D. |
|---|---|---|---|---|---|
| 1. Problem-solving | 3.31(2) | 0.67 | 1. Quantity of output | 3.65 (2) | 0.79 |
| 2. Smoothing | 3.10 (4) | 0.71 | 2. Quality of output | 3.57 (3) | 0.76 |
| 3. Compromise | 3.23 (3) | 0.95 | 3. Efficiency in production | 3.28 (5) | 0.80 |
| 4. Forcing | 2.75 (5) | 1.05 | 4. Rapidity of adjustment | 3.33 (4) | 0.85 |
| 5. Withdrawing | 3.50 (1) | 0.97 | 5. Prevalence of adjustment | 3.22 (6) | 1.04 |
| | | | 6. Flexibility | 3.77 (1) | 0.85 |
| | | | Productivity (overall) | 3.49 | 0.64 |
| | | | Adaptability (overall) | 3.27 | 0.83 |
| | | | Flexibility (overall) | 3.77 | 0.85 |
| | | | Overall effectiveness | 3.52 | 0.64 |

[a]N = 60 for all measures.

fact that the managers made maximum use of withdrawing behaviour in the management of conflicts is somewhat unexpected and inconsistent with the findings of earlier research studies. This particular situation may be attributed to the managerial philosophy and corporate culture of the organisation studied. The smaller values of standard deviations computed for different conflict management methods (varying from a minimum of 0.67 to a maximum of 1.07) lend more of reliability to the research findings obtained regarding the conflict management behaviour of managers.

With respect to the effectiveness dimensions of Organisation 1, it can be seen that the flexibility of the organisation to meet emergency situations such as quick work schedules, breakdown in the flow of work, crash programmes, etc., is the most significant one with a mean value of 3.77, and it is followed by productivity and adaptability with mean values of 3.49 and 3.27, respectively. As regards the specific aspects of productivity, it was found that the quantity aspect of output received greater weightage than the quality and efficiency aspects. The overall productivity of the organisation can, however, be described as being moderately high. It may be further noted that the adaptability aspect of effectiveness did not seem to be satisfactory with the lowest mean value of 3.27 as against the overall flexibility and the overall productivity of the organisation. In fact, the organisation does not seem to be well prepared to adapt to environmental changes in terms of both promptness of adjustment and prevalence of adjustment.

The mean values and ranks of conflict management methods presented in Table 7.2 indicate that the problem-solving mode of resolving conflicts is the most prominent one followed by compromising, smoothing, withdrawing, and forcing behaviours. The predominant utilisation of problem-solving, smoothing, and compromising methods by managers along with their insignificant use of withdrawing and forcing

**Table 7.2:** Conflict management styles and organisational effectiveness dimensions in organisation 2[a] (cement industry)

| Conflict management styles | Mean | S.D. | Organisational effectiveness dimensions | Mean | S.D. |
|---|---|---|---|---|---|
| 1. Problem-solving | 4.03 (1) | 0.87 | 1. Quantity of output | 3.25 (5) | 0.68 |
| 2. Smoothing | 3.69 (3) | 1.03 | 2. Quality of output | 3.58 (3) | 0.62 |
| 3. Compromise | 3.72 (2) | 0.70 | 3. Efficiency in production | 3.28 (4) | 0.70 |
| 4. Forcing | 2.83 (5) | 1.07 | 4. Rapidity of adjustment | 3.84 (2) | 0.77 |
| 5. Withdrawing | 3.40 (4) | 0.90 | 5. Prevalence of adjustment | 3.25 (5) | 0.66 |
| | | | 6. Flexibility | 4.12 (1) | 0.65 |
| | | | Productivity (overall) | 3.36 | 0.51 |
| | | | Adaptability (overall) | 3.57 | 0.68 |
| | | | Flexibility (overall) | 4.12 | 0.65 |
| | | | Overall effectiveness | 3.68 | 0.46 |

[a]N = 57 for all measures

behaviour has been demonstrated in a number of previous research studies too.[26] In contrast to the findings of some earlier research studies, however, the present study has shown that the managers in both Organisation 1 and Organisation 2 utilised more of compromising than smoothing behaviour in resolving work related conflicts with their subordinates for reasons discussed beforehand. The fact that the managers made considerable use of problem-solving, compromising, and smoothing behaviours together with their much lower utilisation of withdrawing and forcing behaviours was true of managers belonging to different levels of the organisational hierarchy, i.e., top management, middle management, and lower level management.

In regard to the organisational effectiveness dimensions of Organisation 2, it can be noticed from Table 7.2 that the flexibility dimension received the highest weightage with a mean value of 4.12, and it was followed by adaptability and productivity with mean values of 3.57 and 3.36, respectively. Thus, it can be stated that both Organisation 1 and Organisation 2 exhibited the highest level of flexibility or ability to handle emergency situations. An analysis of the specific aspects of productivity in Organisation 2 indicates that the quality aspect of output was much more prominent than the efficiency and quantity aspects. However, the overall productivity of Organisation 2 has been lower than that of Organisation 1 whereas the overall adaptability of Organisation 2 has been much higher than that of Organisation 1. In fact, the higher level of adaptability of Organisation 2 has been possible mainly due to the fact that its members demonstrated their ability to quickly accept and adjust to changes in work routines, equipment, etc. In other words, the members of this organisation showed higher level of the adaptability aspect of rapidity of adjustment than prevalence of adjustment. With regard to overall organisational effectiveness, both the organisations appear to be really effective with the mean values of their overall effectiveness scores being 3.52 and 3.68, respectively.

The intercorrelations among the five conflict management methods as used by the managers in Organisation 1 in resolving conflicts with their subordinates have been presented in the triangle portion of Table 7.3. The intercorrelations among these five different methods varied from a minimum of – 0.43 a maximum of 0.38 with nine of them being significantly different from zero. These results further indicate that the problem-solving, smoothing, and compromising modes of resolving conflicts have significant correlations among themselves and tend to move together in the positive direction. This means that the managers who made greater use of problem-solving were also likely to utilise more of smoothing and compromising behaviours in resolving job related conflicts. As emphasized earlier, these three methods or styles of conflict management are somewhat democratic in character and do assign primacy to the human relations aspects of the job or to both the production and the human relations aspects. It can be further noticed that the managers who are making greater use of problem-solving, smoothing, and compromising are also likely to make lesser utilisation of forcing and withdrawing behaviours. In addition, it can be noted that the senior managers' use of forcing behaviour is positively related to their withdrawing behaviour.

Table 7.3: Intercorrelations among conflict management styles and organisational effectiveness dimensions in organisation-1[a]

| | 1 | 2 | 3 | 4 | 5 |
|---|---|---|---|---|---|
| **Conflict management strategies** | | | | | |
| 1. Problem-Solving | | | | | |
| 2. Smoothing | 0.12* | | | | |
| 3. Compromise | 0.38*** | 0.20** | | | |
| 4. Forcing | -0.39*** | -0.24** | -0.42*** | | |
| 5. Withdrawing | -0.43*** | -0.00 | -0.17** | 0.33*** | |
| **Organisational effectiveness dimensions** | | | | | |
| 6. Quantity of output | 0.09 | -0.05 | -0.05 | -0.20** | -0.10 |
| 7. Quality of output | 0.09 | -0.29*** | -0.06 | -0.19** | -0.27*** |
| 8. Efficiency in production | -0.09 | -0.15* | -0.03 | -0.07 | -0.08 |
| 9. Rapidity of adjustment | 0.20** | -0.10 | -0.02 | 0.02 | -0.01 |
| 10. Prevalence of adjustment | 0.11 | -0.06 | -0.06 | -0.05 | -0.04 |
| 11. Flexibility | -0.08 | 0.11* | -0.03 | -0.02 | 0.15* |

[a]N= 60 for all correlations. $^{*}p < 0.10$ $^{**}p < 0.05$ $^{***}p < 0.01$

In regard to the intercorrelations between the conflict management methods and various dimensions of organisational effectiveness in Organisation 1, it was found that only 8 of the correlations had significant coefficient values. While the problem-solving mode had positive significant relationship with rapidity of adjustment, the smoothing mode was negatively related to both the quality and efficiency aspects of production. These research findings are somewhat unexpected and, therefore, need to be interpreted in the light of additional research evidences. The smoothing mode of conflict management was, however, positively related to the flexibility aspect of organisational effectiveness. As expected, the forcing mode of managing conflicts was negatively related to both the quantity and the quality aspects of output. While the withdrawing mode had negative relationship with the quality of output, this mode was positively related to the flexibility aspect of effectiveness.

The intercorrelations among the conflict management methods used by managers in Organisation 2 (as shown in Table 7.4) indicate that the problem-solving, smoothing, and compromising modes have positive relations among themselves. As mentioned earlier, the managers made considerable use of these three methods in this organisation as against their lower degree of utilisation of withdrawing and forcing behaviours. Surprisingly, however, the smoothing mode showed positive relationship with the forcing mode while these two modes of managing conflicts had negative significant correlation in Organisation 1. This inconsistency in research finding needs to be appropriately interpreted in the light of additional research evidences. The remaining correlations among the conflict management methods as shown in the triangle were not the significant ones. With regard to the intercorrelations between the conflict management methods and effectiveness dimensions in Organisation 2, it can be observed that both the problem-solving and the smoothing modes showed positive and significant relationships with the quality aspect of output as well as with both the dimensions of adaptability, i.e., rapidity of adjustment and prevalence of adjustment. Similarly, the compromising mode was positively related to the quality of output and the adaptability aspect of rapidity of adjustment. The fact that the forcing mode of managing conflict was positively related to the quality of output and prevalence of adjustment, was somewhat inconsistent with the research findings obtained in Organisation 1. Again, quite unexpectedly, the withdrawing mode showed positive relationship with the adaptability aspect of rapidity of adjustment.

**Table 7.4:** Intercorrelations among conflict management styles and organisational effectiveness dimensions in organisation-2[a]

| | 1 | 2 | 3 | 4 | 5 |
|---|---|---|---|---|---|
| **Conflict management styles** | | | | | |
| 1. Problem-Solving | | | | | |
| 2. Smoothing | 0.68** | | | | |
| 3. Compromise | 0.64*** | 0.40*** | | | |
| 4. Forcing | 0.19 | 0.54*** | 0.07 | | |
| 5. Withdrawing | 0.00 | 0.13 | 0.02 | 0.21 | |
| **Organisational effectiveness dimensions** | | | | | |
| 6. Quantity of output | 0.18 | 0.19 | 0.08 | –0.01 | 0.21 |
| 7. Quality of output | 0.41*** | 0.56*** | 0.34*** | 0.29** | 0.18 |
| 8. Efficiency in production | 0.21 | 0.19 | 0.10 | 0.15 | 0.19 |
| 9. Rapidity of adjustment | 0.34*** | 0.40*** | 0.22* | 0.18 | 0.25* |
| 10. Prevalence of adjustment | 0.45*** | 0.53*** | 0.16 | 0.43*** | 0.15 |
| 11. Flexibility | 0.11 | 0.07 | 0.08 | 0.00 | 0.06 |

[a]N= 60 for all correlations. *$p < 0.10$ **$p < 0.05$ ***$p < 0.01$

The multiple regression results showing the relationships between conflict management methods and the specific dimensions of organisational effectiveness in Organisation 1 are presented in Table 7.5. These results indicate that the problem-solving mode of resolving conflicts is positively related to rapidity of adjustment (B = 0.28, P < 0.10) but this mode did not indicate any significant relationships with the other effectiveness variables. The smoothing mode was found to have negative significant relationships with the quality of output (B = –0.33, P < 0.05) but it had no significant relationship with the other effectiveness dimensions. It must be pointed out that these research findings obtained with respect to problem-solving and smoothing behaviours in Organisation 1 need to be interpreted in the light of additional research evidences obtained for both the organisations with respect to the composite measures of organisational effectiveness such as productivity and flexibility, as presented in Table 7.7. In keeping with the findings of previous research studies, it was found that the forcing behaviour adopted by managers in Organisation 1 had negative relationships with both the quantity and the quality aspects of output. It was, however, noted that the flexibility aspect of organisational effectiveness was not explained by any of the conflict resolution methods to a significant degree. In addition, the results of multiple regression analysis indicate that that conflict management methods, considered together, explained 22 per cent of the variance in quality of output while their predictive power was comparatively low for other effectiveness variables such as quantity of output (7%), efficiency in production (6%), rapidity of adjustment (6%), prevalence of adjustment (3%) and flexibility (4%).

**Table 7.5:** Conflict management styles and organisational effectiveness dimensions: multiple regression results for organisation-1[a]
(Organisational effectiveness measures as dependent variables)

| Conflict management styles | Regression coefficients | | | | | |
|---|---|---|---|---|---|---|
| | (1) Quantity of output | (2) Quality of output | (3) Efficiency in production | (4) Rapidity of adjustment | (5) Prevalence of adjustment | (6) Flexibility |
| 1. Problem-solving | 0.05 | -0.01 | -0.18 | 0.28* | 0.15 | -0.04 |
| 2. Smoothing | -0.08 | -0.33** | -0.17 | -0.09 | -0.07 | 0.10 |
| 3. Compromising | -0.18 | -0.15 | -0.01 | 0.06 | -0.14 | -0.05 |
| 4. Forcing | -0.27* | -0.27* | -0.16 | -0.04 | -0.08 | -0.09 |
| 5. Withdrawing | -0.01 | -0.21 | -0.11 | -0.10 | -0.02 | 0.15 |
| $R^2$ = | 0.07 | 0.22 | 0.06 | 0.06 | 0.03 | 0.04 |

[a]N= 60 for all correlations. *p < 0.10 **p < 0.05 ***p < 0.01

As against the multiple regression results analysed above for Organisation 1, the results shown in Table 7.6 for Organisation 2 reveal certain contrasting features especially with regard to the impact of problem-solving and smoothing modes of resolving conflicts on certain specific aspects of organisational effectiveness. While problem solving indicates positive and significant relationship with both rapidity of adjustment (B=0.36, P <0.10) and organisational flexibility (B=0.52, P <0.05), the smoothing mode is positive and significantly related to the quality of output (B = 0.54, P < 0.01). In fact, these positive effects of problem solving on certain effectiveness aspects have been shown by the findings of some earlier empirical studies too.[27] The findings obtained with regard to smoothing behaviour in Organisations 1 and 2 do not lead us to any definite conclusions. In addition, it can be noted that the forcing mode of resolving conflicts is positively related to rapidity of adjustment (B = 0.24, $P < 0.10$). This is possible because the forcing or pressure tactics used by senior managers perhaps make the organisation's members show obedient behaviour and quickly accept and adjust to changes made in work routines, equipment, etc. The withdrawing behaviour, however, is negatively related to the quantity aspect of output (B = -0.23, $P < 0.10$). It can be further noticed that the proportions of variance explained by the conflict management methods, taken together, with respect to the specific aspects of effectiveness have been on the higher side for rapidity of adjustment (36%), quality of output (35%), and organisational flexibility (18%), and on the lower side for quantity of output (11%), efficiency in production (9%), and prevalence of adjustment (2%).

**Table 7.6:** Conflict management styles and organisational effectiveness dimensions: multiple regression results for organisation 2[a]
(Organisational effectiveness measures as dependent variables)

| Conflict management styles | Regression coefficients | | | | | |
|---|---|---|---|---|---|---|
| | (1) Quantity of output | (2) Quality of output | (3) Efficiency in production | (4) Rapidity of adjustment | (5) Prevalence of adjustment | (6) Flexibility |
| 1. Problem-solving | 0.11 | –0.06 | 0.26 | 0.36* | 0.12 | 0.52** |
| 2. Smoothing | 0.22 | 0.54*** | –0.03 | 0.21 | –0.01 | –0.22 |
| 3. Compromising | –0.06 | 0.16 | –0.06 | –0.17 | 0.01 | –0.05 |
| 4. Forcing | –0.20 | –0.02 | 0.09 | 0.24* | –0.02 | 0.12 |
| 5. Withdrawing | –0.23* | 0.11 | 0.17 | 0.07 | 0.07 | 0.17 |
| $R^2$ = | 0.11 | 0.35 | 0.09 | 0.36 | 0.02 | 0.18 |

[a]N= 57 for all correlations. *$p < 0.10$ **$p < 0.05$ ***$p < 0.01$

The multiple regression results shown in Table 7.7 for both the Organisations (1 and 2) indicate the relationships between the conflict management strategies or methods and the composite measures of organisational effectiveness such as productivity, adaptability and flexibility. An interpretation of these multiple regression results in conjunction with the multiple regression results obtained and analysed earlier lead us to certain meaningful conclusions as described below:

1. Although the multiple regression results analysed earlier showed that the problem-solving mode was positively related to rapidity of adjustment in both the organisations, the results presented in Table 7.7 bring out the fact that problem solving indicated no significant relationship with the composite measure of organisational adaptability in both these organisations. The problem-solving mode of managing conflict was, however, positively related to the flexibility aspect of organisational effectiveness in Organisation 2.

2. In regard to the impact of the smoothing mode of managing conflicts on the composite measures of organisational effectiveness, it can be seen from Table 7.7 that this mode showed negative relationship with productivity in Organisation 1 (B = –0.23, P < 0.10). This finding is consistent with the fact that the smoothing mode was previously found to be negatively related to the quality of output in Organisation 1 as shown in Table 7.5. Although the smoothing mode had positive significant relationship with the quality aspect of output in Organisation 2 (Table 7.6), this mode indicated no significant relationship with productivity or any other composite measure of organisational effectiveness in this organisation.
3. It is significant to note that compromising indicated no significant relationship with any of the specific measures as well as with the composite measures of organisational effectiveness as shown in Tables 7.5, 7.6, and 7.7.
4. As observed earlier, the forcing mode of resolving conflicts was negatively and significantly related to both the quantity and the quality aspects of output in Organisation 1. Accordingly, the findings presented in Table 7.7 indicate that the forcing behaviour was negatively related to the composite measure of productivity in Organisation 1 (B = – 0.28, P < 10). Although the forcing mode indicated positive and significant relationship with rapidity of adjustment in Organisation 2 as noted earlier, this mode was related to none of the composite measures of effectiveness in this organisation, as the findings shown in Table 7.7 indicate.
5. As regards the efficacy or effectiveness of the withdrawing mode of managing conflicts, the findings presented in Table 7.6 indicated that this mode had negative relationship with the quantity of output in Organisation 2. However, according to the multiple regression results shown in Table 7.7, the withdrawing behaviour showed positive relationship with productivity in Organisation 2.

**Table 7.7:** Conflict management styles and organisational effectiveness dimensions: multiple regression results for organisation-1 and organisation-2
(Organisational effectiveness measures as dependent variables)

| Conflict management styles | Regression coefficients for organisation 1[a] | | | Regression coefficients for organisation 2[b] | | |
|---|---|---|---|---|---|---|
| | **Productivity** | **Adaptability** | **Flexibility** | **Productivity** | **Adaptability** | **Flexibility** |
| 1. Problem-solving | –0.05 | 0.05 | –0.04 | 0.14 | 0.02 | 0.52** |
| 2. Smoothing | –0.23* | –0.09 | 0.10 | 0.30 | 0.18 | –0.22 |
| 3. Compromising | –0.14 | –0.05 | –0.05 | 0.01 | –0.07 | –0.05 |
| 4. Forcing | –0.28* | –0.08 | –0.09 | –0.05 | 0.14 | 0.12 |
| 5. Withdrawing | –0.14 | –0.03 | 0.15 | 0.22* | -0.04 | 0.17 |
| $R^2$ = | 0.13 | 0.01 | 0.04 | 0.22 | 0.07 | 0.18 |

[a]N= 60 for all correlations. [b]N= 57 for all correlations. *p < 0.10 **p < 0.05 ***p < 0.01

## 7.5 DISCUSSION AND CONCLUSION

As mentioned before, a large volume of literature exists in the management discipline on different aspects of organisational conflict and its management. While most of the management experts have offered their viewpoints or perspectives on this only at a theoretical level, it has been noted that there is a paramount need to conduct empirical research studies especially on the management aspects of organisational conflict. In the preceding paragraphs, it was stated that the organisational behaviour experts have proposed different methods or styles of managing interpersonal and inter-group conflicts in organisations and also offered their viewpoints regarding the comparative effectiveness of different methods or styles of conflict management. In addition, it was noted that the few empirical research studies which do exist on the relative effectiveness of these methods or styles suffer from certain methodological inconsistencies or limitations. Although some empirical research studies in this regard have been conducted by researchers[28] in the context of Indian industrial situations and some conclusive research evidences also obtained in relation thereto, the author decided to make further investigations of different aspects of senior-subordinate conflict management in some additional Indian industries. As discussed in Chapter 5, the investigations conducted by the author in a public sector electricity generating and distributing company situated in the NCR region of Delhi provided some meaningful results regarding various issues and sources of senior-subordinate conflict as well as the conflict management behaviours of senior managers in resolving work related conflicts with their subordinates. The present chapter is, however, more specifically directed towards examining the conflict management behaviours of senior managers and, more significantly, towards evaluating the efficacy or effectiveness of conflict management methods in terms of their impact on various organisational performance or effectiveness measures. The research evidences obtained through this study are expected to enhance the reliability of the conclusions obtained regarding the relative effectiveness of different conflict management methods or styles.

It may be mentioned that for purposes of the present study, perceptual data were obtained from 60 and 57 managers of two private cement manufacturing firms. It may be mentioned that a comparative study of these two organisations having similar characteristics such as nature of production, ownership, industry-affiliation, etc., was made to derive certain meaningful information regarding the important research objectives as mentioned in the preceding paragraphs. An analysis of data revealed that the managers of both the organisations made considerable use of problem-solving, compromising, and smoothing behaviour while their utilisation of forcing behaviour was somewhat insignificant or negligible. These patterns of utilisation of conflict management behaviours have been noticed in some earlier research studies too. These findings signify that the Indian managers tend to adopt democratic approach to the management of conflicts at the workplace and place primacy on sound human relations in an organisation or on both the production and the human relations aspects of the job. The fact that the senior managers made greater utilisation of compromising than smoothing behaviour in resolving work related conflicts with their subordinates, indicates that the senior managers do give importance to the knowledge, expertise, and viewpoints of their subordinates on a variety of organisational issues and problems. This development can be attributed to a number of significant factors such as change in industrial ethos, change in management philosophy, increasing education and income levels of subordinates, growing awareness of subordinates regarding their basic democratic rights or privileges at the workplace, etc. Very surprisingly, however, the findings of the study indicated that the senior managers in Organisation 1 made maximum use of withdrawing in behaviours resolving conflicts with their subordinates although the managers' utilisation of withdrawing behaviour in Organisation 2 was somewhat on the lower side as compared to problem solving, compromising, and smoothing behaviours. The maximum use of withdrawing behaviour in Organisation 1 is perhaps due to the individual inclinations of managers to behave in this manner or due to the corporate culture of this organisation.

A comparative analysis of the organisational effectiveness dimensions indicates that the flexibility of both the organisations in the cement industry has been the most predominant one as compared to the productivity and the adaptability aspects of organisational effectiveness. The predominance of the flexibility aspect of organisational effectiveness was noticed even in certain selected manufacturing organisations in the steel and paper industries in a comprehensive research study previously conducted by the author. Thus, the flexibility of various organisations across Indian industries to handle emergency situations such as disruption in the flow of work, breakdown in machinery, moving through crash work programmes, etc., appears to be remarkably high. The productivity of Organisation 2 was the least significant one as compared to its flexibility and adaptability. To raise the productivity levels of both these organisations, there is a particular need to improve the efficiency aspects of output in Organisation 1 and in both the quantity and the efficiency aspects of production in Organisation 2. In addition, it was noted that the ability of Organisation 2 to adapt to various environmental changes was low in terms of both rapidity of adjustment and flexibility of adjustment. Organisation 2, however, showed moderately high degree of overall adaptability as its members exhibited higher level of capability to rapidly adjust to various changes in work routine, equipment, etc. It was, however, noticed that the adaptability aspect of prevalence of adjustment in Organisation 2 was quite low in terms of the proportion of its members accepting and adjusting to organisational changes. Therefore, there is a need for both these organisations to enhance their adaptability to changes occurring in both their internal and external environments.

The multiple regression results analysed for both the organisations with respect to the relationship between their conflict management strategies or methods and various effectiveness dimensions brought out certain important facts. As it was observed, the conflict management methods, considered together, explained 13% of variance in the productivity of Organisation 1 but merely 4% and 1% of variance in its flexibility and adaptability, respectively. In the case of Organisation 2, however, the conflict management methods explained 22%, 18%, and 7% of variance in productivity, flexibility, and adaptability, respectively. Thus, the conflict management strategies taken together had significant impact on all the three composite measures of organisational effectiveness in Organisation 2 while these methods had noticeable impact on productivity only but not on adaptability and flexibility in Organisation 1. With regard to the impact of each individual mode of conflict management on the specific organisational effectiveness measures, it was found that: (1) the problem solving mode was positively related to rapidity of adjustment in Organisation 1; it was also positively related to rapidity of adjustment and flexibility in Organisation 2; (2) the smoothing mode was negatively related to quality of output as well as to productivity in Organisation 1; it was, however, positively related to quality of output in Organisation 2; (3) the forcing mode was negatively related to both the quantity and the quality aspects of output as well as to overall productivity in Organisation 1; and it had positive significant relationship with rapidity of adjustment in Organisation 2; and (4) the withdrawing mode was negatively related to the quantity of output in Organisation 2 but it showed positive relationship with the overall productivity of Organisation 2.

The findings of the present study obtained with regard to the role, importance and effects of conflict management in organisations have been well established in certain organisations across Indian industries. These findings have been largely consistent with those of some previous research studies conducted by the author as mentioned earlier.[29] It was clearly established that 'conflict management' is a crucial organisational variable having noticeable effects on the effectiveness of organisations. An examination of the effects of individual conflict management methods on various organisational effectiveness dimensions as described above leads us to draw some significant inferences regarding the relative efficacy or effectiveness of conflict management strategies or methods in the context of Indian industrial environment. The findings of the studies have amply demonstrated the fact that problem-solving is the most effective method of conflict management. The positive effects of problem-solving have been emphasized by many leading organisation experts as this method values both the production and the human relations aspects of an organisation equally well. Lawrence and Lorsch's[30] conclusion that forcing may be viewed as an effective backup mode to problem solving has not been substantiated by the findings of our previous research studies as well as by the present one. In fact, the research analysis conducted at the organisation level largely indicated that the forcing mode of managing conflicts has detrimental effects on organisational effectiveness. The senior managers may force their viewpoints or decisions on their subordinates through their power, position, or expertise and pressurise the latter to produce as much as possible. However, it must be pointed out that this condition of low morale and high productivity cannot be maintained for long unless the subordinates are duly consulted by their seniors and given the freedom to exercise their innovative thinking and initiative at the work situation. The findings of the present study further indicate that the smoothing and the withdrawing modes of resolving conflict seem to have mixed effects on certain aspects of organisational effectiveness. The compromise mode was found to be related to none of the effectiveness dimensions.

In the light of the research findings as described above, some useful suggestions may be made for the improvement of the conflict management behaviours of Indian managers in the organisational settings. The research data, by and large, indicated that the managers are making immense use of problem-solving, compromising, and smoothing modes of managing work related conflicts while their utilisation of forcing and withdrawing behaviours has been somewhat negligible. The managers' maximum use of problem-solving in resolving conflicts with subordinates augurs well and needs to be enhanced further especially when the income, education, and expertise levels of subordinates have significantly improved over time. In fact, the subordinates have demonstrated their ability and willingness to participate equally with their senior managers in the decision-making process and find amicable solutions to a number of organisational issues and conflicts. Although the present study indicates the mixed effects of smoothing behaviour on the effectiveness dimensions, the findings of the previous empirical research studies conducted by the author[31] have mostly shown the positive effects of this mode of managing conflicts. Therefore, the managers' higher level of utilisation of smoothing behaviour seems to be justified although there is no particular need to enhance it further. It was further noted that the compromising mode of conflict management did not indicate significant relationships with any of the effectiveness dimensions. Therefore, the managers' frequent use of compromising behaviour with their subordinates in resolving work related conflicts doesn't seem to be justified. Although the compromising mode emphasizes upon both the production and the human relations aspects of the job to a moderate degree, this mode has adverse effects on the innovative skills and creativity of employees and on any improvements in organisational performance. The research findings have amply demonstrated the negative effects of forcing behaviour on several dimensions of organisational effectiveness. Thus, it is quite encouraging to note that the Indian managers have shown their sagacity in their infrequent use of this conflict management mode. The analysis of data further revealed that the withdrawing mode of managing conflicts seemed to have mixed effects on certain aspects of organisational effectiveness. Therefore, the managers should not be encouraged to frequently withdraw or escape from the conflict situations in organisations.

## REVIEW QUESTIONS

1. The empirical research findings conducted by researchers on the relationship between conflict management methods or styles and organisational effectiveness have brought out some significant findings. Discuss.
2. The available research studies on the relationship between conflict management styles and organisational effectiveness have certain limitations. Discuss.
3. State the major findings of the research study conducted by the author in the cement industry with regard to the effects of conflict management styles on various effectiveness dimensions.

## REFERENCES


1. Samantara, R. Conflict management strategies and organisational effectiveness, *Indian Journal of Industrial Relations*, 39(3), January, 2004, pp. 298-323.
2. Blake, R.R., and Mouton, J.S., *The Managerial Grid*, Gulf, Houston, 1964; Walton, R.E., Theory of conflict in lateral organisational relationships, J.R. Lawrence, (Ed.), *Operational Research and the Social Science*, Tavistock, London, 1966; Thomas, K.W., Conflict and conflict management, M.D. Dunettee, (Ed.), *Handbook of Industrial and Organisational Psychology*, Rand McNally, 1976, pp. 889-935; Likert, R., and Likert, J.G., *New Ways of Managing Conflict*, McGraw Hill, New York, 1976; Pareek, U., *Managing Conflict and Collaboration*, Oxford-IBH, New Delhi, 1982; Rahim, M.A., *Rahim Organisational Conflict Inventory*, Consulting Psychological Press, Alto Calif, 1983.
3. Blake, R.R., and Mouton, J.S., 1964, *op. cit.*
4. *Ibid.*
5. Lawrence, P.R. and Lorsch, J.W., *Organisation and Environment: Managing Differentiation and Integration*, Division of Research, Harvard Business School, Harvard University, Boston, 1967.
6. Burke, R.J., Methods of resolving inter-personal conflict, *Personnel Administration*, July-August, 1969, pp. 48-55.
7. Blake, R.R., and Mouton, J.S., 1964, *op. cit.*
8. Thomas, K.W., 1976, *op. cit.*
9. Aram, J.D., Morgan, C.P., and Esbeck, E.S., Relation of collaborative interpersonal relationships to individual satisfaction and organisational performance, *Administrative Science Quarterly*, 16(3), 1971.
10. Dutton, J.M., and Walton, R.E., Interdepartmental conflict and cooperation: Two contrasting studies, *Human Organisation*, 25(3), 1966.
11. Sharma, R.A., and Samantara, R., Conflict management in an Indian firm: A case study, *Decision*, 21(4), 1994.

12. Samantara, R., 2004, *op. cit.*
13. Lawrence, P.R., and Lorsch, J.W., 1967, *op. cit.*
14. Burke, R.J., 1969, *op. cit.*
15. Lawrence, P.R. and Lorsch, J.W., 1967, *op. cit.*
16. *Ibid.*
17. Sharma, R.A. and Samantara, R., 1994, *op. cit*; and Samantara, R., 2004, *op. cit.*
18. Blake, R.R., and Mouton, J.S., 1964, *op. cit.*
19. Steers, R.M., *Organisational Effectiveness*, Goodyear, Santa Monica, CA, 1977.
20. Samantara, R., Management of superior-subordinate conflict: An exploration, *Indian Journal of Industrial Relations*, 38(4), 2003, pp. 444-459.
21. Blake, R.R., and Mouton, J.S., 1964, *op. cit.*
22. Mott, P.E., *The Characteristics of Effective Organisation*, Harper and Row, New York, 1972.
23. *Ibid.*
24. *Ibid.*
25. Sharma, R.A., and Samantara, R., 1994, *op. cit.*; Samantara, R., 2004, *op. cit.*
26. Burke, R.J., 1969, *op. cit.*; Sharma, R.A. and Samantara, R., 1994, *op. cit.*; Samantara, R., 2003, *op. cit.*; and Samantara, R., 2004, *op. cit.*
27. Sharma, R.A., and Samantara, R., 1994, *op. cit.*; Samantara, R., 2004, *op. cit.*
28. Sharma, R.A., and Samantara, R., 1994, *op. cit.*; Samantara, R., 2003, *op. cit.*; and Samantara, R., 2004, *op. cit.*
29. *Ibid.*
30. Lawrence, P.R., and Lorsch, J.W., 1967, *op. cit.*
31. Sharma, R.A., and Samantara, R., 1994, *op. cit.*; Samantara, R., 2004, *op. cit.*

# 8

# A Contingency View of Managing Conflicts

## 8.1 INTRODUCTION

The management literature has traditionally been dominated by scholarly writings focusing upon the effectiveness of a manager, the management process, or the organisation. Therefore, the classical and neoclassical schools of management thought (including the scientific management theory, the human relations approach, the social system theory, etc.) developed with certain concepts and ideas rooted in different fundamental assumptions about rationality, efficiency, productivity, governance, the nature of work, motivation, etc. During the last few decades, however, the emphasis in management writings has shifted from the universalistic principles to the changing "situational" character of management. Most of the management scholars now agree that "at the moment, contingency theory is perhaps the most powerful current sweeping over the organisations. The history of many fields of knowledge or enquiry shows a movement from universalistic principles to situational relationships and principles. The current prominence of contingency theory suggests that organisation theory is entering a period of scientific maturity. Therefore, it must be emphasised that the contingency theory of management has developed essentially due to certain limitations of classical organisation theories such as Weber's[2] bureaucracy, Taylor's[3] scientific management theory, etc. These theories failed to take cognizance of the fact that the organisation's structure, process, technology, etc. were influenced by various environmental or situational forces. Some of the prominent contingency theorists who explicitly recongised and studied the relationship between the organisation's structure and various environmental conditions or forces impacting on it, were Woodward, Burns and Stalker, Thompson, and Lawrence and Lorsch.[4] Their classic contingency studies of organisation and environment relationship laid the foundation for the development of the contingency theory of management, as would be discussed later.

In the light of the above-mentioned observations, the present chapter examines various aspects of the contingency concept, especially in the context of conflict management issues. In the first place, this chapter analyses the historical evolution of the contingency concept within the management discipline. In this regard, some of the classic studies made by organisational behaviour experts on the organisation and environment nexus have been discussed. Second, this chapter critically examines certain contingency approaches to conflict management as suggested by some leading management experts. Third, an attempt has been made to discuss the role of various processes and structural contingencies which do impact the dynamics of a conflict episode or the management of specific conflict situations.

## 8.2 HISTORICAL BACKGROUND OF THE CONTINGENCY CONCEPT

It may be noted that several contingency approaches to management were developed by management experts during the 1960s. These pioneering contingency studies basically sought to explain how the organisations made suitable changes in their structures in response to various changes taking place in their internal as well as external environments. In fact, it would be worthwhile to discuss the findings of these research studies and also see how these valuable research findings have immensely contributed to the development of the contingency theory of management. In fact, the contingency concept originated with the famous research work of Woodward[5] who studied 100 English manufacturing firms to find out if the traditional principles of organisation were followed in these organisations. After finding that these principles of organisation were ignored by these companies, Woodward attempted to examine the relationship between the structure of different firms and the types of technologies employed by these firms. As noted by her, the utilisation of different technologies by different firms resulted in different types of organisation structures. For example, two different technologies calling for continuous process production and custom manufacturing respectively, resulted in different organisation structures. She also found that successful firms with similar production technologies tended to display similar organisation structures. Therefore, the technology employed by an organisation was an important "situational" variable that determines the nature of its structure.

Burns and Stacker[6] studied twenty British firms operating in the electronics industry. The authors classified these firms in two categories on the basis of management structures and styles: mechanistic and organic. The mechanistic organisation possessed many of the characteristics comparable to those of Webber's[7] bureaucratic organisation. The mechanistic form of organisation was most suitable for organisations operating in relatively stable environments with predictable conditions prevailing therein. Such organisations are clearly programmed with emphasis on close supervision and control, hierarchically structured authority in decision-making, clearly defined task and role expectations, etc. The organic form of organisation, on the other hand, was most effective in organisations operating in relatively dynamic and unstable environmental conditions. These organic organisations have a flat organisation structure rather than a hierarchy of authority, limited structure in terms of organisational processes and rules. Therefore, Burns and Stalker[8] concluded that stable or unstable environmental conditions were the most significant "situational" variables that determined the most effective form of organisation structure.

Lawrence and Lorsch's[9] contributions towards the development of the contingency theory of management are really significant. In their empirical study of ten organisations operating in three different industries such as plastics, consumer foods, and standardized containers, the researchers found that different types of organisations faced different types of industrial environment. The different characteristics of the environment (i.e., uncertain to certain, homogeneous to diverse) resulted in different types of structures and processes in the organisations studied. Organisations facing an uncertain and diverse environment were composed of differentiated and integrated subsystems. Each organisation needed differentiated subunits as each subunit performed different type of task posed by the diverse environment of the organisation. In addition, the researchers noted that with a differentiated organisation structure, the integration of subunits was equally needed to achieve unity of efforts. In contrast to these organisations operating in uncertain and diverse environments, those organisations which functioned in certain and homogeneous environments tended to operate in the mechanistic fashion. Therefore, the authors concluded that the certainty or uncertainty of the environment and its diversity or homogeneity were the most critical "situational" variables in determining the most efficient and effective form of organisation structure.

In addition to the above-mentioned pioneering efforts of researchers who specifically dealt with the organisation and environment relationship, and thus dealt with the contingency perspective on management extensively. The significant role of the contingency theories of leadership in this regard needs to be highlighted with equal emphasis. Fiedler[10] proposed his contingency theory of leadership that attempts to identify the most effective style of leadership (task-oriented versus relationship-oriented) with varying combinations of three situational variables such as: (1) the task structure; (2) the leader-member relations; and (3) the leader's positional power. According to Fiedler, a task-oriented manager is most effective in situations that are highly favourable or unfavourable to him. On the other hand, a relationship-oriented manager is most effective in situations that have intermediate favourableness or unfavourableness to him. In addition to Fiedler's contingency theory of leadership, it must be noted that certain other contingency theories of leadership have also emerged in the management literature, emphasising upon different contingency variables. The Path-Goal theory of leadership emphasises upon four possible leader behaviours (directive, supportive, achievement oriented and participative) which interact with two specific situational variables: (1) subordinate characteristics, and (2) environmental factors so as to determine the most effective leadership beavhiour.[12] Tannenbaum and Schmidt's[13] leadership continuum specifies two types of leadership styles, i.e., boss-centred versus subordinate centred that interact with four categories of situational variables: (1) forces in the manager; (2) forces in the subordinates; (3) forces in the situation; and (4) forces in the environment, to determine the effectiveness of the leadership style or behaviour.[13]

Thus, it may be observed that there are two schools of thought existing in regard to the flexibility of leadership styles. One school argues that leadership styles are inherent in individuals and cannot be modified at all. Therefore, the leadership styles of particular managers and the situational variables in organisations must be properly studied so that a manager can be selected whose leadership style fits the specific requirements of a particular organisational situation. The second school of leadership thought argues that the leadership styles of managers are flexible and vary according to the needs of specific situations. Thus, the best managers are described as those who can identify the demands of specific situations and vary their leadership styles accordingly.

## 8.3 CONTINGENCY THEORY OF MANAGEMENT

The contingency theory of management can be regarded as an extension of the open system concept which is based on the interdependence of various parts of the system and their relationship to the system as a whole. While there is mutual dependence among the functional parts or subunits in an organisational system, the subsystems are also dependent upon the organisation as a whole for their continued existence or survival. In addition to this interdependency relationships within the organisational system, the open system approach also concentrates on the mutual dependence and exchange relationship between the organisation and its external environment. In fact, the organisation receives resource inputs such as men, materials, money, and other resources from the broader environment and supplies output to the society composed of various parts or functionaries. On the other hand, the contingency theory of management involves an analysis of internal changes or adjustments of the organisation (e.g., changes in organisation's structure, technology, leadership and decision processes, etc.) as it seeks to meet the changing demands of its external or internal environment. This recognition of changing conditions both within the external and the internal environments of an organisation indicates that the contingency theory of management is situational in character. As Luthans and Stewart have stated, a contingency theory of management can be defined as "identifying and developing functional relationship between environment management and performance variables."[14] The above-mentioned explanations regarding the conceptual meaning and implications of the contingency theory of management point to the fact that this new management theorem or perspective is based upon the following important assumptions or features:

1. There is no one best way of managing or organising.
2. All organisations are open systems.[15]
3. The organisational structure or design and its subsystems must match with its environment.

4. The performance level of an organisation is essentially determined by the match between its internal conditions and processes, and the external requirements.
5. Effective organisations are characterized by a proper fit or match not only with the environment but also among its subsystems.
6. Different leadership styles are appropriate for different problem situations.
7. Organisational needs are better satisfied when the organisation is properly designed and the management styles adopted are appropriate to both the tasks to be performed and the nature of the work group.

Thus, it may be stated that the emergence of the open system theory has removed many conceptual barriers and propagated the notion that "the behaviour of an organisation is contingent upon the social field of forces in which it occurs and must be understood in terms of the organisation's interaction with that environmental field."[16] Katz and Kahn have classified the major fields of forces in the external environment which determine the contingencies impacting on an organisation, as mentioned below:[17]

1. Cultural forces (e.g., affirmative action, social standards of excellence, ethical values, etc.).
2. Political forces (e.g., public participation in decision-making, community satisfaction, public service codes, etc.).
3. Economic forces (e.g., job market, union budget, CSR funding, etc.).
4. Physical forces (e.g., organisational space, transportation equipment, etc.).
5. Informational and technical forces (e.g., communication network, state of knowledge and skills, etc.).

## 8.4 CONTINGENCY APPROACHES TO MANAGING CONFLICTS

The normative theories of conflict management are generally advocated in favour of one best style of conflict management. Therefore, many researchers have attempted to examine the functionality of conflict handling behaviours in the context of individual, group or organisational effectiveness.[18] The results of these studies have broadly shown that problem-solving is the most effective style or method of managing conflicts, and it is followed by smoothing behaviours. These empirical research studies have further suggested that the functionality or desirability of problem-solving and smoothing behaviours should be considered suitable to all industrial situations. In contrast to these normative viewpoints, however, many leading organisational behaviour experts have argued that a particular method or style of managing conflicts may be regarded as being functional or dysfunctional depending upon the prevailing situational variables.[19] Therefore, Robbins[20] suggested that for the effective management of conflicts, one conflict handling style or method may be considered more effective than another depending upon the situation. Similarly, Van de Vliert *et al.*,[21] viewed that appropriate conflict management "can best be determined in the light of situational realities." Thus, according to the contingency viewpoints regarding conflict management, the manager must try to identify and analyse the situational factors or variables before choosing the most appropriate style of conflict management to be used in a particular conflict situation. Although different contingency theorists have suggested and analysed different sets of situational variables influencing the choice of most appropriate or most effective conflict management methods, it is significant to note that it has not been possible so far to develop a well-accepted contingency theory of conflict management. In the light of these observations, an attempt has been made in this section to review the existing literature regarding various contingency approaches to conflict management, as suggested by leading management experts.

## Blake and Mouton

In their Managerial Grid, Blake and Mouton[22] explained managerial behaviour in terms of two dimensions: concern for production, and concern for people. Along these two dimensions of human behaviour, they enumerated five methods of handling conflicts such as problem-solving, smoothing, compromise, withdrawing and forcing. According to Blake and Mouton,[23] an individual's managerial styles including his styles of managing conflicts as mentioned above are determined by certain forces and pressures including those arising (1) from within himself such as his family and cultural background, personality traits, value system, etc.; (2) from the immediate external surrounding or situation; and (3) from the organisational characteristics such as established practices or procedures, traditions, etc. Blake and Mouton[24] stated that every individual has a dominant style of conflict management which he tends to use habitually or continuously. However, when the dominant style of managing conflicts fails to work in a particular situation, he tends to fall back upon a back-up style. The fact that an individual is driven by a dominant style of managing conflicts in a particular situation is determined by one or more of the situational variables as described above.

In addition, Blake and Mouton[25] put forth his viewpoints regarding the effectiveness or ineffectiveness of different conflict management styles or methods as enumerated by him. When the problem solving approach is used by the conflicting parties in a genuine sense through open exchange of viewpoints and opinions, it helps in eliminating their personal bias or prejudices against one another and thus leads to the creative solution of conflicts in organisations. This process ultimately helps to achieve organisational objectives while at the same time promoting sound human relations in an organisation. Although the smoothing approach helps in ensuring harmonious working relationships in an organisation, it often stifles creativity and innovation. As a result, the real problems or issues that require open discussion or exchange of views are set aside, thus leading to possible losses in productivity. Compromising as a method of managing conflicts is less likely to lead to significant innovation or creativity in an organisation. It often promotes small improvements that do not move far away from the current ways of doing things. The use of withdrawing mode of resolving conflicts does not lead to individual or organisational growth. Such withdrawing behaviour not only reflects on an individual's apathetic attitude towards organisational goals but also appears to be a failure for the organisation as individual efforts are not properly and adequately integrated with sound human relations in the organisation. At the end, it may be stated that although the forcing behaviour sometimes proves to be effective in resolving conflicts, it often does not remove the underlying sources or causes of conflict. Thus, unresolved conflicts are likely to surface again and thereby affect cooperative relationships and obstruct the attainment of organisation's objectives.

## Thomas

A two-dimensional model of conflict behaviour was developed by Thomas[26] on the basis of two independent dimensions of interpersonal behaviour: (i) assertiveness defined as behaviour intended to satisfy one's own concerns; and (2) cooperativeness defined as behaviour intended to satisfy another's concerns. Along these two dimensions of assertiveness and cooperativeness, Thomas enumerated five different conflict management strategies that included avoiding, accommodating, compromising, competing, and collaborating. In regard to the efficacy or effectiveness of different conflict handling behaviours, Thomas observed that although people typically have a preferred conflict resolution style, different conflict management styles were most useful in different situations. The avoiding style may be appropriate when the conflict or controversy is trivial, when victory is impossible or when someone else is in a better position to solve the problem. However, in many situations, this approach is a weak or ineffective one to be adopted. The accommodating style of conflict management is high on cooperativeness (but not on assertiveness), indicating a willingness to meet other's needs at the expense of one's own needs. Although the accommodating style is not likely to yield the best possible outcomes, but seems appropriate when the issues are more important to the other party or when peace is more valuable than winning. People who prefer a compromising style try to find a solution that will at least partially satisfy the needs of each party involved in the conflict. This approach is particularly useful when there is a prolonged deadlock over the conflict or when there is a deadline to be met. The competing style can be particularly useful when there is an emergency and the decision has to be made fast. However, this approach can make people feel dissatisfied and resentful when it is used in less urgent situations. People who are highly assertive as well as cooperative tend to use the collaborating style with a view to meeting the needs of all people or parties involved. The collaborating style is most effective when divergent viewpoints have to be considered or put together in order to get the best possible solution.

It is equally significant to know that Thomas[27] also proposed a structural model of dyadic conflict that explains the pressures and constraints acting upon the parties involved in a conflict. According to Thomas,[28] the conflict handling behaviour of each party is determined by four types of such pressures and constraints (described by Thomas as "structure variables": (1) behavioural predispositions; (2) social pressure; (3) incentive structure; and (4) rules and procedures. In the first place, the parties in conflict have certain behavioural predispositions that emanate partly from their motives and abilities. Second, both the parties involved in conflict operate under certain pressures from their social surrounding or environment. Third, the parties have certain conflict of interest or stakes in their relationship and, therefore, respond to the incentive structure existing in the conflict situation. Fourth, the parties function within a framework of rules and procedures constraining their behaviour such as negotiating procedures, procedures for third party involvement and decision rules.

## Rahim

Rahim and Bonoma[29] differentiated the conflict handling styles on the basis of two dimensions: (1) concern for self; and (2) concern for others. The first dimension explains the degree to which an individual attempts to satisfy his own concern while the second one explains the degree to which an individual seeks to satisfy the concern of others. Along these two dimensions of human behaviour, Rahim and Bonoma[30] enumerated five styles of handling interpersonal conflict such as integrating, obliging, dominating, avoiding, and compromising. All these five styles and the specific situations in which they are considered appropriate or inappropriate are shown in Table 8.1. As discussed by Rahim[31] (1985), the integrating style is suitable for dealing with complex issues that require the integration or combination of skills, information and ideas possessed by different parties so as to develop better solutions to a problem. This style is also useful for dealing with strategic issues related to long-range planning, organisational objectives and policies, etc. It may be noted, however, that the integrating style is considered inappropriate when there is no time for problem solving or when the task or problem involved is relatively trivial or simple, or when the other parties do not have sufficient training and experience required for problem solving. The obliging style is appropriate when the party does not possess adequate knowledge regarding the issues involved or when the issues are more important to the other party. This style of handling conflicts may be suitable when the person is dealing from a weaker position or when he believes that maintaining relationship with the other party is important. The obliging style, however, seems to be inappropriate when the issue involved is important to the party himself. It may also be appropriate when the party believes that the other party is wrong or unethical. It may be noted that the dominating style appears to be effective when the issues are important to the party itself or when certain unpopular schemes or ideas have to be implemented. This style may also be used for dealing with routine matters or when fast decision making is required. However, the dominating style may prove to be inappropriate when certain complex

**Table 8.1:** Styles of handling interpersonal conflict and situations where they are appropriate or inappropriate

| Conflict style | Situations when appropriate | Situations when inappropriate |
|---|---|---|
| Integrating | 1. Issues are complex<br>2. Synthesis of ideas is needed to come up with better solutions.<br>3. Commitment is needed from other parties for successful implementation.<br>4. Time is available for problem solving.<br>5. One party alone cannot solve the problem.<br>6. Resources possessed by different parties are needed to solve their common problems. | 1. Task or problem is simple.<br>2. Immediate decision is required.<br>3. Other parties are unconcerned about the outcome.<br>4. Other parties do not have problem-solving skills. |
| Obliging | 1. You believe that you may be wrong.<br>2. Issue is more important to the other party.<br>3. You are willing to give up something in exchange for something from the other party in the future.<br>4. You are dealing from a position of weakness.<br>5. Preserving relationship is important. | 1. Issue is important to you.<br>2. You believe that you are right.<br>3. The other party is wrong or unethical. |
| Dominating | 1. Issue is trivial.<br>2. Speedy decision is needed.<br>3. Unpopular course of action is implemented.<br>4. Necessary to overcome assertive subordinates.<br>5. Unfavourable decision by the other party may be costly to you.<br>6. Subordinates lack expertise to make technical decisions.<br>7. Issue is important to you. | 1. Issue is complex.<br>2. Issue is not important to you.<br>3. Both parties are equally powerful.<br>4. Decision does not have to be made quickly.<br>5. Subordinates possess high degree of competence. |
| Avoiding | 1. Issue is trivial.<br>2. Potential dysfunctional effect of confronting the other party outweighs benefits of resolution.<br>3. Cooling-off period is needed. | 1. Issue is important to you.<br>2. It is your responsibility to make decision.<br>3. Parties are unwilling to defer; issue must be resolved.<br>4. Prompt attention is needed. |
| Compromising | 1. Goals of parties are mutually exclusive.<br>2. Parties are equally powerful.<br>3. Consensus cannot be reached.<br>4. Integrating or dominating style is not successful.<br>5. Temporary solution to a complex problem is needed. | 1. One party is more powerful.<br>2. Problem is complex enough, needing problem-solving approach. |

*Source:* Rahim, M.A., (1983). *Rahim organizational conflict inventories: Professional manual*. Palo Alto, CA: Consulting Psychologists Press, p. 21. Reprinted with permission.

issues are involved in the conflict situation, and enough time is available for making a sound decision. Similarly, the use of this style may be resisted by subordinates who possess high level of job competence or expertise. The avoiding style of handling conflict may be effectively used to deal with minor or trivial issues or when a cooling off period is required before certain complex problems or issues can be dealt with. This style is, however, inappropriate when the party is responsible for making some decisions or when quick action is needed. The compromising style may be used effectively when the parties are equally powerful and have reached a deadlock in their negotiations. Since the parties could not reach any consensus, they have to make compromise in order to find some temporary solution to a complex issue. The compromising style is, however, not suitable for handling complex problems or issues that require the use of the problem-solving approach. Similarly, this style may be inappropriate if one party is stronger than the other and believes that its stand is always right.

### Pareek

Pareek[32] proposed a contingency model of approach-avoidance modes of conflict management. According to him, there are two dimensions which influence the choice of a particular conflict management mode: integration of the in-group and criticality of the conflict issues. These two dimensions may vary from low to high as shown in Figure 8.1. It may be further observed that the approach modes of conflict management (including compromise, arbitration, and negotiation) become more and more useful or appropriate as both these dimensions increase. However, when there is a decrease in either or both of these two dimensions, avoidance modes (including resignation, withdrawal, diffusion, appeasement, and flight) become more and more important. Pareek's contingency model of conflict management further signifies that a group may begin with the adoption of an appropriate conflict management mode and then gradually move towards the negotiating mode by strengthening itself on both the dimensions: in-group integration and criticality of the conflict issue. In fact, the negotiation mode is considered the most appropriate for managing conflicts, as it can be seen in Figure 8.1. The negotiation mode is usually approached by a conflicting group through compromise or through arbitration by a third party.

### Philip and Cheston

Philip and Cheston[33] studied 52 incidents of conflict, the methods used to resolve these conflicts, and the effectiveness of these conflict resolution methods. They noticed that there was no "bad result" in 12 incidents in which problem-solving was used. However, there were 11 bad results out of 23 incidents in the use of forcing method, 2 out of 5 in compromise and 10 out of 12 in avoidance. In addition, Philip and Cheston[34] found that problem-solving and forcing were the most important methods of conflict resolution. The problem-solving method was most effective under such conditions as

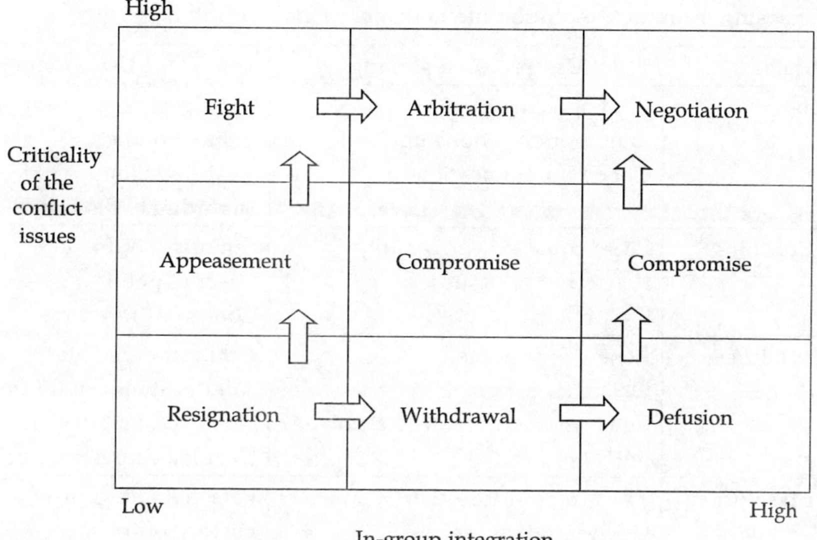


**Figure 8.1:** Contingency model of approach-avoidance modes of conflict management
*Source*: Pareek, U. *et.al.*, *Managing Conflict and Collaboration*, Oxford-IBH, New Delhi, 1982, p. 42.

interdependence, open-minded attitudes, mutual awareness of conflicts, willingness to ignore power issues, and the existing problem-solving procedures. On the other hand, forcing was effective when organisational objectives and policies supported one solution, in-work value conflicts, and refusal to cooperate because of old issues. Phillip and Cheston[35] suggested that the following situational indicators were responsible for the choice of problem solving and forcing methods, as shown in Table 8.2.

## Derr

Derr[36] suggested three important methods of conflict resolution: power play, bargaining and collaboration. According to him, power play may be seen as a means for achieving a dynamic balance of competing forces. In fact, power-play is often the only possible way to resolve ideological disputes. The bargaining method seems to be most effective in establishing power parity among the competing groups or people. It is often utilised as a means of distributing scarce resources of the organisation and is most useful in reaching a formal agreement to a common dispute. Collaboration may be most effectively used when work relationships are likely to be affected by unresolved disputes, and when the parties in conflict are willing to confront their differences and resolve them.

Thus, in the preceding discussion, an attempt has been made to present and explain certain contingency approaches for managing organisational conflicts. In these approaches, the authors have basically suggested certain methods or styles of managing conflicts in organisations and also described the specific situations where

**Table 8.2:** Choosing a conflict resolution method: situational indicators

| Indicator | Use problem-solving | Use forcing |
|---|---|---|
| Conflict issues | Goal agreement<br>Joint work relationship<br>Good communication | "One best way"<br>Values conflict<br>Scarce resources<br>Subordinate discipline |
| Power relationships | Peers equal power coalition<br>Power not an issue | Senior-subordinate<br>unequal political power<br>Control of resources |
| Existing procedures | Renew committee<br>Objective criteria<br>Equal representation of involved parties | Arbitration method<br>Adjudication Committee<br>No agreement on criteria<br>Unequal representation of parties |
| Climate for resolution | Trust, regard for others<br>Open-mindedness<br>History of problem solving<br>No previous history of conflict<br>Group goals oriented to corporate goals | Personal antagonism<br>History of forcing<br>Continuing and bitter conflict<br>Strong adversary relationship |
| Potential for recurrence of conflict | Conflict inherent in structure of situation<br>Need for ongoing conflict resolution | Eliminate recurrence by task change or removal or transfer of personnel |

*Source*: Udai Pareek, *et al.*, *Managing Conflict and Collaboration*, New Delhi: Oxford-IBH (1982): pp. 43-44.

these methods would be appropriate or inappropriate. Thus, according to the contingency viewpoint, there is no best style of managing conflicts and, in fact, different methods or styles may be considered effective or ineffective depending upon the prevailing situational variables or factors. This contingency approach for conflict management has been supported by both theoretical perspectives provided by management experts and the research evidences provided by researchers on the efficacy or effectiveness of various conflict management styles or methods. In spite of the accumulating body of knowledge regarding the contingency perspectives on conflict management, the fact remains that a well-accepted contingency theory of conflict management is yet to be developed in the management literature. In this context, it must be emphasized that there is a need to conduct many more research studies focusing on the role of specific organisational, psychosocial and other contingency variables impacting the effectiveness or ineffectiveness of various conflict management methods or styles.

## 8.5 A CONTINGENCY FRAMEWORK FOR ANALYSING CONFLICT MANAGEMENT ISSUES

The present section is devoted to an analysis of various conflict management issues in a contingency framework, as described by Beres and Schmidt.[37] This analysis can be regarded as an extension of previous reviews of conflict research,[38] through the association of conflict management issues with specific conflict contingencies. The present analysis is based on the definition of conflict as "incompatible differences" existing between individuals or parties,[39] or as the process through which latent incompatibilities are perceived and acted upon.[40] This interaction perspective of conflict emphasises upon incompatible differences between people and thus leads to identification of three general elements in the conflict situation : parties, some kind of discord, and causes. In addition, all conflicts occur in some social context, and are also concerned with certain functional and normative issues that reflect values. Thus, social context and values should also be regarded as two additional general elements in the conflict situation. These five elements involved in a conflict situation provide a contingency framework for analysing various conflicts and conflict management issues.

The dominant themes in conflict research in four different settings (social, international, industrial, and organisational) in terms of the five general elements of conflict as described above, have been presented in Table 8.3.[41] This Table also identifies major conflict management concerns existing in the four different settings. It can be seen that the commonalities and differences identified in this comparative study provide a contingency description of conflict that includes five general elements and their alternative manifestations. Parties range from individuals to large groups or classes. Stages of discord vary from incompatible differences to overt interference behaviour. Causes include conditions that lead to incompatible differences, perception of differences and dominant behaviour shown by the parties. Social contexts range along two dimensions: stage of development, and dominant norms of interaction. Social contexts vary, developmentally, from established and acceptable relationships to unacceptable relationships. However, from normative point of view, social contexts range from cooperative to adversarial interaction patterns. Values also range along two dimensions: outcome values, and process values. Outcome values vary in terms of the preferred beneficiary whose interests are served due to the interaction -self, other, relationship, or system. Process values are concerned with the outcomes of an interaction and emphasise upon distributive and integrative modes of handling conflicts.[42]

It may be noted that Beres and Schmidt[43] classified the above-mentioned five general elements of a conflict situation into two different categories: process contingencies, and structural contingencies. While the process contingencies include parties and stages of discord, the structural contingencies include causes, social context, and values. Although Beres and Schmidt[44] analysed the conflict management issues from a contingency perspective in four different settings (social, international, industrial, and organisational), the present discussion is limited to an analysis of such conflict issues in the organisational setting only.

**Table 8.3:** Dominant themes in conflict research specific to setting

| Elements of Conflicts | Research Settings | | | |
|---|---|---|---|---|
| | Social | International | U.S. Industrial | Organisational |
| Parties | Interest groups<br>Classes | Nations<br>National elites | Organized labour/ management groups | Individuals<br>Small groups<br>Groups represented by individuals |
| Stages of discord | Interference behaviour<br>Incompatible differences | Interference behaviour<br>Incompatible differences | Interference behaviour<br>Incompatible differences | Incompatible differences<br>Process composed of stages<br>Interference behaviour |
| Causes | Dominance resulting in scarcity of positions and resources | Scarcity of resources<br>Ideological differences<br>Dominance | Structural differentiation | Perception<br>Differentiation<br>Communication<br>Personality differences |
| Social context | Established societal system | Loosely defined and flexible community | Established adversarial system | Established cooperative system |
| Values | Clarification of group identity<br>Social change<br>System maintenance | Advancement of national or subnational interests | Resolution of disputes<br>Reduction of latent tension<br>Organisational maintenance | Innovation<br>Organisational change<br>Organizational maintenance |
| Conflict management concerns | Mobilization of groups<br>Social control<br>Management of power | Prevention of war<br>Development of alternatives to war | Balance of power<br>Collective bargaining | Managing perceptions<br>Strategies for handling incompatible differences<br>Problem solving |

*Source*: Beres , M.E. and Schmidt, S.M., The conflict carousal : A contingency approach to conflict management, G.B.J. Bomers and R.B. Peterson, (Ed.), *Conflict Management and Industrial Relations*, Nijhoff Publishing, Boston, 1982, p. 46.

## Process Contingencies

As mentioned earlier, process contingencies affect the internal dynamics of a conflict episode. While the conflict or conflict management behaviours depend upon the types of parties involved in a conflict situation, the differences in the stages of discord affect the decision-making issues related to the conflict events or situations. In other words, the process contingencies raise certain conflict management issues, depending upon the types of parties involved in conflict and the timing of an interaction strategy.

**Parties:** The parties in conflict vary from independent individuals to large groups. As groups comprise of individuals, the conflicts always involve psychological and interpersonal aspects which influence the actions of individuals. Therefore, the literature on conflict management emphasises upon the processes of perception, attribution, and communication. When the individuals function in groups, intragroup processes become active and are added to the psychological and interpersonal influences already in action. In this context, the social conflict theorists have focused upon the significance of mobilisation processes through which energies of individuals are focused into collective effort. As the mobilisation process involves unification and direction of individual efforts, the development and maintenance of cohesiveness and leadership are additional conflict management issues in group conflict episodes.[46]

**Stages of discord:** As stated earlier, a conflict starts with incompatible differences and will lead to interference behaviour if such differences are not resolved. At the early stage, a suitable strategy is to be selected for handling incompatible differences.[47] The parties involved in conflict are free to choose any of the available strategies. The parties may decide to: (1) terminate conflict by withdrawing from the conflict situation; (2) to submit to the other party thereby allowing the latent conflict to remain and reappear at a later stage; (3) pursue goals at the cost of the other party so that the conflict escalates further; and (4) collaborate to achieve a solution acceptable to both the parties, thereby ending the conflict altogether. It may be noted, however, that if the conflict is allowed to escalate to interference behaviour, the managers have to select and make appropriate use of conflict tactics. Such selection of conflict tactics involves cost-benefit analysis in order to determine how alternative tactics will promote the interests of a party.[48] Thus, the parties will become committed to a particular course of action as conflict increases. Therefore, appropriate intervention behaviours are required to influence the choice of strategies at the early stage of a conflict episode and the choice of tactics if interference behaviour has already occurred.

## Structural Contingencies

Structural contingencies refer to the conditions prevailing in a conflict situation that influence the conflict process itself and also the management of conflict. Causes are the specific conditions in individuals and in the environment that create conflict. Social contexts are the conditions in the environment that reduce, intensify or control the expression of conflicts. Values are intra-individual conditions that provide justification for certain strategies or tactics to be used to handle incompatible differences. The causes determine the specific issues involved in a conflict while social contexts and values determine the socially and individually desired approaches towards the management of conflicts.

**Causes:** The research studies have identified the causes leading to the perception of conflict or incompatible differences as well as to the adoption of interference behaviour. There are a number of environmental and interpersonal conditions that lead to incompatible differences. Structural differentiation and personality differences can generate inconsistent goals or expectations.[49] In fact, the resolution of these conditions relates to the issues of coordination and interpersonal development, respectively. Scarcity can be a cause of conflict when the total available resources cannot fulfil the needs of interdependent parties.[50] The resolution of this conflict situation can be regarded as an issue of distribution. Ideology causes conflict when parties with incompatible worldviews seek to impose their ideas on each other.[51] In this case, commitment to a certain ideology can neutralise the influence of interdependence and lead to the use of socially undesirable tactics. The resolution of this ideology-based conflict can be regarded as an issue of power. Dominance represents unequal distribution of power that can produce incompatible differences. Since power distribution is involved in this case, the management of dominance is clearly an issue of power. Aggression dispositions can be another cause of conflict which leads to interference behaviour directly. Aggression is an unique condition that resides within an individual or party rather than in the relationship between the parties, and it is satisfied only by continued conflict behaviour. In this case, conflict management involves the treatment to eliminate the dispositions or channel the conflict behaviour in socially acceptable direction.

**Social contexts:** Social contexts refer to the network of relationships within which conflicts arise. In fact, the social contexts can vary depending upon the developmental level and the dominant norms. As explained by Thibaut and Kelly[53] model of norm formation, norms do not exist in a newly formed social relationship. Therefore, the parties need to use their personal influence to negotiate over incompatible differences and reach a settlement. In a developing social context, the conflict management issues will revolve around power while in established social relations, the earlier agreements are institutionalized into shared norms that facilitate social control over interactions between the parties. In established social contexts, conflict management is based upon the appropriate application of institutionalized control procedures. In this context, it may be stated that the dominant norms for interaction can vary among established social contexts or relationships. As suggested by Bonoma,[54] when one party dominates, conflict involves the direct use of power. When the parties have counterbalancing power, conflict is controlled by mutually accepted rules.[55] When the parties have mutually valued relationship, conflict will be controlled by such relationship between them. Therefore, it must be emphasized that the dominance structure of social context is related to various issues of conflict and its management.

**Values:** Thomas[56] and Thomas *et al.*[57] made systematic attempts to identify the impact of values on conflict and conflict management. In Thomas's[58] model, the values have been classified into outcome preferences and process preferences. According to him, outcome values are related to the strategies for managing conflicts. While self-interest leads to efforts to dominate, other interest leads to appeasement and relationship interest leads to joint outcome strategies. A party with system interest will select a conflict management strategy depending upon the social context. In terms of process values, the parties will prefer either integrative modes or distributive modes of managing conflicts. In this regard, it may be further stated that if the value systems of the parties are complementary, they will pursue complementary strategies. If their value systems are parallel, both of them will use the same strategies. On the other hand, if the value systems of the parties are opposing in nature, their conflict will have both substantial and procedural levels.

## 8.6 SUMMARY AND CONCLUSION

This chapter focuses on certain contingency perspectives on the management of organisational conflict. The contingency approach to management emerged primary due to certain limitations of classical organisation theories such as Taylor's[59] scientific management theory, Weber's[60] bureaucracy, and so on. These theories simply emphasised upon the improvement of organisational efficiency and productivity, scientific selection and training of employees, rationality, efficiency in administration, and so on. They failed to recognise the fact that the organisation's structure, processes, technology, etc., were influenced by various forces and pressures operating in the environment. Some of the classic and pioneering studies on the contingency relationship between the organisation and its environment were made during the late 1950s and the 1960s by Woodward, Burns and Stacker, Thompson, and Lawrence and Lorsch . Since then, many other contingency studies have continued to pour in and contribute to the development of the contingency theory of management. This theory essentially seeks to analyse various internal organisational changes or adjustments that do take place as the organisation attempts to meet the changing demands of its internal and external environments.

It may be pointed out that the contingency approaches to management have had their visible impact in the area of organisational conflict and its management too. The normative theories of conflict management generally argued in favour of one best style of conflict management. Therefore, many empirical research studies were made by experts to examine the relative effectiveness or ineffectiveness of various conflict management methods or styles. The results of these studies broadly indicate that problem solving should be seen as the best style of managing conflicts and it is followed by smoothing behaviour. In contrast to these normative viewpoints regarding conflict management, the contingency theorists have argued that different conflict management methods should be seen as effective or ineffective depending upon the prevailing situational variables. As discussed earlier, some of the well-known contingency approaches to conflict management in organisations were made by such famous authors as Blake and Mouton, Rahim, Pareek, Philip and Cheston, and so on. These contingency approaches to conflict and its management have been corroborated by both theoretical knowledge and the valuable findings of empirical research studies.

In addition, it may be pointed out that the present chapter provids an immensely useful analysis of various conflict and its management issues in a contingency framework, as suggested by Beres and Schmidt.[61] The contingency perspective on conflict and its management builds upon the previous contributions of such famous theorists as Pondy,[62] Fink,[63] Thomas,[64] Kilmann and Thomas,[65] and so on. The contingency description includes an analysis of both process contingencies (i.e., parties and stages of discord) and structural contingencies (i.e., causes of conflict, social context, and values) prevailing in a conflict situation that significantly influences the conflict process itself as well as various conflict management issues. In spite of such valuable contributions of leading contingency theorists in the areas of conflict and conflict management, the fact remains that it has not been possible so far to develop a well established theory of conflict management in organisations. In fact, there is a need to conduct many more meaningful research studies of conflict management styles or methods and their efficacy or effectiveness in the context of various organisational, psychosocial, and other contingency variables.

## REVIEW QUESTIONS

1. The contingency theory of management developed essentially due to certain limitations of the classical organisation theories. Do you agree?
2. Several contingency approaches to management were developed by management experts during the 1960s. Discuss.
3. Explain the contingency theory of management and its implications.
4. Discuss the contributions of well-known organisation theorists towards the development of the contingency approaches to conflict management.
5. Analyse the dominant themes in conflict research within the contingency framework suggested by Beres and Schmidt.

## REFERENCES


1. Khandwall, P., *The Design of Organisations,* Harcourt Brace Tavanovich, New York, 1977, p. 248.
2. Weber, M., *The Theory of Economic and Social Organisation*, Trans. AM Henderson and Talcott Parsons, New York, 1947.
3. Taylor, F.W., The Principles of Scientific Management, New York, 1911.

4. Woodward, J., *Industrial Organisation: Theory and Practice*, Oxford University Press, London, 1965; Burns. T. and Stalker, G.M., *The Management of Innovation*, Tavistock, London, 1961; Thompson, J.D., Organisations in Action, McGraw HIl, New York, 1967; and Lawrence, P. and Lorsch, J., *Organisational Environment: Managing Differentiation and Integration*, Harvard University, Graduate School of Business Administration, Boston, 1967.
5. Woodward, J., 1965, *op. cit.*
6. Burns, T. and Stalker, G.M., 1961, *op. cit.*
7. Weber, M., 1947, *op. cit.*
8. Burns, T. and Stalker, G.M., 1961, *op. cit.*
9. Lawrence, P. and Lorsch, J., 1967, *op. cit.*
10. Fiedler, F.W., The contingency model – New directions for leadership utilisation, *Journal of Contemporary Business*, 1974.
11. *Ibid.*
12. House, R. and Mitchell, T., Path-Goal theory of leadership, Journal of Contemporary Business, 1974.
13. Tannenbaum, R. and Schimdt, W., Retrospective commentary, *Harvard Business Review*, May-June, 1973; Idem, How to choose a leadership pattern, *Harvard Business Review*, March-April, 1958.
14. Luthans, F. and Steward, T., *A general contingency theory of management*, Academy of Management, Review, 2, 1977, p. 187.
15. Katz, D. and Kahn, R.L., *The Social Psychology of Organisations*, (2nd Ed.), John Wiley and Sons, New York, 1978, p. 2.
16. *Ibid*, p. 3.
17. *Ibid*, pp. 124-130.
18. Bruke, R.J., Method of resolving interpersonal conflict, *Personnel Administration*, 32(4), 1969, pp. 48-55; Sharma, R.A. and Samantara, R., Conflict management in an Indian firm: A case study, *Decision*, 21(4), 1994, pp. 235-249; and Samantara, R., Conflict management strategies and orgagnisational effectiveness, *Indian Journal of Industrial Relations*, 39(3), 2004, pp. 298-323.
19. Thomas, K.W., Conflict and conflict management, M.D. Dunettee, (Ed.), *Handbook of Industrial and Organisational Psychology*, Rand McNally, Chicago, 1976, pp. 889-935; Rahim, M.A., A strategy for managing conflict in complex organisations, *Human Relations*, 38(1), 1985, pp. 81-89; and Pareek, U.N., *Managing Conflict and Collaboration*, Oxford & IBH Publishing Company, New Delhi, 1982.
20. Robbins, S.P., *Managing Conflicts: A Non-traditional Approach*, Prentice Hall, NJ, 1974.

21. Van de Vliert, E., Nauta, A., Giebels, E. and Janssen, O., Constructive conflict at work, *Journal of Organisational Behaviour*, 20(4), 1999, pp. 475-491.
22. Blake, R.R. and Mouton, J.S., *The Managerial Grid*, Gulf Publishing, Houston, 1964.
23. *Ibid.*
24. *Ibid.*
25. *Ibid.*
26. Thomas, K.W., 1976, *op. cit.*
27. *Ibid.*
28. *Ibid.*
29. Rahim, M.A. and Bonoma, T.V., Managing organisational conflict: A model for diagnosis and intervention, *Psychological Reports*, 44(3), 1979, pp. 1323-1344.
30. *Ibid.*
31. Rahim, M.A., A strategy for managing conflict in complex organisations, *Human Relations*, 38(1), 1985, pp. 81-89.
32. Pareek, U.N., 1982, *op. cit.*
33. Philips, E., and Cheston, R., Conflict resolution: What works?, *California Management Review*, 21(4), 1979, pp. 76-83.
34. *Ibid.*
35. *Ibid.*
36. Derr, C.B., Managing organisational conflict: Collaboration, bargaining and power approaches, *California Management Review*, 21(2), 1978, pp. 76-83.
37. Beres, M.E., and Schmidt, S.M., The social carousal: A contingency approach to conflict management, G.B.J. Bomers and R.B. Peterson, (Ed.), *Conflict Management and Industrial Relations*, Nijhoff Publishing, Boston, 1982, pp. 37-59.
38. Fink, C.F., Some conceptual difficulties in the theory of social conflict, *Journal of Conflict Resolution*, 12, 1968, pp. 412-460; Thomas, K.W., 1976, *op. cit.*; and Kilmann, R.H., and Thomas, K.W., Four perspectives on conflict management: An attributional framework organising descriptive and normative theory, Academy of *Management Review*, 3, 1978, pp. 59-68.
39. Thomas, K.W., Introduction, *California Management Review*, 21, 1967.
40. Pondy, L.R., Organisational conflict: Concepts and models, *Administrative Science Quarterly*, 12, 1967, pp. 296-320.
41. Beres, M.E. and Schmidt, S.M., 1982, *op. cit.*
42. Thomas, K.W., 1976, *op. cit.*
43. Beres, M.E. and Schmidt, S.M., 1982, *op. cit.*
44. *Ibid.*

45. Oberschall, A., Theories of social conflict, *Annual Review of Sociology*, 4, 1978, pp. 291-315.
46. Blake, R.R., and Mouton, J.S., Reactions to intergroup competition under win-lose conditions, *Management Science*, 7, 1961, pp. 420-435.
47. Derr, C.B., 1978, *op. cit.* and Kilmann, R.H. and Thomas, K.W., 1978, *op. cit.*
48. Kipnis, D., Schmidt, S. and Wilkinson, I., Interorganisational influence tactics: Explorations in getting one's way, *Journal of Applied Psychology*, 65, 1980, pp. 440-452.
49. March, J.G., and Simon, H.A., *Organisations*, Wiley, New York, 1958.
50. Schmidt, S.M., and Kochan, T.A., Conflict: Towards conceptual clarity, *Administrative Science Quarterly*, 17, 1972, pp. 359-370.
51. Converse, E., The war of all against all, *Journal of Conflict Resolution*, 16, 1972, pp. 471-550.
52. Caser, L., *Functions of Social Conflict*, Free Press, New York, 1956.
53. Thibaut, J.W., and Kelley, H.H., *The Social Psychology of Groups*, Wiley, New York, 1959.
54. Bonoma, T., Conflict, cooperation and trust in three power systems, *Behavioural Science*, 21, 1976, pp. 499-514.
55. Kerr, C. Industrial conflict and its mediation, *American Journal of Sociology*, 60, 1954, pp. 230-245.
56. Thomas, K.W., 1976, *op. cit.*; and Thomas, K.W., Towards an evaluative paradigm of conflict management within organisations, *Twenty-fourth International Meeting of the Institute of Management Science*, Honolulu, 1979.
57. Thomas, K.D., Jamieson, D.W., and Moore, R.K.., Conflict and collaboration: Some concluding observations, *California Management Review*, 21, 1978, pp. 56-60.
58. Thomas, K.W., 1976, *op. cit.*
59. Taylor, F.W., 1911, *op. cit.*
60. Weber, M., 1947, *op. cit.*
61. Beres, M.E., and Schmidt, S.M., 1982, *op. cit.*
62. Pondy, L.R., 1967, *op. cit.*
63. Fink, C.F., 1968, *op. cit.*
64. Thomas, K.W., 1976, *op. cit*; and Thomas, K.W., Introduction, *California Management Review*, 21, 1978, pp. 56-60.
65. Kilmann, R.H., and Thomas, K.W., 1978, *op. cit.*

# 9

# Ethical and Cultural Issues in Conflict Management

## 9.1 INTRODUCTION

The issue of ethical behaviour in organisations should be seen as more than a subject of academic interest as the growing body of literature shows that unethical business practices have adverse effects on the profitability of business firms.[1] Kotey and Meredith[2] noted that business firms whose managers or leaders have no respect for the values of honesty and truth are lower performing than firms whose leaders value honesty and truth adequately. In spite of the importance of ethics and morality in organisations, the fact remains that ethical values have not been adequately explored in the area of conflict management in organisations. Soutar *et al.*,[3] reported that about 75% of managers report conflicts related to ethics. The inappropriate application of conflict management styles or methods may intensify an existing conflict or create one that was not existing before. As suggested by Rahim, Garrett and Buntzman,[4] positive results for organisations are associated with ethical rather than unethical applications of certain styles of handling conflict. Although managers have to deal with different conflict situations on a day-to-day basis, there is an absence of explicit guidelines to help them to do their jobs ethically. In view of this, the present chapter provides some guidelines so that the organisation's members can handle different conflict situations with their seniors, subordinates, and peers effectively and ethically. More specifically, the chapter examines certain ethical issues involved in conflict and its management. This chapter also discusses the specific situations where the use of different conflict management styles will be considered ethically appropriate or inappropriate. In addition, it discusses certain ethical criteria or considerations that might be borne in mind while choosing appropriate strategies to be used for managing cross-cultural ethical conflicts. It may be further noted that the second part of this chapter analyses certain cultural issues involved in conflict situations in organisations along with the management aspects of multicultural group conflict, as would be seen later.

## 9.2 CONCEPTUAL MEANINGS OF ETHICS AND MORALITY

The term 'ethics' derives from the Greek word 'ethikos', and it signifies the existence of certain norms or codes of conduct. As explained by Rahim,[5] while morality refers to certain rules and standards of conduct in a society and is concerned with practices defining right and wrong, the term 'ethics' is often restricted to rules and norms relating to specific codes of conduct for specialised groups. Applied to organisations, the concept of ethics refers to various guidelines, principles and codes of conduct which determine the manner in which the members of an organisation should behave at the workplace. In a broader sense, organisational ethics include policies, procedures, and culture of doing the right things in the face of various challenging and often controversial organisational, social, and environmental issues. In view of the importance of the concept, ethical behaviour in organisations has been a central theme of study for both academicians and practising managers

## 9.3 ETHICAL ISSUES IN CONFLICT

As the business activities have expanded significantly cutting across national boundaries, it has been noticed that conflicts have developed over certain ethical issues in organisations such as product safety, financial reporting, treatment of employees, protection of the environment, etc. The experts and social scientists have, therefore, emphasized upon the significance of such concepts or issues as protection of consumer rights, transparent accounting systems, human and democratic approach towards employees, sustainable development, contribution towards social welfare, and so on. In fact, these ethical issues and challenges have arisen due to a number of individual, social, cultural, and organisational factors. The increasing emphasis on ethical values in organisations is manifested in the form of many scholarly writings on this subject. In addition, many research studies have focused on the differences in ethics and moral reasoning in a cross-cultural context. According to organisational behaviour experts, the international transactions of corporate entities have significantly increased over the years and led to many ethics based conflicts across different cultures. In fact, these differences or conflicts have occurred over a number of ethical concerns or issues affecting the broader society and can be attributed mainly to different social and cultural factors across nations.[6] Therefore, many organisational behaviour experts have attempted to address these challenges regarding the ethical norms or codes of conduct to be followed by decision makers in multinational corporations (MNCs). While some authors have proposed certain broad moral values that can be applied equally to all MNCs,[7] it must be noted that these universal norms or codes of conduct have been criticized as being too narrow, abstract, and insensitive to other possible ethical perspectives and practical considerations.[8] In fact, the more recent empirical studies of cross-cultural ethics point to the existence of different ethical standards or values across national cultures on a number of specific issues such as financial reporting, bribery, software piracy, and certain other business practices. Thus, it must be pointed out that cross-cultural differences in ethics have made it difficult to develop universal moral standards that can be applied across national frontiers. While certain general ethical standards or principles may be shared across cultures, cross-cultural differences in ethics are bound to exist over particular issues.

The management theoreticians and researchers have presented their theories and research findings in order to explain ethical behaviour in competitive interactions or conflicts. One approach has attempted to define and explain certain basic values and value systems which give rise to unethical behaviour in conflict situations. The second approach attempts to explain personality types or styles that may be responsible for unethical conduct in conflict situations. Finally, the third approach has endeavoured to describe both similarities and differences in individual approach towards conflicts and their management. The research findings of some studies conducted on these three different approaches may be presented as given below.

**Individual values and value systems:** It may be mentioned that two major research efforts have been made regarding the nature of individual values and value systems. Rokeach[9] suggested that values refer to "enduring beliefs that a specific mode of conduct or end-state of existence is personally or socially preferable to an opposite or converse mode of conduct or end-state of existence". According to Rokeach,[10] values can be classified into two types: terminal and instrumental. While terminal values are end-states that have meaning and significance to individuals, instrumental values refer to the modes of conduct to achieve particular end-states. Rokeach[11] proposed two lists containing eighteen instrumental and terminal values. It is significant to note that subsequent research studies have attempted to relate these two groups of values to researches on individual attitudes and behaviours, political ideologies, and processes of change in values. A similar research effort was made by England,[12] and England, Dhingra, and Agarwal,[13] who classified 66 values into 5 groups : personal goals of individuals, goals of business organisations, groups of people, ideas associated with people, and ideas about general topics. The managers rated these values according to their perceived importance and then proceeded to specify whether a particular value was important because it was right (morale scale), because it was pleasant (feeling scale), or because it contributed to personal success (pragmatic scale). After analysing the priorities assigned by groups and individuals to particular values and the reasons for endorsing these values, England[14] drew conclusions about the values of particular groups and cultures. At this point, it must be mentioned that although the research works of both Rokeach[15] and England[16] enable us to make certain generalizations regarding individual value sets, hierarchies, means-ends concerns, etc., they do not allow us to make precise predictions about ethical judgements in specific situations.

**Personality types and styles:** In regard to the impact of personality types and styles on ethical or unethical conduct in conflict situations, the research efforts made by Bixenstine and his associates[17] may be discussed. The authors have reported about a test developed by them to measure the ethical sensitivity of various participants in competitive decision making. Twenty brief scenarios were presented in which the key actor was asked to choose between pursuing a course of action for ethical or unethical reasons (i.e., personal self-interest versus broad social utilitarianism). These twenty scenarios were counterbalanced in order that half of these depicted the hero figure as male or female. Similarly, half of these scenarios were resolved ethically while the other half were resolved selfishly. For each scenario, the respondent was asked to evaluate his own reaction to the resolution by endorsing one of the four rationales as mentioned below:[18]

1. "Normal" - approval of the ethical hero based on reasonable, workable, equitable standards (act utilitarianism).
2. "Freudian neurotic" - approval of the ethical hero based on adherence to rules or obedience with rules (rule utilitarianism).
3. "Disassociation" - approval of a selfish hero based on a denial of the validity of the conflict situation.
4. "Obsociative" - approval of a selfish hero based on the assertion that selfish choices are really ethical.

According to Bixenstine and his associates,[19] the first two categories represented possible approval of ethical behaviour while the last two largely disapproved of ethical behaviour. It may be further noted that categories one and three measured the relative concern for outcomes based on a pragmatic orientation while categories two and four reflected a strong rule orientation. The authors constructed these two indices to measure relative disposition towards ethicality versus selfishness and relative emphasis on pragmatism versus rule obedience. Although these indices have been employed in a number of subsequent research studies, it must be noted that the results have not been satisfactory.

Another significant research has been conducted by Christie and Geis[20] on the Machiavellian orientation. The researchers created three groups of test items on the basis of the writings of Machiavelli and other similar political philosophies. The first group of test items related to interpersonal tactics or the prescribed ways of dealing with people. The second group reflected perspectives on human nature and human conditions. The third group included certain items or statements regarding morality. It may be noted that the authors developed several forms of the Mach scale through the testing and development of these test items. Each version of the Mach scale was designed to measure a subject's overall agreement with Machiavelli's philosophy and political strategy. Although, the Mach scale has been validated and correlated with measures of attitude, intelligence, personality, etc., there is a need to conduct research on high and low Mach and ethical standards or behaviour.

**Individual differences in conflict management:** It has been extensively discussed earlier that the organisational behaviour experts[21] have proposed different styles or methods of managing conflicts. While the normative theories on conflict management have argued in favour of one best style of managing conflicts, the contingency theorists view that different conflict management styles will be considered effective or ineffective depending upon the prevailing situational factors or variables. Irrespective of these opposite viewpoints on conflict management, the management theorists broadly agree that the conflicting parties exhibit a particular behavioural disposition to use different conflict management styles. These individual differences in conflict management behaviour need to be analysed in the context of ethical concerns of individual parties in conflict. Thomas and Kilman[22] developed an instrument to measure individual dispositions to utilise these conflict management styles and suggested that these styles are effective in different conflict situations. The fact that different types of conflict, different possible resolutions of conflicts, and variations in the effects of such conflict resolutions do exist, individuals with varying preferences for using the conflict management styles or modes will dominate in these situations. In addition, Thomas and Kilman[23] have shown that the use of particular conflict management styles is related to other personality variables too (e.g., high scores on Machiavellianism relate to a preference for utilising the compromising style or behaviour). Although Thomas and Kilman[24] have not discussed the ethical standards or behaviours of individual parties with particular preferred modes of managing conflicts, it is suggested that the specific relationship between preferred conflict management styles and ethical judgement or conduct needs to be investigated.

## 9.4 ETHICS AND CONFLICT MANAGEMENT

The literature on organisational theory has emphasised upon the usefulness or effectiveness of various conflict management styles or methods in different possible circumstances. The research studies on the functionality of conflict management styles or approaches have utilised various criteria of individual, group and organisational effectiveness to form appropriate judgements in this regard. While these approaches to conflict management are most essential from the viewpoint of continued survival and growth of organisations, there is a need to consider certain broader organisational, social, and environmental issues too. To be more specific, there is a need to maintain an appropriate balance between the functional and the ethical aspects of conflict management in organisations. Although the managers have to handle various conflict situations continuously or in a routine manner, it is significant to know that explicit guidelines or codes of conduct do not exist in the literature to help them manage conflicts ethically. In spite of these, an attempt has been made in this section to present or discuss the limited perspectives or viewpoints available on the ethical aspects of conflict management in organisations.

It may be mentioned that Buller, Kohls and Anderson[25] developed a decision-tree model for managing cross-cultural ethical conflict. This model is based on previous theory and research on conflict management[26] and international ethics,[27] and is designed to provide useful aid to decision makers for handling such ethical conflicts. The researchers viewed that the key variables influencing the choice of appropriate strategies for handling such conflicts include power, urgency and moral significance. While power and urgency can be regarded as pragmatic criteria in decision-making, moral significance involves ethical criteria to be followed in the choice of appropriate strategies. It may not be possible to use negotiating, problem-solving and forcing strategies in situations of very low power. However, as power increases, it will become possible to use these strategies. In regard to urgency as a decision variable, the decision-makers' options may be constrained in highly urgent situations. In fact, less urgent situations provide more of time to consider and implement other conflict management strategies. About moral significance, it may be stated that the level of moral significance is determined by two factors: centrality and social consensus. While the centrality of values refers to the importance of the issues to the decision maker and to cross-national cultures, social consensus is concerned with the extent to which a particular value is widely shared within those cultures. Thus, central moral values that are widely shared will be considered high in moral significance. In their decision tree model, Kohls, Buller, and Anderson suggested that the decision-makers should be guided by the following ethical criteria in deciding about the choice of conflict management strategies:

1. The higher the moral significance of the values or standards at stake in the conflict, the more one is justified in pressing for conformity with one's views especially when it appears that the issues have less significance for the other party to the conflict.
2. The less the moral significance, the more one is justified in accommodating or compromising, especially when the issue appears to be highly significant for the other party to the conflict.
3. As far as possible, the position of the other party, especially when it represents fundamental values of the culture, must be treated respectfully. This requires careful listening, empathy and attempting to understand the value priorities of the other party to the conflict.
4. As far as possible, the freedom and autonomy of those who differ should be respected.[28]

Another significant effort has been made by Rahim[29] who discussed five conflict management styles and their ethical appropriateness or inappropriateness in different possible circumstances. Thus, the managers must utilise different conflict handling styles which are not only effective but are also ethical in different situations. The question regarding whether the utilisation of particular conflict management styles is ethical or not is a complex one, and it depends on various factors including the individual motives of managers employing them, the extent to which organisational objectives are being satisfied, satisfaction of the varying claims of organisational stakeholders, the specific situations in which these styles are being used, and so on. All these ethical issues have been addressed by Rahim[30] in a systematic and comprehensive manner, as shown in Table 9.1. In fact, the author discussed five different conflict handling styles such as integrating, obliging, dominating, avoiding and compromising, and the specific situations in which their utilisation will be ethically appropriate or inappropriate.

**Table 9.1:** Ethically appropriate or inappropriate uses of the conflict styles

| Conflict style | Ethically appropriate | Ethically inappropriate |
|---|---|---|
| Integrating | 1. Generally appropriate | |
| Obliging | 1. When a subordinate is in a healthy organization.<br>2. When supervisor has a subordinate with better grasp of what needs to be done. | 1. When subordinates ignore own needs.<br>2. When superior's decisions go against the proper end of the organization.<br>3. When subordinates have the needed expertise. |
| Dominating | 1. When decisions support the organization's proper end.<br>2. When supervisors take into account subordinates' concerns as well as the organization. | 1. When exploitative of others. |
| Avoiding | 1. Temporarily, when other matters have greater moral claim. | 1. When motive is to avoid morally correct but personally painful processes. |
| Compromising | 1. Sometimes when one is a weaker party.<br>2. When required to avoid protracted conflict. | 1. When one is right in principle.<br>2. When one is wrong.<br>3. Compromise of an intellectual sort. |

*Source*: Adapted from Rahim, M.A., Garrett, J.E., & Buntzman, G.F. (1992). Ethics of managing interpersonal conflict in organizations. *Journal of Business Ethics, 11*, pp. 423-432.

**Integrating style:** This style of managing conflicts is considered to be the most ethical one as it treats all parties involved in conflict most respectfully. This style can be adopted most effectively and most ethically only when all the participants possess necessary knowledge, expertise and leadership skills. In reality, however, these ideal conditions do not always exist, and, therefore, a command structure will exist in which the superiors will decide about the tasks to be performed by their subordinates. It is, therefore, necessary for senior managers to take their subordinates into confidence who can really comment upon the adequacy of their judgement and practical reasoning. At the organisation's level, it is also essential to promote wider dialogue and discussions in which various stakeholders including, for example, consumer groups, workers' unions and environmentalists can interact with business leaders.

**Obliging style:** This style of conflict management may be ethically correct in some situations and not in others. As the party in conflict lacks necessary education or expertise to frame organisational policies, it will be most suitable for him to participate only by implementing the policies framed by others. In adopting this conflict handling style, the party neglects his own concerns and tries to satisfy the concerns of the leaders or superior authorities. It is, however, also possible that the subordinate may apprise his superiors of his own needs for fair pay, for more challenging and satisfying work, for healthy work environment, and so on. In fact, it is not ethically advisable for him to ignore his needs, and it is also not compatible with the organisation's professional ethics that they be ignored. Another possible situation is that it may be wrong on some occasions to oblige a senior who is lacking in competence or expertise, or is out of touch with the organisational ethics. In this situation, the ethically optimum response for the senior authority may be to oblige his subordinate who possesses the relevant knowledge or expertise. Alternatively, a long-term optimum choice may be to promote or elevate the subordinate to a level equal to one's own position in the command hierarchy.

**Dominating style:** This style is considered unethical when it is characterized by the party's high concern for self and low concern, including low respect for others. The use of this approach to conflict management is contrary to organisational ethics which include proper justice and respect for other persons. It may be noted, however, that the dominating style may be ethically justified as an expression of firm and sound leadership if all the following conditions are satisfied:

1. The leaders have made essentially wise decisions in accordance with the firm's professional ethics.
2. Some subordinates do not understand this wisdom.
3. There is insufficient time to resolve the impasse using other styles.[31]

In keeping with the principles of organisational ethics, the use of dominating style must consider the needs and interests of subordinate members of the organisation. Although the superiors may not show much concern for the values of subordinates, they should not ignore the individual needs, aspirations and sensitivities of subordinate members. Therefore, it is necessary to distinguish exploitative domination from respectful domination in the context of ethical behaviour - the former being ethically justified and the latter being not.

**Avoiding style:** This style may be ethically justified if there are certain other organisational issues requiring the urgent attention of the individuals or the parties involved in conflict. This style may also be ethically defensible when a deadlock exists, and no solution is clearly visible immediately. It has been observed that the cultural ethics of certain nations have led to the extensive use of this conflict management style. If the avoiding style is rightly used, it will reflect high concern for doing morally justifiable things, and such high concern will lead to rationally justifiable respect for all the parties concerned.

**Compromising style:** The use of compromising may differ in ethical values depending upon whether the party is giving up the best course or not. If a party's demands are wrong and his opponent's demands are right, then compromising may be somewhat justified. However, if the party's demands are right and his opponent's demands wrong, then compromising may be ethically wrong as it might require one to violate consumer safety, environmental and other regulatory laws. If compromising requires cooperation to harm the interest of common citizens or the social well-being, it would be wise to choose such alternatives as quitting, whistle blowing, etc.

Rahim[32] also conducted a field study to investigate the relationship between the stages of moral development and the five styles of handling conflicts with superiors, subordinates, and peers. While Rest's[33] Defining Issues Test (DIT) was used to assess moral development, the five conflict management styles were measured by ROCI-II.[34] It may be mentioned that the study utilised Kohlberg's concept of moral development which classifies individuals on the basis of their moral development into six different stages: two each at the pre-conventional, conventional and post-conventional levels. The pre-conventional stages of moral development are based on the concepts of right or wrong, good and bad, etc., which have connotations of physical power, or pleasure and pain consequences. Therefore, the pre-conventionals are often prevented from possible misconduct or wrongdoings through their fear of the consequences. At the conventional stages of moral development, the individuals are expected to show conformity behaviour and thereby meet social expectations. At these stages, helpful attitude towards others, good behaviour, respect for authority and rules become important. At the post conventional level of moral development, concepts such as justice, morality, reciprocity, utilitarianism, etc., are considered extremely significant for the concerned individuals. In fact, individual actions are judged on the basis of the extent to which they conform to designed ideals. Thus, while the conventional individuals respect social norms and rules, the post-conventionals are more concerned with universal principles such as distributive justice and respect for life. The findings of the study were summarised by Rahim as follows:

1. The highest stage of moral development is associated with the use of the integrating style of handling interpersonal conflict.
2. A moderate stage of moral development is associated with the use of the compromising style of handling interpersonal conflict.
3. A low stage of moral development is associated with the use of dominating and avoiding styles of handling interpersonal conflict.[35]

It must be emphasized that the findings of the study have important implications for both practising managers and researchers. The study highlighted the fact that there is an intimate relationship between moral development of individuals and their uses of different styles of managing conflicts. The integrating style is generally considered the most effective approach to conflict management and is associated with the highest stages of moral development. Therefore, the policy-makers have to decide whether it would be wise to recruit persons at higher levels of moral development or provide moral training to the organisation's existing employees so that the integrating style of handling conflicts can be widely used. In the present-day organisational ethos regarding accommodating the varied needs of the workforce, ensuring greater equality at workplace, adopting teamwork approach to solve organisational problems, etc., it must be ensured that the utilisation of dominating and avoiding approaches to conflict management is minimised as far as possible. Since the individuals at lower stages of moral development tend to use the dominating style quite frequently, and some of them are placed in authority position over others, the managers and the employees of organisations feel really concerned about the moral reasoning and ethical behaviour being practised at the workplace. There is some research evidence to show that moral reasoning can be improved through educational intervention.[36] Therefore, the organisations should utilise these intervention techniques as far as possible. Similarly, training programmes that focus on the usefulness of the integrating style of managing conflicts as compared to the other approaches or styles, will encourage employees with higher levels of moral development to use this style more frequently. Since the organisational behaviour experts have viewed the integrating style as being most effective and ethically appropriate, the outcomes of these training programmes will be more beneficial for the organisation and its employees.

## 9.5 SUMMARY AND CONCLUSION

The preceding discussion has thrown light on the importance of morality and ethical behaviour in organisations. In view of the expansion of business activities and the all-pervasive role of MNCs, the ethical issues and challenges have emerged over various organisational, social and environmental issues such as consumers' rights, product safety, human and democratic approach towards the treatment of employees, compliance with government rules and regulations, protection of the natural environment, and so on. Despite the importance of ethics and morality in organisations, it must be pointed out that ethical and moral values have not been adequately explored in the areas of conflict and conflict management in organisations. Therefore, an attempt has been made in the preceding sections to explain certain issues involved in conflict such as individual values and value systems, personality types and styles, and individual differences in conflict. More significantly, attempts have been made to provide certain guidelines to managers regarding the effective and ethical application of different conflict management styles in different possible situations. In this context, the decision-tree model of Buller, Kohls, and Anderson[37] was extensively discussed in relation to the management of cross-cultural ethical conflicts. Similarly, Rahim's[38] work was also analysed to show that different conflict management styles, may be considered ethically appropriate or inappropriate depending upon the prevalence of certain specific situations. Rahim[39] broadly argued that the integrating style of managing conflicts is the most ethical one and, therefore, suggested that this style should be maximally used by the organisation members. At the same time, there is a need to discourage the use of the dominating and the avoiding styles which are being frequently used by individuals operating at lower stages of moral development.

In the end, it must be stated that the question of ethical management of conflict in organisations has been relatively less explored in the management literature. It is generally presumed that conflict management styles are basically used for ethical purposes in organisations whereas in reality, such styles can be used for unethical purposes too. A determination of whether the conflict management approaches are being ethically or unethical used is a complex one depending on many factors including the situational variables, the motives of persons employing them, and the extent to which the objectives of the organisation are being served, etc. In fact, there is a problem of reconciling the often-conflicting claims of various stakeholders connected with the organisation. In addition, it is also difficult to know whether the ultimate ends of the organisation are being really served by a conflict management decision. A solution to a conflict may appear to be harmful in the short-run, but this may prove to be good in the long run. Or, conversely, a solution which appears to be good in the short run may turn out to be harmful in the long run. At this point, it must be emphasized that there is no simple means to ensure the ethical use of conflict management styles in organisations. A wise leader is, however, never expected to behave ethically and in so doing, he should be open to new information and ideas and be flexible in the use of various conflict management techniques. Similarly, the subordinates and other stakeholders have an ethical duty to express themselves against the senior's decisions when the consequences of such decisions are likely to be detrimental to organisation's objectives.

## 9.6 CULTURAL ISSUES IN CONFLICT MANAGEMENT

It is commonly observed that formation of diverse task groups has become a part of common culture in organisations due to globalisation of trade and business activities, advancement of technology, the need for combining varied talents of the workforce, etc. Individuals hailing from different ethnic and racial backgrounds work together in local companies, multinational corporations (MNCs) or international organisations. Therefore, cooperation among different multicultural groups has become a critical part of the cosmopolitan character of modern organisations. In fact, these significant changes have created a new work environment at the workplace, requiring radical changes in management styles and practices. While teamwork is often adopted as a solution to various challenges arising due to multinational and multicultural character of organisations, a number of problems will undoubtedly arise in dealing with such conflicts at the workplace. In fact, the formation of diverse groups composed of people with different racial, ethnic, and national backgrounds will naturally lead to such multicultural group conflicts in organisations. In this context, it must be stated that the traditional methods or styles of managing conflicts such as problem-solving, smoothing, compromising, forcing, etc., are longer be adequate to handle such multicultural conflicts occurring in the modern organisations. In fact, management should make use of the advantages of cultural diversity rather than see it as a negative impediment.[40] Similarly, Kirchmeyer and McLellan[41] have also suggested a creative approach to utilise the potential of the cultural minority at the workplace. They have also suggested that cultural diversity should be used constructively.

Against the backdrop of the above-stated observations, the second part of this chapter examines different cultural aspects of conflict and its management in organisations. In addition to reviewing the literature on the subject, an attempt has been made to explore issues related with the relationship between culture and cultural diversity, and between cultural diversity and conflicts. Attempts have also been made to highlight certain significant aspects of the management of multicultural group conflicts in organisations.

## 9.7 REVIEW OF LITERATURE

The present section focuses on the role and effects of cultural values in the management of organisational conflicts. It may be mentioned that there are two types of cultural influences on conflict management: (1) culture of the organisation itself including its values, belief systems, traditions, people's ways of behaving, etc.; and (2) cultural influences originating from the external environment. In regard to the influences of organisational culture, DeDreu and Weingart[42] found that task conflict may be moderated by the type of task being performed by the organisation's members and by the team work culture. De Dreu and Weingart[43] seem to suggest the possibility of a contingency approach for the study of outcomes of conflict types: task and relationship conflicts. Similar to these research efforts, Guerra, Martinez, Munduate and Medina[44] attempted to analyse the effects of conflict types (task and relationship conflicts) on employee's satisfaction and well-being. More significantly, the researchers tried to examine the moderating role of organisational culture in this relationship. The researchers studied and compared the effects of task and relationship conflicts in two culturally different organisations: a public service organisation and a private service organisation. While the private service organisations generally have a high goal orientation with emphasis on rationality, accomplishments, client satisfaction, and profit, the public service organisations have a higher support orientation and are essentially governed by rules and regulations and are driven by the service motive, i.e., providing a service to the general public.[45] The researchers found that relationship conflict was negatively related to the satisfaction and the well-being of the employees of both public and private organisations. Their findings also showed that organisational culture moderates the relationship between task conflict and the employees' satisfaction and well-being. Although task conflict had negative effects on employeess' satisfaction and well-being in private organisations, it did not have such negative effects when it was combined with high goal orientation. Task conflict did not negatively affect members' satisfaction and well-being in public organisations when such conflict was combined with highest support orientation in work teams. Thus, it can be observed that conflict can have positive effects when it is stimulated in situations where team culture is a significant variable. Another interesting finding of the study was that the employees of public sector organisations who experienced least conflict in the organisation were the most satisfied ones. This situation may be explained by the fact that cultural characteristics of public organisations are characterized by harmony and cooperation rather than conflict and competitiveness.

A case study was conducted by Darr[46] to examine both conflict and its resolution in a democratically managed taxi cooperative organisation (known as Nir taxi station) that had been functioning for sixty-six years at Tel Aviv, Israel. The researchers found that conflicts at the taxi cooperative emanated from such important sources as ethnic origin, local division of labour, etc. The first major source of conflict occurred due to changes in the balance of power between two ethnic groups. The Nir taxi station was originally founded by Jew immigrants from Europe called, Ashkenazi Jews. These station founders propagated such qualities or values as cleanliness, punctuality, and discipline that are generally associated with German Jews. They did not accept any new member or hired labourer in the taxi station up to the late 1950s. Towards the late 1970s, however, the Sepharadic Jews formed the majority of members and hired labourers. This change in the balance of power between the two ethnic communities gave rise to conflicts between them continuously. It was also observed that conflict between the two ethnic groups sometimes resulted in aggression. In addition, local division of labour was another important source of conflict. The dispatcher was responsible for assigning jobs to the taxi drivers according to a certain system. In fact, the despatcher's discretion was a significant source of conflicts between the dispatcher and the taxi drivers. The findings suggested that these conflicts were partly rooted in the larger cultural and economic environments that was beyond the Nir taxi station's boundaries. However, most of these conflicts and their manifestations occurred due to the Nir's social structure. It may be mentioned that both formal and informal means of conflict resolution were used to resolve conflicts. Conflicts were resolved informally through different forms of social interactions among the taxi drivers such as gossip networks, joke telling, rituals, direct criticism of drivers, etc. In fact, these informal means of conflict resolution were used as per the demands of different situations and in an escalating manner. Thus, it can be seen that conflict management at Nir station was deeply embedded in its social structure. Conflicts were manifested and resolved through social interactions among taxi drivers on a day-to-day basis. When all these informal mechanisms failed, the conflicts were resolved through a formal tribunal consisting of judges elected by the Nir taxi station's members. The tribunal provided equal treatment to both its members and hired taxi drivers. These democratic features contributed to the legitimacy and wide acceptance of the tribunal system in Nir station. Therefore, it can be said that democracy at Nir was implemented in the process of conflict resolution itself.

The study of cross-cultural differences in conflict management has assumed considerable significance in the management literature on account of the increasing number of MNCs, international alliances, and international transactions. Most of the studies conducted on this subject have compared Americans with Asians.[47] These studies generally show that as compared to Americans, the Asians generally react to conflict in a less direct manner. These studies further showed the influence of the national cultures of some countries (e.g., Japan, Korea, and China) on conflict management styles. It may be noted, however, that a few studies have been made to examine the differences among East Asians in terms of their use of different conflict management styles. Ting Toomey *et al.*,[48] examined the conflict management styles being followed by the under-graduate students and found that Korean and Chinese students were more likely to utilise the integrating style of managing conflicts than Japanese counterparts. The researchers further noted that Koreans used more of compromising behaviours than the Japanese whereas the latter tended to use the obliging style to a greater extent. Although the findings of these studies pointed to some significant differences among East Asians in terms of their utilisation of different conflict management styles or methods, it has been noted that these studies did not specifically address the question as to how East Asians differed in resolving interpersonal conflicts with their immediate supervisors. As noted by Rahim[49] and Hold and De Vone,[50] people tend to use different styles of managing conflicts depending upon the authority level of the other party in conflict. While the superiors are more likely to use forcing, the employees generally prefer compromise with their peers as well as seniors.

In view of this, Kim, Kondo and Kim[51] conducted a research study to examine how Chinese, Japanese and Korean subjects resolved interpersonal conflicts with their immediate superiors and also how cultural values mediated the relationship between nationality and the use of conflict management styles. The researchers chose these three East Asian countries for purposes for their study due to some special reasons. Although these three countries have geographical proximity to one another, they have different historical and cultural backgrounds that affect their behaviour. In addition, these countries are the most frequently examined countries in the current cross-cultural conflict management studies. The researchers broadly found that the Chinese, Korean and Japanese somewhat differed from one another in dealing with interpersonal conflicts with their supervisors. The Koreans, for example, are more likely to compromise with their supervisors in solving their interpersonal conflicts as compared to the Chinese and the Japanese. Similarly, the Japanese are more likely to compromise with their supervisors and less likely to dominate over them as compared with the Chinese and the Koreans. The findings of this study further revealed that cultural values played a significant role in explaining some country differences in the use of conflict management styles among East Asians.

Thus, it can be seen that cross-cultural research studies generally focused on studying country-wise differences in the use of different conflict management approaches or styles. At the same time, there is a need to conduct studies on how people with diverse cultures interact so as to strengthen cross-cultural collaboration.[52] In this connection, it is significant to note that Ting Toomey and colleagues developed the face negotiation theory that relates different face concerns to conflict management styles across cultures varying in collectivist and individualist values.[53] The authors suggested that collectivism is positively associated with other face, which leads to the avoiding and the integrating styles of managing interpersonal conflicts. On the other hand, individualism is associated with self-face leading to the dominating style of managing conflicts. Thus, face concerns are assumed to be important variables or factors that account for the effects of cultures on the choice of conflict management styles.[54] It must be noted, however, that self-face and other-face are not mutually exclusive to each other; people who are high on self-face may also have high other-face.[55] Peng and Tjosvold[56] examined how the face negotiation theory applied in cross-cultural interactions between managers and employees at the workplace. The researchers found that the associations between social face concerns and avoidance behaviour were stronger among Chinese employees who interacted with the Chinese managers as compared to the Chinese employees working for Western managers. Thus, the findings of the study suggested that a manager's cultural background moderates the influence of face concerns on the use of avoiding styles or strategies. The Chinese employees were influenced by social concerns to a greater extent when they worked with the local manager than when they were working with the Western managers. These research results seem to confirm the findings of cross- cultural adjustment research that people can modify their behavioural pattern to be more in line with their expectations of the other culture.[57]

## 9.8 CULTURE AND CULTURAL DIVERSITY

In order to have a proper understanding of conflict and conflict management processes in multicultural task groups, it is necessary to study the relevance of culture and cultural diversity in such groups. Adler[58] viewed culture as consisting of six dimensions which can be stated in the form of the following equations:

1. What is the nature of people ?
2. What is a person's relationship to nature ?
3. What is a person's relationship to other people ?
4. What is the primary mode of activity ?
5. What is the conception of space ?
6. What is a person's temporal orientation ?[59]

According to Alder,[60] diversities between different cultures can be observed in the form of differences on these six dimensions. Thus, Alder's[61] descriptions of culture and cultural diversity provide insights into the fact that each individual member of a multicultural task group has certain differences with other group members on his outlook regarding himself, his relationship with others, the world and nature.

The literature on multicultural studies suggests that group processes are significantly influenced by cultural values. The studies also indicate that different group variables such as cohesiveness, leadership, confirmity, etc. are affected by the values within different cultures. This kind of cultural diversity has been found to exist within different task groups in organisations. As defined by Vechhio and Appelbaum,[62] the primary dimensions of diversity include "inborn differences or differences that have an ongoing impact throughout one's life. These include learning style, types of intelligence, age, ethnicity, gender, physical abilities, race and sexual orientation. These dimensions are core elements through which people shape their self image and worldview." On the other hand, the secondary dimensions of diversity can be acquired and changed throughout a person's lifetime. The secondary dimensions have comparatively lesser impact than the primary ones on a person's self image and worldview, and include such characteristics as education, income, marital status, professional or work background, religious beliefs, etc. Thus, it can be stated that different groups consisting of organisation's members can be rightly described as diverse groups characterized by cultural diversities. The research studies have shown that these cultural diversities have a significant impact on group life and development in organisations.

## 9.9 CULTURAL DIVERSITY AND CONFLICT

Cultural diversity in task groups has a significant influence on how conflict is perceived and handled by group members. The management literature shows that cultural diversity can lead to conflicts in two important ways: trust building, and communications. It is really difficult to develop trust in multicultural task groups. The research findings have shown that group members often agree with other group members of their own culture rather than with those of different cultures.[63] In the absence of communication among group members, the development of trust-based relationship becomes almost impossible. Mistrust among group members precipitates the conditions further due to lack of understanding of one another's viewpoints in groups. Similarly, miscommunication can be another significant source of conflict among group members. Although they have to communicate among themselves, cross-cultural communication problems often do occur.

Adler[64] has pointed out that there are three barriers to cross-cultural communication: (1) cross-cultural misperception; (2) cross-cultural misinterpretation; and (3) cross-cultural misevaluation. Cross-cultural misperception refers to a condition in which our perceptual patterns are culturally determined, selectively focused, and inaccurate as the group members tend to perceive what they expect to perceive. Cross-cultural misinterpretation means that the group members often generalise the behavioural norms of their own ethnic and national groups to other countries. In cross-cultural misevaluation, the members use their own culture as a measurement standard or reference criterion in order to judge other cultures. Anderson[65] studied the management of the mixed cultural workgroup with the New Zealand white managers as subjects and concluded that "cultural differences and the possible resulting communication problems may intensify the difficulty of manager's job as he attempts to manage people's work and attempts to produce an effective test strategy for the group." In their extensive investigation of multinational joint ventures, Newman[66] attempted to study the interaction patterns between organisations and individuals who had different cultures. The researcher noticed cross-cultural hurdles in the processes of collaboration between different international companies. In fact, certain difficulties were encountered at the planning and negotiation stages on account of differences in business practices, legal institutions and languages being used. For example, the Chinese often maintain secrecy about business affairs, are polite and tend to avoid open arguments with others. These Chinese traits are in sharp contrast to the Americans' bluntness and straightforwardness in their dealings with others. Thus, it can be observed that achieving common agreement among individuals or parties hailing from different countries and cultures often creates obstacles in communicating, conceiving of new ideas and operations, and in reconciling different values, beliefs and viewpoints regarding organisational issues. Similarly, at the execution stage, several problems were encountered in promoting the desired behaviour among group members, ensuring the accountability of employees, and measuring their job performance.

Gardenswarlz and Rowe[67] suggested that cultural lenses have a strong influence on team work among group members. The author suggested four elements that need to be examined to explain this relationship:

1. **Desire for harmony:** It has been found that although North Americans are somewhat reluctant to handle conflict, they will do it in team building sessions particularly if it is related to productivity. In other cultures such as Central America, Mexico, the Middle East, etc., maintaining harmony or smooth interpersonal relation is considered supreme. Therefore, differences or conflicts are resolved through the informal network of relationships rather than through team building sessions.
2. **Social status based on family connections:** While the Western societies perceive teamwork as a significant means of promoting collaboration in task groups, many other societies or cultures do not perceive things in this manner. In these societies, factors such as seniority, gender, family connections, social status, etc., have a significant impact on the expectations of team members who

have been brought up in different cultures. In this situation, it becomes necessary to be sensitive to such differences in upbringing and cultural norms of the organisation or group members.

3. **Emphasis on group:** Cultural overlap and homogeneity among group members provide opportunities to bring the group together and promotes team building processes with a view to cultivating good relationships and building trust. This conducive situation encourages individual growth and development that can be channelled towards group attainments and rewarded accordingly.
4. **Fatalism and external locus of control:** In some cultures, it is presumed that certain organisational or group issues are beyond the control of human beings. This trust in fatalism or predestination often acts as an innovating factor and obstructs team building and problem solving efforts in groups. A manager, for instance, notices that a person or group of persons is sabotaging group efforts when they are actually responsive to cultural upbringing and belief.[68]

The research studies have further shown that cultural diversity can intensify or inhibit conflicts in task groups. Hofsteade[69] studied differences in job related attitudes of manager and employees working in an American MNC and suggested that cultures can fall into four different pairs of opposite dimensions: (1) high power distance/low power distance; (2) high uncertainty avoidance/low uncertainty avoidance; (3) individualism/collectivism; and (4) masculinity/femininity. Following Hofstede's[70] line of research, we can discuss the inherent conflicts that do exist in task groups. It is commonly observed that the Chinese hail from a culture of large power distance (or more of unequal power distribution in groups and organisations), work uncertainty avoidance, collectivism and masculinity. The Americans and Canadians are seen as hailing from small power distance, weak uncertainty avoidance, individualist and masculine cultures. The Germans are said to belong to a culture of small power distance (or lesser degree of inequality in power distribution), strong uncertainty avoidance, individuality and masculinity. Although some common cultural dimensions may exist among the group members, conflicts and in-group fightings are bound to occur due to high uncertainty avoidance, individualism and masculinity in such groups. High uncertainty refers to a condition in which group members feel threatened by uncertain and ambiguous situations and, therefore, try to avoid these situations. Individuality refers to maximum concern for the fulfilment of individual needs rather than group needs whereas masculinity emphasizes upon materialistic acquisitions of money and other things without much of concern for human relations. However, these inherent conflicts in groups can be minimised to some extent if the group has some members hailing from collectivist and feminine cultures which emphasise upon group members' common needs and interpersonal relationships respectively.

Hofstede[72] rightly stated that cultural differences among members of work groups in MNCs have important implications for managerial practice. Managers in many companies all over the world have been making efforts to make work more challenging and satisfying to the workers. The American companies, for example, have focused on job restructuring or job enrichment programmes, thereby fulfilling the workers' needs for individual achievement, greater recognition and a sense of fulfilment. In European countries such as Sweden, Norway, etc., the management's efforts to make work more interesting have focused on developing and adopting the team approach to work, thus emphasizing upon interpersonal relationships over individual achievements. It must be noted, however, that such differences in national culture have important implications for managers in MNCs. Management practices that are suitable for a particular nation may not be appropriate or effective abroad. Even within a nation's boundaries, regional differences in culture do play a prominent role.

## 9.10 MANAGEMENT OF MULTICULTURAL GROUP CONFLICT

As discussed earlier, people from different cultural backgrounds have different norms of behaviour at the workplace. Therefore, the managers need to acknowledge the cultural impact on conflict and build on it.[72] Adler[73] has suggested that cultural differences should be handled by defining the issues from the viewpoints of the cultures of both the parties in conflict. The underlying idea is to come up with cultural interpretations of certain specific issues and then develop a 'cultural synergy' that works for the benefit of both the groups. In fact, both formal and informal mechanisms can be used to discover the cultural differences that motivate individuals or groups at the workplace. An informal method may be to ask the intermediaries or leaders to find out such cultural differences between people.[74] At the same time, more formal methods may also be used depending upon the nature of organisation, the stage of group development, and other situational variables. The responsibility for discovering and handling such cultural differences through the use of formal methods may be assigned to managers or formal task groups in the organisation.

Abbassi and Hollman[75] have offered certain useful recommendations for the use of managers of multicultural organisations as given below:

- Managers should recognise and acknowledge that people from various backgrounds and ethnic groups with different values and unorthodox attitudes make up corporate life.
- Managers should communicate and show respect for the culture and values of others. They should listen to the views of minority workers and make sure that they are included in their formal and informal networks.
- Managers should avoid stereotyping anyone from any culture.
- Managers should provide workers with a sense of psychological safety, assist them when needed in the accumulation process.
- Managers should be empathetic, but be themselves, they should not try to be "one of them". In addition, they should avoid projecting or imposing their own culture and value system onto others.

- Finally, managers should trust their instincts in dealing with foreign employees.[76]

Thus, it can be stated that for managing multicultural groups effectively, the managers must recognise and respect cultural differences between groups and people, avoid stereotyping of different cultures, and be empathetic towards other cultures. There is also a need for them to adopt a balanced approach so as to accommodate all unique cultures and analyse group and organisational issues from the viewpoint of multiple cultures. While both formal and informal mechanisms may be adopted to better manage cultural differences, the managers should be open minded and be flexible enough to promote the utilisation of collaborative behaviours in the management of multicultural group conflicts.

## 9.11 SUMMARY AND CONCLUSION

In the second part of this chapter, attempts were made to analyse the role and importance of certain significant cultural issues in conflict and its management. In view of expansion and globalisation of trade and business activities, adoption of advanced technology in business, the need to utilise the multifarious talents of the workforce, it has become absolutely necessary to form multicultural task groups in organisations including MNCs and international organisations. A natural consequence of the formation of such diverse task groups consisting of people with different national, ethnic and racial backgrounds naturally leads to multicultural group conflicts. In this changing organisational scenario, the traditional methods of handling conflicts may not be adequate to handle such multicultural group conflicts arising in the modern organisations. There is a need for managers to adopt a changed outlook and to seek to realise the benefits of cultural diversity rather than seeing it as a negative phenomenon within organisations. In addition to reviewing the literature on this subject, the present chapter focused on the relationships between culture and cultural diversity as well as between cultural diversity and conflicts in organisations. Finally, efforts were also made to highlight the management aspects of multicultural group conflicts existing in organisations. The review of literature broadly indicated that national cultures have a profound influence on conflict management or on the adoption of various conflict management styles. Therefore, it was suggested that research studies are needed to examine how people hailing from different ethnic and cultural backgrounds interact to promote cross-cultural collaboration among group members. In regard to the relationship between culture and cultural diversity, it was noted that cultural differences among group members have a strong influence on group life, group development, and group processes in organisations. In this context, both the primary and the secondary dimensions of cultural diversity existing among group members were discussed. In addition, it was observed that cultural diversity in groups plays a significant role in the perception and resolution of conflicts. As shown by the management literature, miscommunication and the consequent lack of trust among group members can precipitate conflicts in groups. The researchers have noticed that cross-cultural diversities often create hurdles in the collaborative processes within task groups. The research studies have further shown that cultural diversities can intensify or innovate conflicts in groups. Regarding the management of multicultural group conflicts, the experts have suggested that cultural differences should be handled by analysing the issues from the viewpoint of the respective cultures of both the parties in conflict. In resolving such conflicts, both formal and informal mechanisms may be utilised to identify the cultural differences that influence the behaviour of individuals or groups at the workplace. In fact, the managers need to be open-minded and adopt a flexible approach so as to promote collaboration among group members in the management of multicultural group conflicts in organisations.

The present analysis of various cultural issues involved in conflict and its management has important implications for both practising managers and researchers. This analysis will help the managers to enhance their understanding of cultural differences among group members hailing from different ethnic, racial, and national backgrounds. This enhanced understanding is expected to help the cross-cultural managers in reducing animosity in managing people from different cultures. In so doing, the managers should be flexible enough to adopt the use of different conflict management styles in dealing with employees with different cultural backgrounds. In managing cross-cultural conflict in groups, the managers may develop training programmes for employees with a view to promoting more open and constructive conflict management practices. Such training programmes will help the members to develop cooperative goals and mutually shared reward systems and also improve their conflict management skills of expressing their feelings and viewpoints, freely restating the other party's arguments and thereby integrating the best ideas so as to reach mutually acceptable and beneficial solutions.

The present research may also be considered an extremely valuable from the viewpoint of future research on cross-cultural conflict management as it suggests opportunities for more meaningful research and theory building in different ways. The study has found that group members with different national cultures tend to use different styles of managing interpersonal conflicts among themselves. These research results have generally extended the findings of current conflict management studies. In addition, the research results do enhance our understanding of cross-cultural differences by highlighting the significant cultural attributes among different "collectivist" cultures that have generally been ignored.

## REVIEW QUESTIONS

1. Business firms than those whose managers or leaders have no respect for ethics and morality are lower performing firms whose leaders value ethics and morality adequately. Discuss.

2. Critically examine the ethical issues involved in conflict and its management in organisations.
3. The decision-tree model represents an useful aid to managers for managing cross-cultural ethical conflict. Explain.
4. Rahim made a significant research effort to explain the ethical appropriateness or inappropriateness of five conflict management styles in different possible situations. Discuss.
5. Explain the role and effects of cultural values in the management of organisational conflicts. Cite necessary research evidences in this regard.
6. Cross-cultural differences play a significant role in the management of conflict in organisations. Explain.
7. Cultural diversity in task groups has a significant influence on the management of conflicts. Discuss.

## REFERENCES


1. Baucus, M.S., and Baucus, D.A., Paying the Piper: An empirical examination of longer-term financial consequences of illegal corporate behaviour, *Academy of Management Journal*, 40 (1), 1997, pp. 129-151.
2. Kotey, B. and Meredith, G.G., Relationships among owner/manager personal values, business strategies, and enterprise performance, *Journal of Small Business Management*, 1997.
3. Soutar, G., McNeil, M.M., and Molster, C., The impact of the work environment on ethical decision making: Some Australian evidence, *Journal of Business Ethics*, 13(5), 1994, pp. 327-339.
4. Rahim, M.A., Garrett, J.E., and Buntzman, G.F., Ethics of managing interpersonal conflict in organisations, *Journal of Business Ethics*, 11(5-6), 1992, pp. 423-432.
5. Rahim, M.A., *Managing Conflict in Organisations*, Quorom Books, London, 2017, p. 182.
6. Vitell, S.J., Nwachukwu, S.L., and Barnes, J.H., The effects of culture on ethical decision-making: An application of Hofstede's typology, *Journal of Business Ethics*, 12, 1993, pp. 753-760.
7. Donaldson, T., *The Ethics of International Business*, Oxford University Press, New York, 1989; DeGeorge, R.T., *Competing with Integrity in International Business*, Oxford University Press, New York, 1993; Badaraco, J.L., The IBM-Fujitsu Conundrum, W.M. Hoffman, J.B. Kamm, R.E. Frederick and E.S. Petry, Jr. (Ed.), *Emerging Global Business Ethics*, Quorom Books, Westport, CT., 1994, pp. 79-88; and Sternberg, E., Relativism rejected: The possibility of transnational business ethics, W.M. Hoffmann, J.B. Kamm, R.E. Frederick and E.S. Petry, Jr. (Ed.), *Emerging Global Business Ethics*, Quorom Books, Westport, CT., 1994.

8. Bowie, N., Moral decision making and multinationals, *Business Ethics Quarterly*, 1, 1991, pp. 223-232; and Velasquez, M., International business ethics, *Business Ethics Quarterly*, October, 5(4), 1995, pp. 865-882.
9. Rokeach, M., *The Nature of Human Values*, Free Press, New York, 1973.
10. *Ibid.*
11. *Ibid.*
12. England, G., Personal value systems of American managers, *Academy of Management Journal*, 10, 1967, pp. 53-68.
13. England, G., Dhingra, O.P., and Agarwal, N.C., *The Manager and his Values*, Ballinger, Cambridge, Mass, 1975.
14. Engalnd, G., 1967, *op. cit.*
15. Rokeach, M,. 1973, *op. cit.*
16. Engalnd, G., 1967, *op. cit.*
17. Bixenstine, E.V., Potash, H.M., and Wilson, K.V., Effects of level of cooperative choice by the other player on choices in a prisoner's dilemma game, Part I, *Journal of Abnormal and Social Psychology*, 66, 1963a, pp. 308-313; Bixenstine, E.V., and Wilson, K.V., Effects of level of cooperative choice by the other player on choices in a prisoner's dilemma game, Part II, *Journal of Abnormal and Social Psychology*, 67, pp. 139-147; and Bixenstine, E.V., Leavitt, D.A., and Wilson, K.V., Collaboration among six persons in a prisoner's dilemma game, *Journal of Conflict Resolution*, 10, pp. 488-496.
18. Lewicki, R.J., Ethical concerns in conflict management, G.B.J. Bomers and R.B. Peterson, (Ed.), *Conflict Management and Industrial Relations*, Nijhoff,, The Hague, 1982, pp. 423-445.
19. Bixenstine, *et. al.*, 1963a, 1966, *op. cit.*
20. Christie, R., and Geis, F., *Studies in Machiavellianism*, Academic Press, New York, 1970.
21. Blake, R.R., and Mouton, J.S., *The Managerial Grid*, Houston, Gulf., Houston, 1964; Lawrence, P.R. and Lorsch, J.W., *Organisation and Environment: Managing Differentiation and Integration*, Division of Research, Harvard Business School, Harvard University, Boston, 1967; Thomas, K.W., Conflict and conflict management, M.D. Dunettee (Ed.), *Handbook of Industrial and Organisational Psychology*, Rand McNally,Chicago, 1976, pp. 889-935; Rahim, M.A., *Rahim Organisational Conflict Inventory*, Consulting Psychological Press, Alto Calif, 1983; and Pareek, U., *Managing Conflict and Collaboration*, Oxford-IBH, New Delhi, 1982.
22. Thomas, K., and Kilman, R., Developing a forced-choice measure of conflict-handling behaviour: The 'Mode' instrument, *Educational and Psychological Measurement*, 37, 1997, pp. 309-435.

23. *Ibid.*
24. *Ibid.*
25. Buller, P.F., Kohls, J.J., and Anderson, K.S., A model for addressing cross-cultural ethical conflicts, *Business and Society*, 36(2), 1997, pp. 169-193.
26. Ruble, T. and Thomas, K., Support for a two-dimensional model of conflict behaviour, *Organisational Behaviour and Human Performance*, 16, 1976, pp. 143-155.
27. Donaldosn, T., *The Ethics of International Business*, Oxford University Press, New York, 1989; and DeGeorge, R.T., Competing With Integrity in International Business, Oxford University Press, New York, 1993.
28. Buller, P.F., Kohls, J.J., and Anderson, K.S., 1997, *op. cit.*
29. Rahim, M.A., 2017, *op. cit.*
30. *Ibid.*
31. *Ibid*, p. 191.
32. *Ibid.*
33. Rest, J.R., *Moral Development: Advances in Research and Theory*, Praeger, New York, 1986.
34. Rahim, M.A., Buntzman, G.F., and White, D., An empirical study of the stages of moral development and conflict management styles, *International Journal of Conflict Management*, 10(2), 1999, pp. 154-171.
35. Rahim, M.A., 2017, p. 194, *op. cit.*
36. Penn, W.Y., and Collier, B.D., Current research in moral development as a decision support system, *Journal of Business Ethics*, 4(2), 1985, pp. 131-136; and Rest, J.R., and Thomas, S.J., Educational programs and interventions, J.R. Rest (ed.), *Moral Development*, Praeger, New York, 1986.
37. Buller, P.F., Kohls, J.J., and Anderson, K.S., 1997, *op. cit.*
38. Rahim, M.A., 2017, *op. cit.*
39. *Ibid.*
40. Adler, N.J., Doktor, R. and Redding, S.G., From the Atlantic to the Pacific century: Cross-cultural management reviewed, *Journal of Management*, 12(2), 1986, pp. 295-318.
41. Kirchmeyer, C. and McLellan, J., Managing ethnic diversity: Utilising the creative potential of diverse work-force to meet the challenges of the future, C. Kirchmeyer (Ed.), *Organisational Behaviour*, 11(5), Administrative Sciences Association of Canada, Canada, 1990, pp. 120-129.
42. De Dreu, C.K.W., and Weingart, L.R., Task versus relationship conflict: A meta-analysis, *Journal of Applied Psychology*, 88, 2003, pp. 741-749.
43. *Ibid.*

44. Guerra, J.M., Martinez, I., Munduate, L., and Medina, F.J., A contingency perspective on the study of the consequences of conflict types: The role of organisational culture, *European Journal of Work and Organisational Psychology*, 14(2), 2005, pp. 157-176.

45. Porter, L.W., and Lawler, E.E., and Hackman, J.R., *Behaviour in Organisations*, McGraw Hill, New York, 1975.

46. Darr, A., Conflict and conflict resolution in a cooperative: The case of the Nir taxi station, *Human Relations*, 52(3), 1999.

47. Ohbuchi, K., Fukushima, O., and Tedeschi, J.T., Cultural values in conflict management: Goal orientation, goal attainment, and tactical decision, *Journal of Cross-cultural Psychology*, 30(1), 1999, pp. 51-57; Tinsley, C.H., Models of conflict resolution in Japanese, German, and American cultures, *Journal of Applied Psychology*, 83(2), 1998, pp. 316-323; Lee, H.O., and Rogan, R.G., A cross-cultural comparison of organisational conflict management behaviours, *International Journal of Conflict Management*, 2(3), 1991, pp. 181-199; and Tinsley, C.H., and Brett, J.M., Managing work place conflict in the United States and Hong Kong, *Organisational Behaviour and Human Decision Processes*, 85(2), 2001, pp. 360-381.

48. Ting-Toomey, S., Gao, G., Trubisky, P., and Yang, Z., Culture, face maintenance, and styles of handling interpersonal conflicts: A study in five cultures, *International Journal of Conflict Management*, 2(4), 1991, pp. 275-296.

49. Rahim, M.A., *Managing Conflict in Organisations*, 2nd Ed., Praeger, Westport, CT, 1992.

50. Holt, J.L. and De Vore, C.J., Culture, gender, organisational role, and styles of conflict resolution: A meta-analysis, *International Journal of Intercultural Relations*, 2(2), 2005, pp. 165-196.

51. Kim, T., Wang, C., Kondo, M., and Kim, T., Conflict management styles: The differences among the Chinese, Japanese and Koreans, *International Journal of Conflict Management*, 18(1), 2007.

52. Bond, M.H., Cross-cultural social psychology and the real world of culturally diverse teams and dyads, D. Tjosvold and K. Leung (Eds.), *Cross-cultural Foundations: Traditions for Managing in a Cross-cultural World*, Ashgate Publishing, Aldershot, 2003, pp. 43-58; and Gelfand, M.J., Erez, M., and Aycan, Z., Cross-cultural organisational behaviour, *Annual Review of Psychology*, 58(1), 2007, pp. 479-514.

53. Ting Toomey, S., Intercultural conflict styles: A face negotiation theory, Y.Y. Kim, and W.GudyKunst (Eds.), *Theories in International Communication*, Sage, Newbury Park, CA, 1998, pp. 213-235; and Ting Toomey, S., and Kurogi, A., Facework competence in intercultural conflict: An updated face negotiation theory, *International Journal of Intercultural Relations*, 22(2), 1998, pp. 187-225.

54. Oetzel, J.G., and Ting Toomey, S., Face concerns in interpersonal conflict: A cross-cultural empirical test of the face negotiation theory, *Communication Research*, 30(6), 2003, pp. 599-624.
55. Ting Toomey, S., and Kurgoi, A., 1998, *op. cit.*
56. Peng, A.C., and Tjosvold, D., Social face concerns and conflict avoidance of Chinese employees with their Western or Chinese managers, *Human Relations*, 64(8), 2011, pp. 1031-1050.
57. Thomas, D.C., and Ravlin, E.C., Responses of employees to cultural adaptation by a foreign manager, *Journal of Applied Psychology*, 80(1), 1995; and Rao, A., and Hashimoto, K., International influence: A study of Japanese expatiate managers in Canada, *Journal of International Business Studies*, 27(3), 1996, pp. 443-466.
58. Adler, N.J., *International Dimensions of Organisational Behaviour*, PWS-Kent Publishing Company, Boston, MA, 1991, pp. 20-21.
59. Appelbaum, S.H., Shaprio, B., and Elbaz, D., The management of multicultural group conflict, *Team Performance Management*, 4(5), 1988, pp. 211-234.
60. Adler, N.J., 1991, *op. cit.*
61. *Ibid.*
62. Veechio, R.P., and Appelbaum, S.H., *Managing Organisational Behaviour: A Canadian Perspective*, Dryden-Harcourt Brace and Co., Toronto, Canada, 1995.
63. Triandis, H.C., Hall, E.R., and Ewen, R.B., Some cognitive factors affecting group creativity, *Human Relations*, 18(1), 1965.
64. Adler, N.J., 1991, *op. cit.* pp. 67-83,
65. Anderson, L.R., Management of the mixed-cultural work group, *Organisational Behaviour and Human Performance*, 31(3), 1983, pp. 303-330.
66. Newman, W.H., Stages in cross cultural collaboration, *Journal of Asia Business*, 11(4), 1995, pp. 69-74.
67. Gardenswarlz, L., and Rowe, A., *Managing Diversity: A Complete Desk References and Planning Guide*, Peffer and Company, Irwing, 1993, pp. 107-108.
68. *Ibid.*
69. Hofstede, G., Motivation, leadership and organisations: Do American theories apply abroad?, *Organisational Dynamics*, 9(1), 1980, pp. 42-63.
70. *Ibid.*
71. *Ibid.*
72. Gardenswarlz, L., and Rowe, A., 1993, *op. cit*, p. 113.
73. Adler, N.J., 1991, *op. cit.*
74. Gardenswarlz, L. and Rowe, A., 1993, *op. cit*, p. 131.
75. Abbassi, S.M., and Hollman, K.W., Managing cultural diversity: The challenges of the 90s, *ARMA Records Management Quarterly*, 25(3), 1991.
76. *Ibid*, pp. 7-11.

# 10

# Concluding Observations

## 10.1 THEORETICAL PERSPECTIVES ON CONFLICT AND CONFLICT MANAGEMENT

The social scientists broadly agree that conflict as a social phenomenon has influenced the course of human history and civilization since times immemorial. In view of the importance of social conflict, the social scientists representing diverse disciplines of knowledge such as philosophy, sociology, psychology, political science, economics, etc., contributed their thoughts and knowledge in explaining the concept of conflict in the context of various social situations. Some of the famous social scientists who contributed quite significantly towards the development of the theory of social conflict include Plato, Aristotle, Locke, Hegel, Marx, Dewey, Simmel, Mayo, Coser, and so on. These scholars essentially tried to pinpoint the root causes of social conflict and also offered necessary remedies for the eradication of conflicts in the social situations. It must be emphasized that their explanations touched upon various subjects and many different ways of looking at the conflict situations in the human society. They analysed social conflict from many different angles, based upon social themes or subjects as varied as maintaining social balance, abolition or retention of private property, lack of order in social relations, government formation, class struggle within the human society, human adaptation to environmental changes, socialisation processes in groups, sound human relations in organisations, and so on.

It must be pointed out that the organisation theorists have taken adequate interest in the study of conflict only in recent times. Apart from recognising the fact that conflict is an important social phenomenon, the organisation theorists began to appreciate the fact that conflict is one of the major organisational phenomena too. In fact, it can be aptly said that the study of organisation theory and behaviour cannot be considered complete without adequately understanding the phenomenon of conflict. It would be appropriate to mention that the views on organisational conflict have undergone significant changes over time. In this context, it would be worthwhile to present a bird's-eye view of the evolution of the concept of organisational conflict through a brief analysis of the contributions made by classical, neoclassical, and modern organisation theorists or experts. In fact, the contributions of these theorists have been already been discussed in detail in the preceding chapters.

The classical organisation theorists regarded conflict as a pathological phenomenon in organisations and therefore sought to avoid it or eliminate it. Therefore, the classicists prescribed organisation structures based on such important features as hierarchy of authority, division of work, chain of command, rationality, rules and regulations, efficiency in administration, systems and procedures, etc. They believed that the organisational structures based on these classical pillars will ensure harmony and cooperation in organisations and restrain the organisation's members from conflict and conflictful behaviour. In the end, the classical organisation structures will lead to maximum possible organisational effectiveness. It may be noted that the contributions made by famous classical organisation theorists in this regard were analysed earlier. Such famous classical authors included Taylor, Fayol, Weber, and Follett.

The neoclassical theorists believed that conflictis were essentially dysfunctional in character and, therefore, attempted to eliminate conflicts in organisations through suitable changes in their social systems. Mayo, a famous neoclassicist, was the father of the human relations movement, which started from late 1920s and early 1930s onwards.[1] Therefore, an extensive analysis of Mayo's[2] research findings and views on various aspects of the social system was made in Chapter 1. Mayo's major finding was that physical conditions alone were not enough to raise the productivity of workers. In fact, the positive social factors such as informal social relations, employee recognition, and teamwork among employees were extremely important in ensuring high levels of employees' productivity and their job satisfaction. About the role of conflict in organisations, Mayo viewed that conflict was essentially negative in character and, therefore, needed to be eliminated or reduced. Mayo sought to achieve this objective through various changes in the social system of an organisation.

While the classical and the neo-classical views on organisational conflict had considerable influence on management thoughts and practices for quite a long time. The modern view of conflict gained prominence especially after the first half of the twentieth century. Some of the well-known management thinkers who propagated the modern perspective of conflict were Litterer, Whyte, etc. These modern thinkers not only viewed conflict as an inevitable part of organisational life but also suggested that conflict may be even desirable in certain conditions. In fact, the healthy organisations not only seek to resolve conflicts but also stimulate them in order to realise their potential benefits. According to the modern viewpoint, conflict, if managed constructively, can lead to many positive outcomes such as increased productivity, creative problem-solving and effectiveness within organisations. The other potential benefits of well-managed conflict as discussed previously, include organisational change and creativity, release of tension of group members, group cohesiveness, productive challenges for organisation's members and groups, enhanced organisational effectiveness, etc.

A critical analysis of organisational conflict revealed an important aspect of conflict management, which should be followed by managers in the real organisational settings. According to the modern organisation theorists, a moderate degree of conflict must be maintained in organisations so as to enhance individual, group, and organisational effectiveness. The management experts including Robbins, Rahim, and Bonama[3] emphasized that a moderate amount of conflict, handled constructively, leads to optimum effectiveness in organisations. In other words, conflict in certain limits is necessary to fully utilise the potential, creativity, and innovative abilities of individuals and groups in organisations. It has been observed that little or no conflict leads to weak decisions, stagnation and ineffectiveness. Similarly, conflict beyond a certain limit has been found to hamper organisational productivity, sound human relations, and employee's job satisfaction. Therefore, it would be right to say that both too less and too much of conflict are detrimental to the attainment of organisational objectives. The modern organisation theorists have further suggested that a moderate amount of substantive or task related conflict (rather than affective or emotional conflict) ought to be maintained so as to attain optimum organisational effectiveness. Regarding the specific relationship between the intensity of conflict and organisational performance, Sharma[4] noted that a low degree of conflict leads to low organisational performance and, therefore, some amount of conflict must be promoted in order to stimulate organisational processes and activities. This stimulation of conflict helps to enhance organisational performance and reaches a particular point beyond which any further conflict stimulation proves to be rather counter-productive. If the intensity of conflict goes on increasing, it results in decreased performance and dysfunctionality of conflict. In this situation, there is an urgent need for resolution of conflict or reduction of conflict.

The available literature on organisational conflict has focused on its management aspects with a view to realising its potential benefits to an organisation. In fact, both the theoretical perspectives and the research findings available on conflict have indicated that conflict can lead to positive or negative consequences in organisations, depending upon its management. In this regard, it may be mentioned that the available literature on the management of organisational conflict has generally moved in two directions. According to the first approach, the researchers have tried to measure the degree or intensity of conflict existing at various organisational levels in terms of stress, anxiety, hostility, tension, etc., and also identify the sources of such conflicts. The underlying purpose is to maintain a moderate degree of conflict by altering the sources of such conflicts so that organisational effectiveness would be enhanced. In the words of Brown,[5] "conflict management can require intervention to reduce conflict if there is too much or intervention to promote conflict, if there is too little." It may be pointed out, however, that this intervention strategy for managing conflict as suggested by Brown appears to be appropriate for substantive conflict but not for affective conflict. The distinction between substantive conflict and affective conflict has been well laid out by Guetzkow and Gir[6] who viewed that substantive conflict is concerned with differences or disagreements between two or more parties over organisational issues or policies and leads to many beneficial outcomes. Affective conflict, on the other hand, consists of incompatible relations among organisation's members arising due to emotional or interpersonal issues and has negative effects on group performance and organisational effectiveness. Therefore, Guetzkow and Gir[7] suggested that a moderate level of substantive conflict should be maintained in organisations while affective conflict is to be minimised as much as possible on account of its deleterious effects. The second approach to conflict management involves the researchers' attempts to study the effectiveness of different conflict management methods or styles in terms of their impact on various dimensions of organisational effectiveness. In fact, a number of research studies have been conducted by researchers to examine the relationship between the conflict handling styles and different criteria of effectiveness. These research studies have not only provided valuable information regarding the present conflict management behaviours of managers but also suggested necessary changes therein so as to enhance organisational effectiveness.

In addition to the traditional approaches to conflict management as described above, it would be worthwhile to note that negotiation as a technique of conflict management has assumed considerable significance in the present-day industrial environment. In fact, negotiation, in its various forms, is frequently used by industry experts and managers for resolving disputes and allocating resources. Although there are certain similarities between negotiation strategies and conflict management, it must be pointed out that the scope of negotiation is much wider, and it goes beyond resolving conflict and can be extremely useful as a managerial skill for enhancing both individual and organisational success. In the modern organisations, the negotiation skills process is commonly observed in the interactions of almost all members in an organisation. The negotiation skills have indeed become very critical to the success of an organisation as the members have to continuously interact among themselves in order to carry on various team-related works and processes. In the context of negotiation, Walton and McKersie[8] distinguished between the two different types of approaches to negotiation in the context of negotiation: distributive bargaining, and integrative bargaining. Distributive bargaining operates under zero-sum conditions, i.e., the gain or profit made by one party is at the expense of the other party. To put it differently, distributive bargaining assumes that there is a "fixed pie" and, therefore, focuses upon negotiating over who gets what share of the fixed pie. Distributive bargaining is often used in the distribution of financial benefits and incentives such as salary, commission, bonus, etc., between individuals or parties. Integrative bargaining, on the other hand, involves an alternative approach that seeks to "expand the pie" with a view to finding win-win outcomes. It is noteworthy that integrative bargaining is often used to settle issues of common interest to both the parties such as allocation of work, greater employee autonomy in work activities, quality of work life, etc. The integrative approach is based on problem-solving or collaboration between individuals or groups.

In regard to the utilisation of negotiation skills and techniques, the negotiators need to understand contemporary issues in negotiation so as to enhance their bargaining strength and problem solving abilities or skills. These significant contemporary issues include the role of personality traits in negotiation, gender differences in negotiation, cultural differences in negotiation, and the use of third parties in the negotiation process. It is generally observed that the negotiators do possess varying personality dimensions, risk taking abilities, attitudes, and so on. The research evidence suggests that these personality traits do not have significant impact on the bargaining process or on the outcomes of negotiation. Therefore, any prior information regarding the personality traits of the rival negotiators will not be useful in predicting their negotiation strategies or tactics. Instead, the negotiator should pay utmost attention to the negotiation issues in each bargaining situation or episode rather than focusing on the personality traits of the opponent. In regard to the role of gender differences in negotiation, it is generally believed that women are more relationship oriented and cooperative than men in the process of negotiating with their opponents. This stereotype held about women in general is perhaps due to lesser power possessed by women in many of the organisations. Research evidence has indicated that both male and female managers with less power tend to use persuasive skills with their opponents rather than using confrontation tactics or direct threats. When men and women possess almost equal amount of power, their negotiation styles or tactics do not vary significantly. Cultural differences among managers and executives have a great impact on their negotiating styles or strategies. It has been observed that these cultural factors tend to influence the preparation for bargaining, the values placed on task versus interpersonal relationships, the negotiation strategies or styles to be used, etc. The role of third-party negotiators becomes necessary when the individual or group representatives are unable to resolve their disputes through direct negotiations. In these deadlock situations, they may approach a third party to help them in settling their disputes or conflicts. As discussed previously, there are four types of third-party negotiators: mediator, arbitrator, conciliator, and consultant.

Chapter 4 included a detailed description of various approaches to conflict management as suggested by the social scientists. In this context, it would be quite useful to make certain critical reflections on the applicability of these different approaches in the real conflict situations in organisations. In fact, these conflict management approaches are essentially based upon different methods or styles of handling conflict in organisations and also indicate the effectiveness of different conflict management methods or styles in different situations. These theoretical perspectives on conflict management have been suggested by such leading management theorists as Blake and Mouton, Thomas, Rahim, Blake, Shepard, and Mouton, Likert and Likert, Luft and Ingham, Hall, Pruitt, and Filley. A critical analysis of these approaches brings out the fact that every manager displays a preference for using a particular style of managing conflict. In spite of having such a dominant method of conflict management, however, every manager tends to fall back upon a backup style when the dominant method or style of managing conflict fails to work in a given situation. In addition, it may be noted that the social scientists have broadly viewed the problem-solving approach as the most effective one in managing conflict in the industrial situations. In fact, the managers following the problem solving approach seek to maintain a proper balance between the the production objectives and the human relations aspect of the job. Although the managers are supposed to achieve the production targets, they have to be equally concerned about the welfare of employees, maintain harmonious and useful relations with them, and also consider their viewpoints and suggestions in the decision making process.

As discussed, a number of empirical research studies have been conducted to examine the effects of conflict handling styles or methods on various dimensions of interpersonal, inter-group, or organisational effectiveness. It would be pertinent to briefly review the findings of some of these significant studies and also make certain observations in this regard. At a theoretical level, Blake and Mouton[9] viewed that individuals or organisations using the problem-solving style of conflict management achieve effective interpersonal relations and enhanced organisational effectiveness. Lawrence and Lorsch[10] examined the effects of confrontation, smoothing, and forcing behaviours in six organisations and found that confrontation or problem-solving was positively related to organisational effectiveness. It was also observed that the presence of forcing as a back-up mode and the absence of smoothing were related to organisational effectiveness. Burke[11] examined the five methods of conflict management as suggested by Blake and Mouton in the context of senior-subordinate relations. The findings in their study suggested that confrontation or problem-solving was the most effective method of conflict resolution and it was followed by smoothing behaviour. In addition, it was noted that withdrawing and forcing behaviours were negatively related to interpersonal effectiveness while compromising was related to none of the effectiveness variables. Thomas[12] noted that managers' satisfaction with inter-departmental negotiations had positive relationship with the utilisation of confrontation and smoothing behaviours by their colleagues in other departments and negative relationship with forcing and withdrawing behaviours by the latter. Aram *et.al.,*[13] conducted a study in research and development teams and found that collaboration was positively related to certain measures of members' self actualization and well-being. On the contrary, Dutton and Walton[14] noticed that managers engaged in competitive inter-departmental relations experienced anxiety and frustration.

It may be further noted that the researchers have conducted a few valuable empirical research studies in the Indian industrial situations on the relationship between the conflict management styles and effectiveness measures. Sharma and Samantara[15] conducted an empirical study in an Indian computer-manufacturing company in order to examine the effects of conflict resolution methods on effectiveness measures such as productivity, adaptability, and flexibility. The findings of the study indicated that confrontation or problem-solving was the most effective method of conflict resolution, and it was followed by smoothing behaviour. While compromising and withdrawing behaviours were somewhat positively related to certain effectiveness measures, the forcing mode of conflict resolution was the most ineffective one. In order to gather additional research evidence concerning the relative effectiveness of conflict management methods or styles and certain other important aspects of organisational conflict, Samantara[16] conducted a comprehensive research study in some organisations in aluminium, steel, and paper manufacturing industries in India. In addition to obtaining valuable information regarding certain significant issues and sources of senior-subordinate conflict in the aluminium-manufacturing organisation, the researcher found that the managers working in different departments and across hierarchical levels of this organisation made considerable use of problem-solving, smoothing and compromising behaviours while their utilisation of forcing and withdrawing behaviours was relatively negligible. This pattern of utilisation of conflict management methods or behaviours was noticed even among managers within the steel and the paper manufacturing units. The findings of this comprehensive study also revealed some important relationships between the conflict management methods and various dimensions of organisational effectiveness such as productivity, adaptability, and flexibility. In general, it was observed that problem-solving was the most effective method of conflict resolution, and it was followed by smoothing behaviour. While the compromising mode produced mixed results with respect to its effects on effectiveness measures, the forcing behaviour was found to have negative impact on several dimensions of organisational effectiveness. The withdrawing behaviour seemed to be related to none of the effectiveness variables.

A significant development in the management literature relates to the fact that during the last few decades, the management writings have undergone changes in emphasis from the universalistic principles of management to situational principles and relationships. The broad consensus among management scholars is that the contingency theory of management is perhaps the most dominant one in the field of organisational behaviour. The growth of the contingency theory of management can be primarily attributed to the inherent limitations of the classical organisation theories such as Taylor's[17] Scientific Management theory, Weber's[18] bureaucracy, etc. These theories failed to recognise the fact that organisation's structure, technologies, processes, etc., were influenced by various situational or environmental forces. In fact, the seminal works of prominent contingency theorists such as Woodward, Burns and Stalker, Thompson, and Lawrence and Lorsch explicitly recognised and explored the organisation and environment relationships and thus laid the foundation for the development of the contingency theory of management. A significant fallout of this development has been that the management experts have suggested several contingency approaches in the area of organisational conflict and its management as well.

It must be highlighted that the preceding discussions of conflict management approaches are based on the normative viewpoints which suggest that there is one best style of conflict management. Therefore, many researchers examined the functionality of conflict management methods or styles in the context of various dimensions of interpersonal, inter-group or organisational effectiveness. As we have seen above, the results of these empirical studies have generally suggested that problem-solving is the most effective method of conflict management, and it seems to be followed by smoothing behaviour. In contrast to these normative approaches to conflict management, the contingency viewpoints suggest that a particular method or style of conflict management may be viewed as more effective than another one, depending upon the situational variables. Thus, according to the contingency viewpoints, the managers must identify and analyse the situational variables before choosing the most appropriate style of conflict management to be used in a particular situation. It is, therefore, significant to note that different contingency theorists including Blake and Mouton, Thomas, Rahim, Pareek, Philips and Cheston, and Derr have identified and analysed different sets of situational variables that do influence the choice of the most effective or the most appropriate methods or styles of conflict management. In spite of the valuable contributions of these contingency theorists, it must be pointed out that it has not been possible so far to develop a well accepted contingency theory of conflict management. In addition, it may be noted that most of the contingency viewpoints on conflict management have been offered by management experts only theoretically although there is a need to examine the appropriateness of conflict management methods or styles in the context of various organisational, psychosocial, and environmental variables.

Ethical considerations in conflict management have been a major area of concern for the social scientists and management experts. With the significant expansion of business activities cutting across national boundaries, conflicts have increased over ethical issues in organisations such as transparent accounting systems, protection of consumers' rights, product safety, protection of the environment, treatment of employees, contribution towards social welfare schemes, etc. The business leaders have come to realize that unethical business practices have adverse effects not only on the profitability and effectiveness of business firms but also on conflict and its management in organisations. It has been observed that positive results for organisations are invariably related to ethical rather than unethical applications of certain methods or styles of managing conflicts. In fact, the unethical or inappropriate application of conflict management methods may escalate the current conflicts and create ones that never existed before. In view of the importance of ethics and morality in organisations, attempts were made in Chapter 8 to address some significant ethical issues in the area of conflict management. In this connection, the organisational behaviour experts have noted the role of such important conflict-related issues as individual values and value systems, personality types and styles, and individual differences in conflict, which lead to ethical or unethical behaviour in conflict situations. In addition, the organisation theorists have attempted to provide certain guidelines to organisations members so that they can handle interpersonal and inter-group conflicts more effectively and more ethically. In this regard, Rahim[19] has made pioneering research works to show that the applications of different conflict management methods or styles may be considered ethically appropriate or inappropriate, depending upon the prevalence of some specific situations. According to Rahim,[20] the integrating style of managing conflicts is the most ethical one, and, therefore, this style should be used by organisation's members to the maximum possible extent. At the same time, Rahim argued for reduction in the use of the dominating and the avoiding styles which are generally being maximally used by individuals operating at lower levels of moral development.

In spite of the relevance of ethical considerations in conflict management, it has been noticed that such significant issues have been relatively less explored in the context of organisations. Although it is generally believed that the conflict management methods or styles are used for ethical purposes, it is quite possible that these methods can be utilised for unethical purposes too. The ethical or unethical use of conflict management styles depends upon many factors such as the situational variables, the intentions of parties using them, the extent to which the goals of the organisation are served, etc. The business leaders and managers have to reconcile the conflicting claims of various stakeholders connected to the organisation. In fact, there is no simple means to ensure that conflict management styles are ethically used in organisations. Nevertheless, the business leaders are expected to be more open to new information and insights and be guided by ethical or moral considerations in their utilisation of various conflict management techniques. At the same time, they must ensure that the ultimate objectives of the organisation are being served by the conflict management decisions made by them.

In view of globalisation, liberalisation, and expansion of business activities, the adoption of advanced technologies in business, and the need to combine and utilise the varied talents of the workforce, etc., the formation of multicultural task groups has become absolutely necessary in the modern organisations. The formation of these diverse task groups composed of people with different national, ethnic, and racial backgrounds are bound to lead to multicultural group conflicts in organisations. In this changed organisational scenario, the traditional approaches to conflict management involving the use of problem-solving, smoothing, compromising, forcing, withdrawing, etc., will no longer be sufficient enough to handle these conflicts occurring in modern organisations. In fact, the managers are supposed to adopt a changed outlook and attempt to utilise the benefits of cultural diversity rather than seeing it as an impediment to the attainment of group and organisational objectives. In managing organisational conflicts, the managers should be guided by two types of cultural influences: (1) culture of the organisation itself including its traditions, values, belief systems, people's ways of behaving, etc.; and (2) cultural influences imposed by the external environment. The research studies have shown that cultural diversity in task groups has a significant impact on the manner in which conflict is perceived and handled by group members. In addition, it has been found that cultural diversity can intensify or inhibit conflicts in task group. On account of these facts, it is broadly suggested that the managers ought to adopt an open-minded and flexible approach so as to promote collaborative group behaviour among group members while managing multicultural group conflicts in organisations.

In the light of the above-mentioned facts, it must be emphasized that multicultural group conflicts occurring in MNCs and international organisations have important implications for practising managers and policy-makers. Managers in many international organisations have been focusing their efforts on how to make jobs more challenging and more satisfying to the workers. The American companies, for instance, have undertaken various job enlargement and job enrichment programmes with a view to satisfying the workers' needs for individual autonomy, sense of fulfilment, and more of recognition at the workplace. In European countries, on the other hand, the corporate leaders' or policy-makers' efforts to make work more challenging and more satisfying have emphasized upon team-oriented approach to work and interpersonal relationships rather than individual accomplishments. It may be noted that these differences in national cultures have great significance for managers operating in multinational organisations. These managers need to adopt management styles and practices that are suitable for the particular nation or culture in which they are operating.

## 10.2 MAJOR RESEARCH FINDINGS OBTAINED

After having examined various conceptual issues relating to organisational conflict and its management aspects, it would be appropriate to present and discuss the valuable findings of the empirical research studies conducted by the author in this regard. In spite of the importance of the subject of conflict and its management in organisations, it has been found that empirical research evidences in these areas have been rather inadequate. Therefore, the author decided to explore certain crucial aspects of conflict in certain selected organisations in the Indian industry. The major questions of organisational conflict examined included certain issues and sources of senior-subordinate conflict, the present conflict handling behaviours of senior managers while dealing with their subordinates, the relative effectiveness of these behaviours in terms of their impact on certain aspects of organisational effectiveness. In addition, it may be noted that certain desirable changes in the conflict management behaviours of managers have also been suggested in order to enhance organisational effectiveness in the Indian industry. The empirical research studies were conducted in two major industries: power generation and distribution, and cement manufacturing industries. The following discussions are intended not only to provide a cursory picture of the major research findings obtained but also to analyse the practical significance of the research findings obtained for both practising managers and researchers.

The empirical research studies were conducted in two distinct but related phases. Initially, the study was conducted in a public sector electricity generating and distributing company having its network spread over different regions of the country. Managers working in different functional areas such as production, engineering, accounting, HR, IT, etc., and across hierarchical levels of this organisation were contacted at the Corporate Office of this company situated in the NCR region of Delhi. The respondent managers had sufficient field experience as they were being intermittently transferred from the Corporate Office to the power generation sites at other places and back to the headquarters. It may be mentioned that questionnaire data were provided by 52 managers out of about 400 managers working in the Head Office of the company. The managers provided perceptual measures of their responses to various questionnaire items that related to certain significant issues and sources of job related conflicts within the framework of senior-subordinate relationships, and the conflict management behaviours of both the senior managers and their subordinates at the workplace. The questionnaire items relating to various issues and sources of conflict were selected after a careful review of the literature. In regard to the measurement of conflict handling behaviours of managers, it may be noted that a Conflict Management Scale developed by the author[21] was used to measure the managers' responses regarding their utilisation of five different conflict management methods or styles as suggested by Blake and Mouton[22] such as problem-solving, smoothing, compromise, forcing, and withdrawing. Subsequently, the perceptual responses provided by the managers were analysed with the help of such statistical techniques as means, standard deviations and correlations with a view to deriving some significant research results and conclusions.

The results of this research study brought out certain important aspects of senior-subordinate conflict at the workplace. Regarding ten different issues of senior subordinate conflict examined in this study, it was found that the most frequently occurring conflict issues included errors or misinterpretation of official orders and carelessness, performance appraisal of subordinates, time spent by them on the job, work standards to be achieved, etc. Thus, these significant issues of conflict were related to certain individual and managerial issues that needed to be sorted out at the workplace. In fact, the managers are supposed to make necessary improvements in such areas as proper management of time, accurate interpretation of official communication and orders by subordinates, achievement of work standards by them, etc. On the other hand, the least important issues of conflict were the physical work environment, wage and salary administration, promotion, leave sanctioned, etc., conflict over job objectives, and utilisation of equipment and facilities within the office complex. These findings can be attributed to the fact that the physical work environment was quite satisfactory with an excellent office layout. In addition, the objectives of each job or position were clearly defined through an efficient administrative system while both the senior managers and their subordinates were generally satisfied with the salary structure as well as promotion and leave rules of the organisation.

An analysis of research data obtained regarding the sources of senior-subordinate conflict indicated that the most significant sources of conflict were differences in knowledge, skills or expertise, differences in personal value systems and beliefs, and unreasonable policies, procedures, rules, etc. Thus, it can be stated that individual differences between seniors and subordinates in terms of job knowledge or expertise and managerial orientations emerged as the underlying sources of conflict. Contrary to our expectations, hierarchical differences in status, power and rewards were also noticed as a major source of senior-subordinate conflict. At the same time, it was noted that the least important sources of conflict included need for tension release, individual drive for autonomy, and personality differences between the seniors and subordinates. In fact, these are certain individual factors that did not seem to have any significant influence on senior-subordinate relations at the work situation.

With regard to the conflict management behaviours of managers, the analysis of research data revealed that both the senior managers and their subordinates made considerable use of problem-solving, smoothing, and compromising modes of resolving conflicts while their utilisation of forcing and withdrawing modes was relatively negligible. It was also noted that both the seniors and their subordinates exhibited this pattern of utilisation of conflict management behaviours irrespective of whether they belonged to the top management, middle management, or lower management level. Thus, the managers, regardless of their organisational position, power, and status, valued the human relations aspect of the job to a great extent. Their management orientations or behaviours indicated that the production objectives of the organisation are to be achieved but only through the voluntary cooperation of subordinates and their participation in organisational decision-making on a variety of task related issues and challenges. The fact that both the senior managers and their subordinates are making maximum possible use of the problem-solving approach indicates that they engage themselves in the rational process of identifying the alternatives, evaluating the alternatives, and finally, selecting the best possible alternative out of the whole lot with a view to finding amicable solutions to work-related problems and conflicts. In addition, it can be stated that the managers' considerable use of problem-solving, smoothing, and compromising behaviours is a clear reflection of their democratic approaches to the management of job related conflicts. In fact, these three methods or styles of conflict management emphasize upon the human relations aspect of the job or upon both the production and the human relations aspects of the job on an equal basis. Finally, the managers' low or insignificant use of forcing and withdrawing behaviours indicates that both the seniors and the subordinates preferred to confront or face conflicts and find productive solutions thereto rather than avoiding the conflict situations.

In the second phase of the research studies conducted by the author, attempts were made to study the managers' utilisation of conflict handling methods or styles and then examine the relative effectiveness of these methods or styles in terms of their impact on well defined measures of organisational effectiveness. These significant research issues were, in fact, investigated in two privately owned cement manufacturing organisations situated in the north-eastern region of India. In this context, it may be mentioned that these research issues were previously examined by the author in two steel manufacturing and two paper manufacturing organisations.[23] Although these earlier studies provided adequate research evidence regarding the present conflict management behaviours of Indian managers and the relative effectiveness thereof, the present research is intended to make further investigation of these important research questions in the cement industry in order to gather some additional evidences in relation thereto. It is expected that these accumulating research evidences will help us in making some meaningful generalisations regarding the effectiveness of conflict management methods and also in suggesting necessary improvements in the conflict management behaviors of Indian managers so as to enhance organisational effectiveness.

It may be mentioned that the present empirical research studies are also intended to improve upon the research inconsistencies and methodological limitations of some previous well-known research studies. As discussed in Chapter 7, Lawrence and Lorsch[24] examined the effectiveness of conflict management methods in high performing, medium performing, and low performing organisations. According to them, a particular method of conflict management was to be regarded as effective or ineffective depending upon whether it was utilised to a greater or smaller extent in the more effective organisation than in the less effective one. However, it is felt that the effectiveness of conflict management methods or styles can be judged more realistically if these methods are explicitly related to certain well-defined measures of organisational effectiveness. In addition, it may be noted that Lawrence and Lorsch[25] examined data obtained at the organisation level and concluded that forcing was an effective method of conflict management and could be considered an effective back-up mode to confrontation or problem-solving behaviour. However, Burke[26] examined data collected at the individual level and inferred that smoothing was to be considered an effective back-up method to problem-solving whereas forcing was not. It was considered necessary to resolve these research inconsistencies and make necessary suggestions in this regard. Finally, it must be highlighted that most of the empirical studies examining the relationship between conflict management methods or styles and various dimensions of effectiveness have been conducted in the American industrial or organisational situations. These studies may not have much of relevance in the Indian context due to differences in education and income levels of managers and employees, their socio-economic conditions, cultural factors, etc. Therefore, there is a need to explore the above-stated research questions regarding conflict management across a wide spectrum of Indian industries so that the research findings obtained can be regarded as generally applicable in Indian industrial situations.

Considering the major research issues as discussed above, the author proceeded to examine different aspects of conflict management behaviours of Indian managers in two cement manufacturing firms situated in North East India. To be more specific, the research study attempted to explore the relationship between the five methods of conflict management suggested by Blake and Mouton[27] and certain perceptual measures of organisational effectiveness. The five conflict management methods or styles examined included: (1) problem-solving; (2) smoothing; (3) compromise; (4) forcing; and (5) withdrawing. In view of multifarious dimensions of organisational effectiveness as mentioned in the management literature, the scope of investigation in the present study has been limited to such selected measures of organisational effectiveness: (1) productivity; (2) adaptability; and (3) flexibility. As mentioned by Steers,[28] these three measures of effectiveness have been most frequently utilised in various models of organisational effectiveness. In this connection, it may be noted that a Conflict Management Scale developed by the author[29] (as given in Appendix 2) was used to measure the managers' responses regarding their utilisation of the five conflict management methods as mentioned above. Similarly, the Organisational Effectiveness Scale developed by Mott[30] was used to measure the three dimensions of effectiveness: productivity, adaptability and flexibility. All these important aspects of effectiveness were measured on a 5-point Likert type scale. It is noteworthy that questionnaire data were obtained from 60 managers and 57 managers of the two cement manufacturing firms labelled as Organisation 1 and Organisation 2, respectively. The respondent managers represented various levels of the organisational hierarchy (top management, middle management, and lower-level management) and belonged to diverse functional areas including production, marketing, HR, finance, etc.

A comparative analysis of data obtained from Organisation 1 and Organisation 2 broadly indicated that the managers of both these organisations made considerable use of problem-solving, compromising, and smoothing behaviour while their utilisation of forcing behaviour was relatively insignificant or negligible. In fact, research evidences regarding this pattern of conflict management behaviour of Indian managers have been obtained in some previous research studies too.[31] These significant findings regarding the conflict management behaviours of Indian managers point to the fact that they tend to adopt democratic approaches to the management of work related conflicts at the workplace while dealing with their seniors or subordinates. The adoption of these conflict management approaches further signifies that the Indian managers value both the production and the human relations aspects of the job and also give due importance to the knowledge and viewpoints of subordinates at the workplace. As discussed in detail in Chapter 5, this significant development in the area of conflict management in Indian organisations can be attributed to such factors as changes in industrial ethos and practices, changes in management orientations, increasing levels of subordinates' income and education, their increasing awareness of their basic democratic rights and privileges in the industrial or organisational situations.

The multiple regression results analysed for both organisations revealed some important aspects of the relationship between the conflict management methods (as used by managers) and various dimensions of organisational effectiveness. It was noticed that the conflict management methods or styles, considered collectively, explained a significant proportion of variance (i.e., 13 per cent) in the productivity of Organisation 1 but not in its adaptability and flexibility aspects. In Organisation 2, however, the conflict management methods, taken together, explained all the three composite measures of productivity, flexibility, and adaptability (i.e., 22 per cent, 18 percent, and 7 per cent respectively). The findings regarding the impact of each individual method of conflict management on specific measures of organisational effectiveness were as follows: (1) the problem-solving mode was positively related to rapidity of adjustment in Organisation 1 and also to rapidity of adjustment and flexibility in Organisation 2; (2) the smoothing mode had negative and significant relationship with both the quality of output and the productivity of Organisation 1 but it was positively related to the quality of output in Organisation 2; (3) although the forcing mode was negatively related to the quantity and the quality aspects of output as well as to the overall productivity of Organisation 1, it was found to have positive significant relationship with rapidity of adjustment in Organisation 2; and (4) the withdrawing mode was negatively related to the quantity aspect of output in Organisation 1 but it indicated positive relationship with the overall measure of productivity in Organisation 2.

The findings of the present research concerning the impact of conflict management methods on different measures of organisational effectiveness have been largely similar to those of some previous studies conducted by the author.[32] It has been clearly established that 'conflict management' is a crucial aspect of organisational behaviour, having noticeable impact on the effectiveness of organisations. The research findings further indicate that problem-solving is clearly the most effective method of conflict management whereas the forcing mode has dysfunctional effects on organisational effectiveness. In addition, the results of the present research study have revealed that the smoothing and the withdrawing behaviours seem to have mixed effects on certain effectiveness dimensions. The compromising mode appears to be related to none of the effectiveness variables.

## 10.3 IMPLICATIONS FOR PRACTISING MANAGERS

The valuable findings of the present study suggest that certain modifications or improvements in the conflict management behaviours of Indian managers are required to enhance various aspects of organisational effectiveness in Indian industry. The research data broadly indicate that the Indian managers are making an immense use of problem-solving and smoothing behaviours in resolving work related conflicts with their subordinates. The managers' maximum use of problem-solving behaviour is certainly to be welcomed and strengthened further especially when the job related knowledge, expertise and income levels of subordinate managers or subordinate employees have improved quite significantly in the recent times. In fact, the subordinates do possess the requisite ability and willingness to work together with their superiors in organisational decision-making and thereby develop constructive solutions to a variety of organisational problems or conflicts. Although the present study has indicated the mixed effects of smoothing behaviour on different aspects of organisational effectiveness, the studies conducted by the author[33] previously have generally shown that this mode of resolving conflict has positive effects on effectiveness dimensions. Therefore, the managers' immense utilisation of smoothing behaviour seems to be somewhat justified although there is no particular need to enhance it further. The managers' emphasis on the human relations aspect alone may not yield the desired results fully as there is a paramount need to focus on the production aspect of the job too.

In addition, it has been noticed that the managers are making considerable use of compromising behaviour in resolving job-related differences or disputes with their subordinates. As discussed in Chapter 5, the subordinates too utilised compromising behaviour to a considerable extent in handling conflicts with their seniors. The results of the present study, however, show that compromising behaviour does not seem to have significant impact on any of the effectiveness aspects. In fact, the organisation theorists have viewed that compromising has adverse effects on individual creativity or innovation or on any significant improvement in organisation's performance. Therefore, a reduction in the managers' dependence on compromising behaviour would be considered desirable.

In regard to the utility of forcing behaviour, the findings of the present study as well as of the previous ones have amply demonstrated the negative effects of forcing behaviour on different aspects of effectiveness. In the contemporary industrial situations and conditions, the managers cannot afford to neglect the increasing needs and aspirations of their subordinates or ignore the latters' suggestions and viewpoints in the decision-making process. In fact, there is an all-important need to treat the subordinates as equal partners in organisational decision-making and utilise their job related expertise or abilities to the fullest possible extent. It is quite encouraging to know that the Indian managers have shown considerable wisdom in their infrequent use of this mode of handling conflicts.

The research findings have, by and large, shown that withdrawing behaviour seems to have mixed effects on dimensions of organisational effectiveness. Therefore, the managers should not be encouraged to frequently withdraw or escape from the conflict situations. Since conflicts are inevitable in organisational life, any attempts made by managers to keep away from the conflict situations do not lead to any productive outcomes or solutions.

## 10.4 AREAS FOR FUTURE RESEARCH

The present research may serve as a benchmark in that it reveals some of the significant issues relating to organisational conflict and its management aspects. In addition to analysing and integrating the theoretical knowledge and insights gained from the review of available literature, the author made endeavours to empirically study the relative effectiveness of different conflict management methods or styles in terms of their impact on effectiveness dimensions and also suggest necessary behavioural modifications required of Indian managers in order to enhance organisational effectiveness. It was broadly suggested that problem-solving may be regarded as the most effective method of conflict management and accordingly, the managers are required to continue with their maximum utilisation of this conflict handling behaviour as is being made by them at present. At the same time, the negative effects of forcing behaviour were amply demonstrated by the results of the present study as well as of the earlier ones. While these research findings may have practical relevance in the Indian industrial situations, it has been pointed out in Chapter 8 equally well that several situational variables do play a significant role in the selection and utilisation of appropriate conflict management methods or styles in organisations. According to the proponents of the contingency viewpoint, different conflict management methods or styles may be considered effective or ineffective depending upon the prevailing situational factors or variables. Therefore, the practising managers in organisations need to understand and consider the situational variables before choosing the most appropriate method of conflict management to be used. As discussed in Chapter 8, the famous contingency theorists including Thomas, Derr, Pareek, Rahim and so on, have analysed different sets of situational variables affecting the choice of conflict management methods or styles and their attendant consequences. In spite of these valuable contributions made by leading contingency theorists, it must be pointed out that so far it has not been possible to develop a well accepted theory of conflict management within the domain of organisational behaviour. Therefore, it is suggested that the researchers need to conduct many more extensive studies of conflict management methods or styles and their effectiveness in the context of various organisational, environmental and other contingency variables.

As discussed quite extensively in Chapter 9, the question of ethical management of conflict in organisations has not been adequately explored in the management literature. Therefore, another significant area of future research relates to ethical values and behaviours of managers that do play a significant role in their selection and use of appropriate conflict management methods or styles in organisational situations. In addition, it has been noted by organisational behaviour experts that cross-cultural conflicts in many organisations do occur over ethical issues or concerns affecting the broader society. These conflicts can be largely attributed to various social and cultural factors across nations. The future researchers need to focus on this nexus between cross-cultural conflicts in MNCs and international organisations and differences in ethical standards or values across national cultures.

Another important aspect of cross-cultural conflict in organisations is that such conflicts do arise due to the formation of diverse work groups comprising of individuals with different ethnic, racial and national backgrounds. As stated earlier, the traditional methods or styles of conflict management will not be adequate enough to handle multicultural conflicts in organisations. In fact, management should try to utilise the benefits of cultural diversities existing in organisations rather than seeing such diversities negatively. In this context, the researchers need to explore various issues relating to the relationship between cultural diversity and conflict in organisations. The researchers should also examine the question as to how the potential of cultural minorities at the workplace can be utilised to manage organisational conflicts constructively.

The present research has shown that members of task groups hailing from different cultural and national backgrounds tend to use different methods or styles of managing interpersonal conflicts among themselves. In addition, it has been observed that these group members with diverse ethnic and cultural backgrounds do interact to promote cross-cultural collaboration among themselves. The findings of the present research do point to possibilities of further research on these important aspects of cross-cultural conflict management as it suggests opportunities for both meaningful research and theory building in many different ways.

## REFERENCES

1. Mayo, E., *The Human Problems of an Industrial Civilisation*, Mcmilan, New York, 1933.
2. *Ibid.*
3. Robbins, S.P., *Managing Organisational Conflict: A Non-traditional Approach*, Prentice-Hall, Englewood Cliffs, NJ, 1974; Rahim, M.A., and Bonama, T.V., Managing organisational conflict: A model for diagnosis and intervention, *Psychological Reports*, 44, 1979, pp. 1323-1344.
4. Sharma, R.A., *Organisational Theory and Behaviour*, Tata McGraw Hill, New Delhi, 2000.

5. Brown, L.D., Managing Conflict at Organisational Interfaces, Addison-Wesley, Reading, MA, 1983.
6. Guetzkow, H., and Gyr, J., An analysis of decision-making groups, *Human Relations*, 1954.
7. *Ibid.*
8. Walton, R.E. and McKersie, R.B., *A Behavioural Theory of Labour Negotiations: Analysis of a Social Interaction System*, McGraw Hill, New York, 1965.
9. Blake, R.R., and Mouton, J .S., *The Managerial Grid*, Gulf, Houston, 1964.
10. Lawrence, P.R., and Lorsch, J.W., *Organisation and Environment: Managing Differentiation and Integration*, Division of Research, Harvard Business School, Harvard University Boston, 1967.
11. Burke, R.J., Methods of resolving inter-personal conflict, *Personnel Administration*, July-August, 1969, pp. 48-55.
12. Thomas, K.W., Conflict and conflict management, M.D. Dunettee, (Ed.), *Handbook of Industrial and Organisational Psychology*, Rand McNally, 1976, pp. 889-935.
13. Aram, J.D., Morgan, C.P. and Esbeck, E.S., Relation of collaborative interpersonal relationships to individual satisfaction and organisational performance, *Administrative Science Quarterly*, 16(3), 1971.
14. Dutton, J.M., and Walton, R.E., Interdepartmental conflict and cooperation: Two contrasting studies, *Human Organisation*, 25(3), 1966.
15. Sharma, R.A., and Samantara, R., Conflict management in an Indian firm: A case study, *Decision*, 21(4), 1994.
16. Samantara, R., Management of superior-subordinate conflict: An exploration, *Indian Journal of Industrial Relations*, 38(4), 2003, pp. 444-459; Samantara, R., Conflict management strategies and organisational effectiveness, *Indian Journal of Industrial Relations*, 39(3), January 2004, pp. 298-323.
17. Taylor, F.W., *The Principles of Scientific Management*, Harper and Row, New York, 1911.
18. Weber, M., The Theory of Social and Economic Organisation (Trans. from German, A.M. Henderson and T. Persons), Oxford University Press, New York, 1947.
19. Rahim, M.A., *Managing Conflict in Organisations*, Quorom Books, London, 2002.
20. *Ibid.*
21. Samantara, R., 2003, *op. cit.*
22. Blake, R.R., and Mouton, J.S., 1964, *op. cit.*
23. Samantara, R., 2004, *op. cit.*
24. Lawrence, P.R. and Lorsch, J.W., 1967, *op. cit.*

25. *Ibid.*
26. Burke, R.J., 1969, *op. cit.*
27. Blake, R.R., and Mouton, J.S., 1964, *op. cit.*
28. Steers, R.M., *Organisational Effectiveness*, Goodyear, Santa Monica, CA, 1977.
29. Samantara, R., 2003, *op. cit.*
30. Mott, P.E., *The Characteristics of Effective Organisation*, Harper and Row, New York, 1972.
31. Burke, R.J., 1969, *op. cit.*; Sharma, R.A. and Samantara, R., 1994, *op. cit.*; Samantara, R., 2003, *op. cit.*; and Samantara, R., 2004, *op. cit.*
32. Sharma, R.A., and Samantara, R., 1994, *op. cit.*; Samantara, R., 2003, *op. cit.*; and Samantara, R. 2004, *op. cit.*
33. *Ibid.*

# APPENDICES

# Appendix 1

## QUESTIONNAIRE

Name :

Designation :

Department :

Hierarchical Level :

## CONFLICT ISSUES

Please rank the following topics or issues in terms of how frequently you have disagreements about them with your subordinates (1 means the most frequent one; 2 the next most frequent one, & so on, up to 10, which is the least frequent one)

(i) Conflict over job objectives ( )

(ii) Work standards to be accomplished (volume of work expected, time limits, etc.) ( )

(iii) Planning of activities (what should be done, how it should be done, who should do it, etc.) ( )

(iv) The question as to how equipment and facilities are to be used or other technical issues are to be dealt with. ( )

(v) Amount of time spent on the job (not meeting deadlines, arriving late, leaving early, etc.) ( )

(vi) Errors, misinterpretation of orders, carelessness, etc. ( )

(vii) Supervision, direction and control (too less or too much of freedom, participation in decision-making, etc.) ( )

(viii) Performance appraisal (evaluation of task execution, goal attainment, etc.) ( )

(ix) Administration of wages, promotions, sanction of leave, etc. ( )

(x) Physical working environment (including noise, space, office temperature, ventilation, etc.) ( )

## SOURCES OF INTERPERSONAL CONFLICT

Also rank the following in terms of how often these are perceived as the reasons for disagreement including you and your subordinates (1 means the most frequent one; 2 the next most frequent one, & so on, up to 9 which is the least frequent one)

(i) Personality differences (such as family background, education, social pattern, etc.) ( )

(ii) Differences in basic values, beliefs or opinions ( )

(iii) Differences in knowledge, skills, or expertise ( )

(iv) Unreasonable policies, procedures, or rules ( )

(v) Barriers to interpersonal communication ( )

(vi) Hierarchical differences in status, power and rewards ( )

(vii) Competition for a particular position, power or recognition ( )

(viii) Drive for autonomy ( )

(ix) Need for tension release ( )

## CONFLICT MANAGEMENT STYLES

### PART A

The following statements represent ways of resolving differences or disagreements arising between individuals in the work situation. Please read each statement and write a number from 1 to 5 in the space provided on the left hand side of the statement to indicate the extent to which it describes the manner in which *you actually resolve conflict with your subordinate(s) on job related matters.*

(1) Describes behaviour which never occurs.

(2) Describes behaviour which seldom occurs.

(3) Describes behaviour which occurs sometimes.

(4) Describes behaviour which occurs frequently.

(5) Describes behaviour which usually occurs.

__________ The argument of the most powerful always carries the most weight.

__________ A fair exchange brings no quarrel.

__________ Conflict can be resolved if the conflicting parties understand each other and jointly search for alternate solutions.

__________ While trying to resolve conflicts, each party should ensure that the other's feelings and emotions are not hurt.

__________ In the face of conflict, the best policy is to remain neutral or stay out of it.

__________ When conflict arises, one should try to identify the reasons for it and resolve the underlying issues.

__________ When conflict arises, one should use all possible means (power, position or expertise) to force acceptance of one's own point of view.

__________ Whenever conflict occurs, one should try to be fair and firm, and try to get an equitable solution.

__________ A person loses least in a quarrel if he avoids arguments, takes no responsibility and tries not to get involved.

__________ In a conflict situation, one should tone down the differences and emphasise common interests to maintain good relations.

__________ A conflict issue should be resolved through the use of knowledge or reason if we want to have sound, creative decisions.

__________ It is easier to refrain than to retreat from a quarrel.

## PART B

You are also requested to indicate, using the scoring procedure as given in Part A (1, 2, 3, 4, & 5), the extent to which each of the following statements describes the manner in which *your subordinates resolve conflict with you on job related matters.*

__________ The argument of the most powerful always carries the most weight.

__________ A fair exchange brings no quarrel.

__________ Conflict can be resolved if the parties involved understand each other and jointly search for solutions.

__________ While trying to resolve conflicts, each party should ensure that the other's feelings and emotions are not hurt.

__________ In the face of conflict, the best policy is to remain neutral or stay out of it.

__________ When conflict arises, one should try to identify the reasons for it and resolve the underlying issues.

__________ When conflict arises, one should use all possible means (power, position or expertise) to force acceptance of one's own point of view.

__________ Whenever conflict occurs, one should try to be fair and firm, and try to get an equitable solution.

__________ A person loses least in a quarrel if he avoids arguments, takes no responsibility, and tries not to get involved.

__________ In a conflict situation, one should tone down the differences and emphasise common interests to maintain good relations.

__________ A conflict issue should be resolved through the use of knowledge or reason if we want to have sound, creative decisions.

__________ It is easier to refrain than to retreat from a quarrel.

# Appendix 2

## QUESTIONNAIRE

Name :
Designation :
Department :
Hierarchical Level :

## CONFLICT MANAGEMENT STYLES

The following statements represent ways of resolving differences or disagreements arising between individuals in the work situation. Please read each statement and write a number from 1 to 5 in the space provided on the left-hand side of the statement to indicate the extent to which it describes the manner in which *you actually resolve conflict with your subordinate(s) on job related matters.*

(1) Describes behaviour which never occurs.
(2) Describes behaviour which seldom occurs.
(3) Describes behaviour which occurs sometimes.
(4) Describes behaviour which occurs frequently.
(5) Describes behaviour which usually occurs.

__________ The argument of the most powerful always carries the most weight.

__________ A fair exchange brings no quarrel.

__________ Conflict can be resolved if the conflicting parties understand each other and jointly search for alternate solutions.

__________ While trying to resolve conflicts, each party should ensure that the other's feelings and emotions are not hurt.

__________ In the face of conflict, the best policy is to remain neutral or stay out of it.

__________ When conflict arises, one should try to identify the reasons for it and resolve the underlying issues.

__________ When conflict arises, one should use all possible means (power, position or expertise) to force acceptance of one's own point of view.

__________ Whenever conflict occurs, one should try to be fair and firm, and try to get an equitable solution.

__________ A person loses least in a quarrel if he avoids arguments, takes no responsibility and tries not to get involved.

__________ In a conflict situation, one should tone down the differences and emphasise common interests to maintain good relations.

__________ A conflict issue should be resolved through the use of knowledge or reason if we want to have sound, creative decisions.

__________ It is easier to refrain than to retreat from a quarrel.

## ORGANISATIONAL EFFECTIVENESS

Given below are statements that relate to various dimensions of organisational effectiveness. Please read each statement and tick your response out of various alternatives given.

### (Production: Quantity)

Thinking of the various products produced by people in your organisation, how much are they producing?

__________ (1) Their production is very low.

__________ (2) It is fairly low.

__________ (3) It is neither high or low.

__________ (4) It is fairly high.

__________ (5) It is very high.

### (Production: Quality)

How good would you say is the quality of products or services produced by people in your organisation?

__________ (1) Their products or services are of poor quality.

__________ (2) Their quality is not too good.

__________ (3) Fair quality.

__________ (4) Good quality

__________ (5) Excellent quality.

### (Production: Efficiency)

Do the people seem to get maximum output from the resources available? That is, how efficiently do they do their work?

___________ (1) They do not work efficiently at all.
___________ (2) Not too efficient.
___________ (3) Fairly efficient.
___________ (4) They are very efficient.
___________ (5) They are extremely efficient.

**(Adaptation: Promptness of adjustment)**

When changes are made in work routines or equipment, how quickly do the people in your organisation accept and adjust to these changes?

___________ (1) Most people accept and adjust to them very slowly.
___________ (2) Rather slowly.
___________ (3) Fairly slowly.
___________ (4) They adjust very rapidly, but not immediately.
___________ (5) Most people accept and adjust to them immediately.

**(Adaptation: Prevalence of adjustment)**

What proportion of people in your organisation readily accept and adjust to these changes?

___________ (1) Considerably less than half of the people accept and adjust to these changes readily.
___________ (2) Slightly less than half do.
___________ (3) The majority does.
___________ (4) Considerably more than half do.
___________ (5) Practically everyone accepts and adjusts to these changes readily.

**(Flexibility)**

From time to time, emergencies arise such as crash programmes, schedules moved ahead, a breakdown in the flow of work, etc. When these emergencies occur, they cause work overloads for many people. Some work groups cope with these emergencies more readily and successfully than others. How good a job do the people in your organisation do at coping with these situations:

___________ (1) They do a poor job of handling emergency situations.
___________ (2) They do not do very well.
___________ (3) They do a fair job.
___________ (4) They do a good job.
___________ (5) They do an excellent job of handling these situations.

# Index